Great Sermons on the Birth, Death, and Resurrection of Christ

Great Sermons on the Birth, Death, and Resurrection of Christ

Edited by

Wilbur M. Smith

VOLUME 3

Jesus' Resurrection

BAKER BOOK HOUSE
Grand Rapids, Michigan 49516

Contents

Appendices

INTRODUCTION

Both the publisher and compiler of this series of volumes cannot but be deeply gratified with the cordial reception and enthusiastic book reviews of the first volume, *Great Sermons on the Birth of Christ*. The present volume is the second in the series. The next one, God willing, will carry the title *Great Sermons on the Death of Christ*.

As in the earlier volume, so here, it has been necessary, of course, to restrict severely the number of texts chosen for the sermons to be included in this selection, inasmuch as there are approximately two hundred eighty verses in the New Testament bearing upon the general subject of the Resurrection, and particularly, the Resurrection of our Lord.

As in the earlier volume, so in regard to this one, I have myself personally read every sermon referred to in the bibliographies, and consequently, these references may be depended upon as containing material directly related to and expounding the text to which they are attached. In regard to biographical sketches, I have taken the liberty of using those which appeared in the earlier volume when the same author appears in this second volume of the series, though I have abbreviated some sketches, and here and there added a few lines.

The bibliographies in this volume, I am glad to say, are more extensive than those that appeared in the earlier volume, because in the preparation for this work, I have spent a great many hours in the theological libraries of the area about Chicago, and also in the Library of Congress in Washington, in the superlatively rich library at Princeton Theological Seminary, as well as in Union Theological Seminary in New York City. After carefully

3

checking sermonic literature on the Resurrection, I must say that I have been increasingly amazed at the mysterious lack of adequate sermon collections in any of the basic theological libraries that I have been able to visit in the last few months. In fact, twelve books dealing directly with the Resurrection and sermons on the Resurrection, I was not able to find in over twenty different libraries whose resources I attempted to examine. I wonder why theological libraries do not have extensive collections of sermons by outstanding preachers, not second-rate and third-rate material which need not clutter up any library.

I regret that I have not been able to examine the literally thousands of volumes of British and American religious journals, where, I am sure, are a number of great sermons on this subject long forgotten. I have, however, carefully gone through the one hundred eighty volumes of the *Christian World Pulpit,* which has only this year ceased publication. As an example of the vastness of sermonic material on the subjects of Resurrection and the Resurrection of Christ, may I simply point to the fact that in the volume of the *Speaker's Bible* that covers the later chapters of First Corinthians, there are twenty columns of references alone to sermons on the Fifteenth chapter of that Epistle.

While in the Library of Congress (and I also discovered a copy in the library of Princeton Theological Seminary), I came upon a separately printed sermon of the greatly gifted late Professor William Lyon Phelps, for many years at Yale University, entitled *Easter, the World's Best News.* Now, I have known for years that Dr. Phelps preached many, many summers in a Methodist Church in Michigan where he spent his vacations, drawing hundreds of people to hear him every Lord's Day, but I did not know before of the existence of this sermon, which has probably become quite scarce. With the kind permission of the publishers, the Fleming H. Revell Company, I am taking the liberty of quoting a few lines here in the introduction:

"On the third day came sunrise — the most magnificent dawn humanity has ever known. The formerly desparing and scattered disciples reunited in triumph. No more doubt, no more questioning, no more uncertainty, no more gloom. The early Apostolic days were marked by a confidence which nothing could dim. Out of their joyous triumphant *certainty* came the Christian church. Never was there in any assemblage a more complete transformation — it was the change from utter and apparent hopeless defeat to the obstreperous joy of victory. . . . There is more and better evidence for the resurrection than for any other miracle. It is encouraging to remember that the story is told in all four Gospels, and that it was the foundation as well as the inspiration of the whole courier of St. Paul."

As in the first volume, so here, I have not felt justified in altering any statement of these authors, even though there are some contradictions. Thus, for example, Dr. G. Campbell Morgan calls attention to the fact that there is no such a phrase as "the second Adam," while Dr. Adolph Saphir, a very careful Bible student, nevertheless, uses that phrase. Nor have I taken any liberty of omitting lines with which I could not agree, as for example, the very strange statement by Dr. G. Campbell Morgan, that priesthood was "never a divine institution or provision." Normally, it is assumed there were ten appearances of our Lord after the resurrection, though Canon Liddon here enumerates eleven. If the references to quoted verses do not appear in the original text, I have not attempted to insert them — it will be profitable for many to look up these references, if they cannot at once recall where they are found in the Scriptures.

The sermons in this volume will inevitably be found to be more theological than those in the volume on the Nativity of our Lord. Most of the passages depicting the birth of Christ are, apart from the Songs of the Nativity, simple historical narratives, whereas many of the passages on the Resurrection of Christ, especially those in the Epistles, present some of the profoundest truths that form part of the Christian faith.

SOME GENERAL CONSIDERATIONS OF THE NEW TESTAMENT DATA RELATING TO THE RESURREC- TION AND THE OBSERVANCE OF EASTER IN THE CHRISTIAN CHURCH

The annual celebration of the Resurrection of Christ in the calendar of the Christian church, and in the Western world in general, extends over a much briefer period of time than does the celebration of the Nativity of our Lord, for which of course, there is a transparent reason. The whole period of Lent emphasizes sorrow, repentance of sin, and the sufferings and death of our Lord, which carries on up through the afternoon of Good Friday, when the whole Western world is remembering the agony of the cross. The celebration of the Resurrection takes place in less than forty-eight hours subsequent to the meditations upon the last Seven Words. In other words, sermons on the Resurrection are hardly ever preached at the Easter season, except on Easter Sunday, whereas the events gathered around the Nativity of our Lord will often be chosen as suitable subjects for meditation and preaching early in December. On the other hand, there is much more material in the New Testament on this subject of the Resurrection than on the birth of our Lord. There are 131 verses in the four Gospels devoted to the events between the visit of the women to the empty tomb and Christ's ascension, and there are some 160 additional verses bearing on these themes in the book of Acts and the New Testament epistles. Indeed, while the actual birth of Christ can be said to be referred to only twice in the New Testament epistles, the subject of Christ's resurrection is referred to by the Apostle Paul alone twenty-two times.

It might be of interest to consider for a few moments some of the similarities in the two narratives of the Nativity and the

Resurrection of our Lord, as well as some contrasts. To begin with, a very elemental matter, Jerusalem and the temple in Jerusalem, appear in the record of both of these episodes. The wisemen, of course, came to Jerusalem asking where the King of the Jews was born (Matthew 2:1); Zacharias was ministering in the temple of Jerusalem when the angel announced that their home would be blessed with a son (Luke 1:8ff); and the Holy Family took the babe to the temple to be dedicated when still in its infancy and where some notable characters were met (Luke 2:22-39).

There is opposition in both of these narratives, though I think possibly we have almost forgotten this. There was the opposition of Herod and the total indifference of the scribes and chief priests to the fact that the Babe had been born in Bethlehem (Matthew 2:1-10, 16-18), and in the same first Gospel, the scribes and elders bribed soldiers to falsify the cause for the body of Jesus disappearing from the tomb of Joseph of Arimathaea (Matthew 28:11-15). I have often wondered if the scribes who quoted the Messianic prophecy of Micah to Herod were, at least some of them, among the scribes who in bewilderment concocted this ridiculous story about the theft of the body of Jesus.

In these two narratives, we have the greatest concentration of angelic ministry to be found in the Gospel records, though strange to say, the angelic participation in the Nativity narrative is found exclusively in Matthew and Luke, while the angels at the time of the resurrection are noted only in the Fourth Gospel (Matthew 1:20 and 2:13, 19; Luke 1:11-20, 28-37; 2:9-12; John 20:12, 13).

In both of these tremendous events, we have the unique combination of fear and great joy. Mary, we are told, "was greatly troubled" at the first greeting of the angel Gabriel (Luke 1:29). The shepherds "were sore afraid" when the glory of the Lord suddenly appeared to them (Luke 2:9). So likewise, are we told, so easy to believe, that the women watching at the tomb were afraid at the appearance of an angel, as they were possessed with fear the second time when Jesus suddenly appeared to them

(Matthew 28:5, 10). At the same time, as we have said above, there is abounding joy because of the birth of one who was to save His people from their sins, and the resurrection of the same one, from which hope is born. The wisemen from the East "when they saw the star rejoiced with exceeding great joy" (Matthew 2:10). The angel in announcing the birth of John the Baptist told Zacharias "thou shalt have joy and gladness; and many shall rejoice at his birth" (Luke 1:14). To the shepherds, some months later, the word of the angel from heaven was "be not afraid; for behold I bring you good tidings of great joy" (Luke 2:10). How perfectly natural that there should be joy among the disciples when they knew that the promises of Christ had been fulfilled, and their redeemer had triumphed over death. In fact, we are told "they disbelieved for joy (Luke 24:41), and after the day spent with the risen Lord, and their watching Him ascend out of their sight, we are told that "they returned to Jerusalem with great joy" (Luke 21:52). Indeed St. John tells us that when the Risen Lord, on Easter night, convinced them that the one standing before them was none other than their own Messiah, "the disciples therefore were glad" (John 20:20; Mt. 28:8).

Not only joy, but peace also, appear in the narratives of both of these events. Peace is announced when the heavenly host praising God exclaimed in words known to all, "Glory to God in the highest, And on earth peace among men in whom he is well pleased" (Luke 2:14). As Luke's Gospel begins with an announcement of peace from heaven, so it ends with our Lord standing in the midst of His disciples saying, "Peace be unto you" (Luke 24:36; John 20:21).

Even the presence of the Holy Spirit is emphasized in both of these events. Luke, calling our attention especially to those who were filled with the Spirit of God at the time of our Lord's birth (1:15, 35, 41, 67; 2:25-27), while our Lord in His appearance to the disciples on Easter night said to them again, "Peace be unto you (John 20:22) and identified Himself as co-equal with the Father and the Holy Spirit in His great commission (Matthew 28:19).

At both the birth and at the resurrection, we have acts of worship recorded. The wisemen in arriving at Jerusalem declared that they had come to worship the King of the Jews (Matthew 2:2) and when at last they came into the presence of the holy family, their journey was consummated "when they fell down and worshipped Him" (Matthew 2:11). Then it was the Babe Jesus that was worshipped, but at the time of the resurrection, some thirty-three years later, it is the Son of God and the Risen Saviour whom the women worshipped, as well as the eleven disciples in Galilee (Matthew 28:9, 17). And in Luke's account of the ascension, how natural to read that when He "was carried up into heaven, they worshipped Him" (Luke 24:51, 52).

I believe there are still two more correspondences in these remarkable pregnant narratives. In both it is often stated that what is happening is in fulfillment of the predictions of the Old Testament. The fact that Christ was conceived by the power of the Holy Spirit is predicted by Isaiah (Matthew 1:22, 23; Isaiah 7:14); that Bethlehem was to be His birthplace was recorded by Micah (Matthew 2:5, 6; Micah 5:2); that they would be compelled to flee into Egypt, later to return, is an event predicted by Hosea (Matthew 2:15; Hosea 11:1); the slaughter of the babes at Bethlehem wrought a remarkable fulfilment of a strange passage in Jeremiah (Matthew 2:17, 18; Jeremiah 31:15). The angel in announcing the coming birth of Jesus referred directly to the great prophecy to David concerning His posterity and His kingdom (Luke 1:32, 33; 2 Samuel 7:11-16). It is our Lord Himself, however, after His resurrection who calls the disciples' attention to the fact that Christ must suffer and enter into His glory "that all things must needs be fulfilled which are written in the law of Moses and the prophets and the psalms" (Luke 24:25-27, 44-47).

Finally, both at the time of our Lord's birth, and at the time of His resurrection, there was a strange urgency to proclaim what had taken place. Thus the simple shepherds, after their visit to Bethlehem, "made known concerning the saying which was spoken to them about this child" (Luke 2:17). It is really surprising how often, both the angels and the risen Lord, urge upon the women and the disciples to "go quickly and tell He is risen from the dead" (Matthew 28:8-10). The Great Commission, of course, begins with this word "go ye therefore" (Matthew 28:19. See also Mark 16:7, 13, 15, 20; and Luke 24:33-35). Over and over again, our Lord told the disciples "ye are witnesses of these things" (Luke 24:48; Acts 1:8). Even to Mary Magdalene, the command was "go unto my brethren," followed by immediate obedience for we read that "Mary Magdalene cometh and telleth the disciples, I have seen the Lord; and *that* he had said these things unto her" (John 20:17, 18).

THE EARLY CELEBRATION OF EASTER

One of the strangest anomalies in the King James version is the appearance of the word *Easter* in the text of Acts. "And when he had apprehended him, he put *him* in prison, and delivered *him* to four quaternions of soldiers to keep him; intending after Easter to bring him forth to the people" (Acts 12:4). Of course, the translators in 1611 felt justified in inserting this word because it was in Tyndale's version in 1525, and the Great Bible of 1539, as well as in the Bishops' Bible of 1568, though the Rheims Bible of 1582 actually transliterated the Greek word here appearing and called it *Pasche*. The Geneva Bible in 1560 and the Revised Versions of 1881 and 1946 all use the word *Passover*. The early church never called the day of our Lord's resurrection Easter. In fact, it is now generally recognized that, as the Anglo-Saxon historian Bede stated, Easter often spelled Ester is a word derived from Eostre, the name of a goddess whose festival was celebrated at the time of the vernal equinox.

In the Greek text of the New Testament, the word is *Pascha* which is the name of the Jewish festival known as Passover, occurring on the fourteenth of the month Nisan, followed by the Feast of Unleavened Bread. This is the meaning of the word in

Luke 22:1 and Mark 14:12. The same word sometimes means the Paschal Lamb, as in Luke 22:7 and I Corinthians 5:7. The time of the full moon for this celebration could vary within the extremes of March 21 and April 25.

While the early church, from the very beginning, celebrated every week the Lord's resurrection on what they called the first day of the week, or the Lord's Day, there was no particular period of the year, as far as we know, when the time of Christ's resurrection was recognized with great celebrations. In fact, Socrates in his *Ecclesiastical History,* written about 440 A.D., is still speaking strongly against the celebration of Easter and regrets the quarrels that had arisen throughout the church as to the time of this celebration. "As we have touched the subject I deem it not unreasonable to say a few words concerning Easter. It appears to me that neither the ancients nor moderns who have affected to follow the Jews, have had any rational foundation for contending so obstinately about it. For they have not taken into consideration the fact that when Judaism was changed into Christianity, the obligation to observe the Mosaic law and the ceremonial types ceased. And the proof of this matter is plain; for no law of Christ permits Christians to imitate the Jews. On the contrary the apostle expressly forbids it; not only rejecting circumcision, but also deprecating contention about festival days. In his epistle to the Galatians he writes, 'Tell me, ye that desire to be under the law, do ye not hear the law?' And continuing his train of argument, he demonstrates that the Jews were in bondage as servants, but that those who have come to Christ are 'called into the liberty of sons.' Moreover he exhorts them in no way to regard 'days, and months, and years.' Again in his epistle to the Colossians he distinctly declares, that such observances are merely shadows: wherefore he says, 'Let no man judge you in meat, or in drink, or in respect of any holy-day, or of the new moon, or of the sabbath-days; which are a shadow of things to come.' The same truths are also confirmed by him in the epistle to the Hebrews in these words: 'For the priesthood being changed, there is made of necessity a change also of the law.'

Neither the apostles, therefore, nor the Gospels, have anywhere imposed the 'yoke of servitude' on those who have embraced the truth; but have left Easter and every other feast to be honored by the gratitude of the recipients of grace. Wherefore, inasmuch as men love festivals, because they afford them cessation from labor: each individual in every place, according to his own pleasure, has by a prevalent custom celebrated the memory of the saving passion. The Saviour and his apostles have enjoined us by no law to keep this feast: nor do the Gospels and apostles threaten us with any penalty, punishment, or curse for the neglect of it, as the Mosaic law does the Jews. It is merely for the sake of historical accuracy, and for the reproach of the Jews, because they polluted themselves with blood on their very feasts, that it is recorded in the Gospels that our Saviour suffered in the days of 'unleavened bread.' The aim of the apostles was not to appoint festival days, but to teach a righteous life and piety. And it seems to me that just as many other customs have been established in individual localities according to usage. So also the feast of Easter came to be observed in each place according to the individual peculiarities of the peoples inasmuch as none of the apostles legislated on the matter. And that the observance originated not by legislation, but as a custom the facts themselves indicate. In Asia Minor most people kept the fourteenth day of the moon, disregarding the sabbath: yet they never separated from those who did otherwise, until Victor, bishop of Rome, influenced by too ardent a zeal, fulminated a sentence of excommunication against the Quartodecimans in Asia. Wherefore also Irenaeus, bishop of Lyons in France, severely censured Victor by letter for his immoderate heat; telling him that although the ancients differed in their celebration of Easter, they did not desist from intercommunion. Also that Polycarp, bishop of Smyrna, who afterwards suffered martyrdom under Gordian, continued to communicate with Anicetus bishop of Rome, although he himself, according to the usage of his native Smyrna, kept Easter on the fourteenth day of the moon, as Eusebius attests in the fifth book of his *Ecclesiastical History*. While therefore some in Asia Minor observed the day above-mentioned, others in the East kept that feast on the sabbath indeed, but differed as regards the month. The former thought the Jews should be followed, though they were not exact: the latter kept Easter after the equinox, refusing to celebrate with the Jews; 'for,' said they, 'it ought to be celebrated when the sun is in Aries, in the month called Xanthicus by the Antiochians, and April by the Romans.' In this practice, they averred, they conformed not to the modern Jews, who are mistaken in almost everything, but to the ancients, and to Josephus according to what he has written in the third book of his *Jewish Antiquities*. Thus these people were at issue among themselves. But all other Christians in the Western parts, and as far as the ocean itself, are found to have celebrated Easter after the equinox, from a very ancient tradition. And in fact these acting in this manner have never disagreed on this subject. It is not true, as some have pretended, that the Synod under Constantine altered this festival: for Constantine himself, writing to those who differed respecting it, recommended that as they were few in number, they could agree with the majority of their brethren. His letter will be found at length in the third book of the *Life of Constantine* by Eusebius; but the passage in it relative to Easter runs thus:

'It is a becoming order which all the churches in the Western, Southern, and Northern parts of the world observe, and some places in the East also. Wherefore all on the present occasion have judged it right, and I have pledged myself that it will have the acquiescence of your prudence, that what is unanimously observed in the city of Rome, throughout Italy, Africa, and the whole of Egypt, in Spain, France, Britain, Libya, and all Greece, the diocese of Asia and Pontus, and Cilicia, your wisdom also will readily embrace; considering not only that the number of churches in the aforesaid places is greater, but also that while there should be a universal concurrence in what is most reasonable, it becomes us to have nothing in common with the perfidious Jews.' "

In spite of Socrates' words here, and the objections of some

Christians, after the year 300, the resurrection was almost universally observed throughout Christendom, when it was variously called "the Day alone Great," "The Most Royal Day of Days," or "The Festival of Festivals." It is not necessary in a work of this kind to enter into details regarding what has been called the Paschal controversies. The early church quarreled over the time of Easter as we have seen, the bitterest quarrel among Christians of Great Britain in the early days of Christianity there was over this matter of the time for the celebration of Easter, to which Bede devotes a great deal of space. Indeed Easter became the most joyous occasion of the whole year for Christians. "All labor ceased, all trades were suspended, the husbandman threw down his spade and plow and put on his holiday attire. The roads were empty of travelers, the sea of sailors. The mother came to church with the whole band of her children and the domestics, the husband and the whole family rejoicing with her. The poor man dressed like the rich, and the rich wore his gayest attire; those who had none of their own borrowed of their neighbors." (Probably as satisfactory an account of the Paschal controversies in the early church that my readers would wish to consult may be found in Philip Schaff's *History of the Christian Church,* Volume II, pp. 209-220 and the rich notes by Dr. A. C. McGiffert in his edition of *The Church History of Eusebius,* pp. 241-245).

THE RESURRECTION OF CHRIST
by
Charles Pettit McIlvaine

"The Lord is risen indeed." — Luke 24:34

These are words of conviction, and of joy. To appreciate them, as uttered by the disciples of Christ, when they became assured that he had risen from the dead, we must enter into their circumstances. Well persuaded that, in Jesus, they beheld him to whom all the prophets had witnessed, who was to sit on the throne of David, and to establish his kingdom over all people, they had forsaken all to follow him, and had embarked all their hopes on his claims. Already had they learned, by painful experience, that it was through much tribulation they were to share in his kingdom; but such trials had not shaken their faith. Accustomed to behold him despised, persecuted, and rejected of men, their confidence was continually sustained, as they heard him speak "as never man spake," and with an authority that controlled the sea and raised the dead. But now, deep tribulation, such as they had not know before, had overtaken them. What darkness had come upon their faith! He, who was once so mighty to give deliverance to the captive, had himself been taken captive and bound to the cross. He, who with a word raised the dead, had been violently, wickedly, put to an ignominious death. He, whom they expected to reign as King of kings and to subdue all nations, had been brought under the dominion of his own nation, and shut up in the sepulcher, and all the people of Israel were now boastfully confident that the death of the cross had proved him a deceiver. O, indeed, it was a season of great heaviness, and

17

dismay, and trial, those days and nights in which their beloved Master was lying in death! The great stone which his enemies had rolled to the door of the sepulcher, lest his disciples should go by night and take away the body, was expressive of the cold, dead weight, which that death and burial had laid upon their hearts. That sepulcher seemed as the tomb of all their hopes. All was buried with Jesus. "For, as yet (it is written), they knew not the Scripture, that he must rise again from the dead." (John 20:9). Had they understood what he had often told them, they would have known "that thus it behooved (the) Christ to suffer, and to rise from the dead, the third day."

The third day was now come. The Jewish Sabbath was over. The first day of the week was breaking. While it is yet dark, faithful women repair to the sepulcher with spices for the embalming. They find the stone rolled away. Wondering at this, they enter the tomb. The body is not there. Enemies have taken it away, is their first thought. Mary Magdalene hastens to say to Peter and John, "they have taken away the Lord out of the sepulcher, and we know not where they have laid him." Angels appear to the women in their alarm, saying, "He is not here, but is risen." "With fear," and yet "with great joy," they ran "to bring his disciples word." But to the latter, "their words seemed as idle tales, and they believed them not." Peter and John had now reached "the place where the Lord lay," and entering in, they found the grave-clothes remaining, but otherwise an empty sepulcher. "They saw and believed." After a little, came Mary Magdalene to the other disciples, and "told them she had seen the Lord," and what things he had spoken unto her. Still, "they believed not." It seemed too good to be true. How was it that they did not remember his words, which even the chief priests and Pharisees repeated to Pilate, as a reason for posting a guard around the tomb, "After three days, I will rise again." (Matthew 27:63). The terrible shock of the crucifixion must have so stunned their faith, and distracted their thoughts, that what they afterward remembered so clearly, was either forgotten, or not comprehended.

That same day, two of them went toward the neighboring village. Their hearts were heavy, and they "talked of all those things that had happened." Jesus "drew near and went with them." He often draws near to those whose hearts are sad, because they feel their need of him. He asked their grief. They told him of Jesus of Nazareth, whom they believed to have been "a prophet, mighty in word and deed;" how he had been put to death — he of whom they expected that "he would have redeemed Israel;" and how it was now the third day since this was done; and of the amazing statement that the sepulcher had been found empty, and that a vision of angels had been seen, "who said he was alive."

Then answered their unknown companion: "O, slow of heart to believe all that the prophets have spoken." "And beginning at Moses and all the prophets, he expounded unto them in all the Scripture the things concerning himself." What an exposition must that have been! Who but must wish we had it to read! No wonder their hearts were inflamed at the touch of such words, and burned within them, while thus the Light of the world was opening to them the Scriptures. Presently, while sitting at meat with them, Jesus *"took bread, and brake it, and gave to them."* It was a sign they could not mistake. Their eyes were opened in that breaking of bread. "They knew him, and he vanished out of their sight." Immediately they returned to Jerusalem with the tidings. They found the rest of the disciples, and others, gathered together — but in what mind? No more in doubt, but saying among themselves, *"the Lord is risen indeed."* The two from Emmaus now added their testimony. Again, and more confidently and joyfully, must they all have said one to another, with a relief of heart, and a return of faith, and a resurrection of hope, like the return of day after a long and fearful night, *the Lord is risen indeed; the Lord is risen indeed.*

Corresponding with the faith and joy of those disciples, is the state of mind in which the church should keep her feast this day — the annual commemoration of the resurrection of the Lord and Head. Eminently is it the Lord's day — that from which all the Sabbaths of the Christian year derive their light and festival. It is "the great day of the feast" — that feast of faith and hope which measures all the life of the true believer.

We began by saying that the words of the text, as uttered by the apostles, are words of *conviction* and words of *joyfulness*. Under these two aspects we will treat the subject they contain.

I. *Words of conviction.* "The Lord is risen indeed."

The apostles had laid aside their doubts and were assured. And what if *we* were not assured that Christ did rise? St. Paul answers, "If Christ be not risen, then is our preaching vain, and your faith is also vain. Ye are yet in your sins. Then they which are fallen asleep in Christ are perished." (I Cor. 15:14, 17, 18). In other words, the great seal and evidence of the victory of Christ over sin and death, as our surety, would be wanting. We could have no confidence in the efficacy of his death as a sacrifice for us. Life and immortality would be still in darkness. Our hope would want its corner-stone, our faith its warrant. Every promise of the gospel would lack the signature of him who alone can fulfill it. But, saith the same apostle, "now *is* Christ risen from the dead, and become the first-fruits of them that slept." (I Cor. 15:20). His resurrection was not only the greatest and most important of his miracles, but the most abundantly and variously attested. We have only space here for a glance at its evidence.

Prophets had for many centuries foretold that Messiah would rise from the dead. Jesus had several times predicted and promised it, both to his disciples and the Jews, who believed not on him. (Matthew 20:18, 19). So well did the chief priests and Pharisees remember his words, and the exact time that he said he would lie in the grave, that it was the alleged ground of their application to Pilate for a guard of soldiers to protect the sepulcher from any attempt of his disciples apparently to make good the prediction, by stealing away his body. But while his enemies remembered so well his saying, his disciples, as if it were so ordered, to increase the evidence, had no recollection, or no idea of the meaning of his words, and therefore no preparation, either to expect his resurrection or to practice the fraud, which the chief priests apprehended; but now that the tomb is empty on the predicted third day, notwithstanding the guard of Roman soldiers, determined, as they valued their lives, to keep it safely, that notorious fact must be accounted for. The grave-clothes are there. The fact of the burial was certain and notorious. Either *friends* or *enemies* must have removed the body; or else it did not rise from death. Enemies of course did not. Their easy and triumphant answer to the preaching of the resurrection, had they done it, would have been to produce the body. Did friends? Who were the friends of Jesus? Eleven apostles, Joseph of Arimathea, and a few women! The first were so overpowered by fear, that when he was taken "all forsook him and fled." (Matthew 26:56). But had they not been too fearful to attempt it, in the face of the Roman guard, was it possible for them to accomplish it, to roll away that great stone, and bear away that burden, so jealously and so strongly watched? Were the soldiers awake or asleep? Of course, the latter, if that robbery was committed. But what less than miracle put to sleep a whole Roman guard, on such a night, with such a trust, and under such responsibility, and kept them all so fast asleep that all the movements of all the men necessary to roll away the stone, and force the tomb, and bear away the body, did not arouse them? Seeing, then, that friends *could* not, and enemies *would* not, remove the body, the empty sepulcher was negative evidence of resurrection. Then, when afterward Jesus was frequently seen and conversed with; when his doubting disciples were allowed to touch him, to place their hands in the print of the wounds in his hands and sides; when, during a space of forty days, they listened to his instructions, recognizing perfectly the well-known countenance and voice, and the teaching as never man taught; when he appeared to "more than five hundred brethren at once" (1 Corinthians 15:6), so that, as a mere historical fact, we must deny the evidence of all history, if we question the evidence of his appearance in the body after his crucifixion; what excuse can be devised for not believing that he has risen indeed? Will any resort to the desperate pretext that the disciples were deceived? But, as men of ordinary sense, must they not have known, during a close conversation and association of forty days, whether it was really a human body, and the body of Jesus, which they beheld, or not? Will you imagine a miracle of blindness, to get rid of a miracle of resurrection? Will you take another expedient, and say they were not deceived, but they practiced a deception? Then you must give a motive to account for such a deception. You must explain how men, so evidently good men, and the teachers of so much goodness, and the influence of whose teaching was, and is, to make all deception abhorred and despised; how such men could have gone out into a world in arms against them and their doctrine, and preached everywhere the resurrection of Christ as the great seal of the gospel and corner-stone of their message; knowing that they would draw upon them the utmost rage and persecution that man could show; unshaken by any dangers, unwearied by any sufferings; cheerfully losing their all, and submitting to tortures and death, that they might preach Jesus and the resurrection; if Christ was not raised, if their teaching was all untrue, then "were they, of all men, most miserable," having nothing but sufferings here, and expecting to answer for a life-long fraud hereafter. Will you imagine a miracle of folly that you may escape the miracle of resurrection? But there was an evidence, if possible more convincing even than the appearance of Jesus to his disciples, and his frequent association with them. It was in "the events of the day of Pentecost."

Here we remark, in general, that his resurrection was the great sign and crowning miracle to which our Lord, all the way of his ministry, to the day of his crucifixion, referred both friends and opposers, for the final confirmation of all his claims and doctrines. He staked all on the promise that he would rise from death. The Jews asked of him a sign, that they might believe. He answered, "There shall no sign be given, but the sign of the prophet Jonas. For as Jonas was three days and three nights in the whale's belly, so shall the Son of man be three days and three nights in the heart of the earth." (Matthew 12:38-40). Again, in answer to the question of the Jews, "What sign showest thou?" he promised the same sign: "Destroy this temple and in three days I will raise it up." "He spake," says the Evangelist, "of the temple of his body." (John 2:19). Thus, on that single event, the resurrection of Christ, the whole of Christianity, as it all centers in, and depends on him, was made to hinge. Redemption waited the evidence of resurrection. Nothing was to be accounted as sealed and finally certified, till Jesus should deliver himself from the power of death. All of the gospel, all the hopes it brings to us, all the promises with which it comforts us, were taken for their final verdict, as true or false, sufficient or worthless, to the door of that jealously-guarded and stone-sealed sepulcher, waiting the settlement of the question, *will he rise?*

It was a wondrous sign to choose. The mere selection of such a sign by Christ himself, was itself a very strong evidence of what its accomplishment was to prove. We do not wonder that the enmity of the Jews was all centered upon the watching of that gate. It was a serious night indeed, to friends and foes, and well appreciated among the powers of darkness, when that great sign was to be seen or else the gospel finally contradicted. But an event so momentous was not left to but one class of evidence. There was a way by which thousands at once were made to receive as powerful assurance that Christ was risen, as if they had seen him in his risen body. Jesus, before his death, had made a great promise to his disciples, to be fulfilled by him only after his death and resurrection; a promise impossible to be fulfilled if his resurrection failed; because then, not only would he be under the power of death, but all his claim to divine power would be brought to naught. It was the promise of the Holy Ghost. "When the Comforter is come *whom I will send unto you* from the Father, even the Spirit of truth which proceedeth from the Father, *he shall testify of me," "he shall glorify me."* (John 15:26 and 16:14).

It was after he had "shown himself alive after his passion by many infallible proofs, being seen of his disciples forty days, and speaking to them of the things pertaining to the kingdom of God," that the day for the accomplishment of that promise came.

The day was that which commemorated the giving of the law on Mount Sinai. It was now to witness the going forth of the gospel from Jerusalem. I need not relate to you the wonderful events of that day of Pentecost, the coming of the Holy Ghost with the "sound as of a rushing mighty wind," that "filled all the house;" the "cloven tongues like as of fire," which sat on each of the disciples; the evidence that it was the Spirit of God which had then come, given in the sudden and astonishing change which immediately came over the apostles, transforming them from weak and timid men to the boldest and strongest; in the change which suddenly came upon the power of their ministry, converting it from the weak agent it had previously been, in contact with all the unbelief and wickedness of men, into an instrument so mighty, that out of a congregation of Jews of all nations, many of whom had probably partaken in the crucifixion of Christ, *three thousand that day* were bowed down to repentance and subdued to his obedience. I need not remind you of the miraculous attestation that all this was from God, in the sudden gift to the apostles of divers tongues, whereby they preached to an audience from all nations, in the several languages in which they were born; nor need I tell you of the immense number of people that witnessed all these things. Thus the power of God testified of Jesus. Thus Jesus made good his word, "I will send the Holy Ghost and he shall testify of me." How could he thus employ the power of God, if the great sign appointed — his resurrection, had failed? How could he thus show himself mighty to raise thousands from the death of sin, and to make his apostles, in a moment, preachers in all languages, if the power of death were still upon him? How could he send the Holy Ghost and show such mighty signs, who was still bound in the sepulcher?

Thus was the day of Pentecost a great day of testimony to the life and divine power, and consequently the resurrection, of Christ. Each of those who heard the divers tongues of the ministry of that day, each of the three thousand, was a witness to the same. "The signs and wonders, and divers miracles, and gifts of the Holy Ghost," by which God bore witness to the preaching of the apostles, as in all their ministry they made the resurrection of Christ the great demonstration of their message, all testified to its reality. For, would God accompany with such powers the constant declaration of a lie? But witnesses have been multiplying by thousands ever since. Every man that receives the Holy Ghost to raise him from the death of sin to the life of righteousness, is a witness. He can testify that Christ now liveth, and is exalted to the right hand of power, and is able to make good all his word, because he hath given him his Spirit. He hath given him a new heart; he hath done that for him which only a power above man could do, and which no faith but a Christian faith ever obtained. And his question is, Can he be dead, lying under the dominion of the grave? Can he have been rejected of God, who hath the living power to do these things? Thus will the evidence of our Lord's resurrection be increasing with every day when he shall "come in the glory of his Father and all his angels with him," and when "every eye shall see him, and they also which pierced him." Then will "the *power* of his resurrection" be known in the universal rising of the dead at his word.

We said, the words of the text, in the mouths of the apostles, were words of *conviction* and of *joyfulness.* Under the latter head we proceed next to consider the subject contained in them:

II. *Words of joyfulness. "The Lord is risen indeed."*

The resurrection of Christ was the resurrection of the faith and hopes of his disciples to a new life and vigor. It made them new creatures, as to all joy and peace in believing. "Blessed be the God and Father of our Lord Jesus Christ, who, according to his abundant mercy, hath begotten us again unto a lively hope, by the resurrection of Jesus Christ from the dead, to an inheritance incorruptible and undefiled, and that fadeth not away." (1 Peter 1:3, 4). "The Lord is risen indeed," was an exclamation of joy equivalent to, His kingdom shall embrace all nations; our faith shall overcome the world; death is conquered; eternal life is the heritage of all believers.

1. Let us consider the resurrection of Christ in its connection with *his death as an atoning sacrifice* for sin. Suppose that after

we have commemorated his crucifixion, in the solemn services of our "Good Friday," we had no resurrection to commemorate in the customary praises of our "Easter Sunday," what consolation would there be to us in the former? You know that Jesus became "obedient unto the death of the cross" as our *surety*. "He was made sin for us." "The Lord laid on him the iniquities of us all." Our sins being thus imputed to him as our representative, he was treated, in his death, by him to whom atonement was offered, as if our guilt were his own. He was held under the arrest of the law of God. Its penalty was required of him. Every jot and tittle was he to pay, and not till all was discharged could he be justified from the imputed sin, and delivered from its bonds. He did satisfy the law to the uttermost, and was justified in behalf of all those in whose place he stood, and for whom he died. But how is that ascertained? Where is the evidence? By what hath God declared it? The only conclusive evidence of justification from the imputation of sin, is the release of him to whose account it is laid. Then if my surety were still under the bonds of death, and lying in its prison, must I not suppose that the arrest of the law which he came to satisfy, is still holding him; that the price of my redemption has not been all paid, or has not been accepted; and, therefore, that my hope is vain, and I am yet under condemnation? But Christ *is risen indeed*. The law has delivered its prisoner. The surety comes forth from the grave. "Death hath no more dominion over him." He is *"justified in the Spirit,"* by the power of his own Spirit raising him from the dead. Thus was his justification from the imputed sins of men, *declared* by the Spirit, that he might be "believed on in the world." (1 Timothy 3:16). In his resurrection, "God hath given assurance unto all men," that the atonement was finished and accepted, the surety discharged, the hand-writing against us nailed to his cross, the way of a free and full remission of sins laid open; that Jesus is "able to save to the uttermost all who come unto God by him," and that in him, whosoever believeth shall be justified perfectly, and have peace with God. Thus you perceive the close connection between his being *"delivered for our offenses and raised again for our justification."*

2. Let us consider the resurrection of our Lord in connection with *his making intercession for us.*

You must not suppose that the whole work of Christ, as the offerer of a propitiation, was finished on the cross. The death of the sacrifice was there finished. All of the office of our atoning priest and victim that pertained to the altar of sacrifice in the court of the sanctuary, was there completed. But there was a work remaining to be done within the vail, in the most holy place of the sanctuary on high, in the presence of God the Father — a work of oblation and intercession, in the presentation of the sacrifice.

Those two chief parts in the Saviour's priesthood were showed in the typical office of the Levitical high priest on "the great day of atonement." In the solemn services of the annual expiation, there were two main acts: the slaying of the victim, and the presentation or oblation of the sacrifice. The former was done only at the altar of burnt-offerings in the court of the temple; the latter only within the inner vail, when the high priest entered the most holy place, with the blood, and sprinkled it before the mercy-seat. The second was as essential as the first. It was only when the oblation in the most holy place had been added to the sacrificing in the court of the sanctuary, that the propitiation became effectual.

This type could be fulfilled in our Lord, only when he who was the Lamb that was slain, should rise from death as our ever-living priest, and ascend *in the body* that was slain to "the tabernacle in the heavens," there to present himself as the Lamb of God, before God, and make intercession for us, in virtue of his having been sacrificed for us. Resurrection was thus essential. How could St. Paul have put forth that triumphant challenge, "who shall lay any thing to the charge of God's elect?" if he could not have said, as the strength of his confidence, "it is Christ that died; yea, rather that is *risen again,* who is even at the right hand of God, who also maketh intercession for us?" Here is first the initiatory work of our justification, *Christ hath died;* then the finishing work on his part, his *intercession for us* at God's right hand; and between them is the connecting fact, he is *risen again.* The cross being thus connected with the throne — the death with the intercession by means of resurrection — we have the one perfect and sufficient oblation and satisfaction for the sins of the whole world.

Thus all the precious mercies that flow down upon a guilty world, through Christ — all that justifies the believer — all that sanctifies the sinner — all the grace by which our weakness is made strong, and our darkness is made "light in the Lord;" every present consolation in Christ, and all that we hope to find in him during the trial of death, amid the solemnities of the judgment-day, and in the everlasting blessedness of the kingdom of God — as all depend on the completion of his office in his everlasting priesthood in heaven, so all combine to teach us the joyfulness of the assurance that "the Lord is risen indeed."

3. Let us next consider the resurrection of Christ, as it is connected with, and insures, *the promised triumphs of his church.*

The church is the mystical body of Christ, inhabited and made alive unto God by the Holy Spirit, as his natural body was inhabited by his human soul. Of the latter, the promise was, that *"his soul should not be left in hell, neither should his flesh see corruption."* Concerning the former, the promise is, *"the gates of hell shall not prevail against it."* In both promises the word *hell* stands, as in the Apostle's Creed, for Hades — *the region and dominion of death.* In the first promise, the meaning was, that the powers of death should not be permitted to keep the natural body of our Lord in their dominions. In the second, the meaning was, that all the powers of darkness, sitting in the gates of the dominion of death, and pouring forth from thence their forces against his mystical body, the church, should not finally prevail against it.

How the powers of hell endeavored, not only to subdue the Captain of our salvation, but after he was shut up within the gates of death, to hold him there, and when he arose from the dead, to persuade men that he was still there, I need not tell you. How impossible it was that he should be holden of them, when the set time to come forth had arrived; how the guard was made to swoon away, and there was a great earthquake, and an angel rolled the stone from the mouth of his tomb, and Jesus came forth, bearing "the keys of death and of hell," the mighty conqueror, to reign forever and ever, I need not tell you. But in that triumph, we read how easily and how certainly he will see that the gates of hell shall not prevail against his church. It is the pledge and earnest that all his glorious promises concerning her shall be fulfilled.

Very precious and glorious are those promises. The church is to embrace all nations. The stone "cut out of the mountains, without hands," is to become a great mountain, and fill the whole earth (Daniel 2:34, 35-45). "The kingdom, and dominion, and greatness of the kingdom under the whole heaven shall be given to the people of the saints of the Most High, whose kingdom is an everlasting kingdom, and all dominions shall serve and obey him." (Daniel 7:27). The long-dispersed of Israel and Judah are to be summoned from out of all nations, gathered to their own land, converted to Christ. Then shall "the fullness of the Gentiles come in," and be "as life from the dead" (Romans 11:25 and 15).

But man demands a sign from heaven to convince him that such things are possible. "What sign showest thou, seeing thou wilt do all these things?" The answer is, the sign has already been given: "I am he that liveth, and was dead; and behold, I am alive for evermore, Amen, and have the keys of hell and death" (Revelation 1:18). Jesus, risen from the dead, is the sign unto the end of the world, to assure the church and the world that not a jot or tittle of what he hath promised by the Scriptures, shall fail. "I am the resurrection and the life," saith the Lord. "Fear not, therefore, little flock, for it is your Father's good pleasure to give you the kingdom." "Because I live, ye shall live also." Great tribulations and persecutions, and falling away from the truth, may yet befall the church, as in times past. It may seem, once more, as if she had gone almost to the grave. Priests of Antichrist, in league with the gates of hell, may conspire to keep her in prison and in darkness, fast bound in chains, such as they well know how to forge. But they shall not prevail. The captive shall be delivered. "The Lord shall be her light," and "the days of her mourning shall be ended." Such, in point of tribulation, has been her history more than once already. Think of the fearful corruption, and darkness, and bondage, and persecution, and spiritual death, with which the Papal dominion, the power of "the man of sin," who, "as God sitteth in the temple of God, showing himself that he is God" (2 Thes. 2:3, 4), did once, and for a long time, oppress the church of Christ, and drove the few faithful witnesses of the truth, that remained, into the wilderness, into prisons, and dens, and caves of the earth, so that it seemed as if there was hardly faith left on the earth. But, though Amalek was thus long victorious, there were a faithful few — a little scattered flock, a remnant, as in the days of Elijah, the prophet — who held up their hands to God in prayer and ceased not till God raised up his faithful witness, Martin Luther, and gave him the trumpet of the sanctuary, to sound an alarm, and proclaim anew his truth. The wonderful awakening of the church, as from the dead, in that day — that manifestation of the power of her risen Head, to be unto her "the resurrection and the life," is a standing and glorious testimony to all ages, and for all future trials, how little her faithful people have to fear, and how certain are the promises of a final possession, by her Lord, of the whole kingdom of this world, in his time. Her grave-clothes shall be laid aside; her sackcloth will be cast away. "As a bride adorned with her jewels," will she come forth, leaning on the hand of her Lord. "Voices in heaven" shall be heard, saying, "The kingdoms of this world are become the kingdoms of our Lord and of his Christ, and he shall reign forever and ever."

Now, it deserves your attention, that when the Scriptures speak of great conversions of nations and millions to the gospel, as connected with the second advent of our Lord, and which are to bring in his millennial reign, the change is represented as one of impossibility to human strength, of hopelessness to human wisdom and foresight, of magnitude, and wonder, and miracle, equal to that of a resurrection of the dead. Read the thirty-seventh chapter of Ezekiel. It is an account of the restoration of the Jews, of the lost ten tribes, as of Judah and Benjamin, to their own land; their being united together again as one nation; their being cleansed from their sins and converted to Christ, so as to have the Son of David for their acknowledged King and Shepherd forever, and his sanctuary in the midst of them forevermore; and all these wonderful changes are described under the figure of the resurrection of a whole nation from the dead. The prophet was "carried out in the spirit of the Lord, and set down in the midst of a valley which was full of bones," and was made to pass round them to observe their state. "There were very many in the open valley, and lo, they were very dry." Then the question was asked him: *Can these bones live?* In other words, what can be more hopeless, to all human view, than the condition of these bones? How is it possible they can be gathered from this wide and promiscuous dispersion, so long exposed and bleached, and mingled together in this open valley, carried by beasts of prey hither and thither? How can they be made to resume their former places, each in its own body, bone to its bone, and stand up alive? The prophet's faith could answer no further than by referring the question to the power of God: "O Lord God, thou knowest." Then came the command: "Prophesy upon these bones; say unto them, 'Hear the word of the Lord.' " How can the dead hear? But the prophet obeyed. "And there was a noise, and behold a shaking, and bones came to bones, *bone to his bone.*" Each resumed its original place in its own body, "and the sinews and the flesh came upon them, and the skin covered them above." But as yet there was no life in them. The prophet, as commanded, prophesied again, and "the breath came into them, and they lived and stood up an exceeding great army." Then came the interpretation of the Lord: "These bones are the whole house of Israel; behold, they say, 'Our bones are dried, and our hope is lost.' Behold, O my people, I will open your graves, and cause you to come out of your graves, and bring you into the land of Israel, and put my Spirit in you, and ye shall live and know that I am the Lord."

Now, what says the unbelief of the world, as it looks over the present condition of the Jews, so widely dispersed, so mixed up among themselves, so mixed up among all nations — the ten tribes so lost that none know where they are — all so hardened against the gospel? "Surely their bones are dried, and their hope is lost." We ask the faith of man, "Can these dry bones live?" Can the promises of the Scriptures, concerning these people, be fulfilled? We do not wonder that many ridicule the idea; that others are unable to entertain it, seeing how few are content with the answer of the prophet: "Lord, thou knowest." The difficulties are as insuperable to human might as the raising of the dead. So was it intended that we should regard them. We have no desire to lessen the appearance of impossibility, except to him who is "the Resurrection and the Life."

But carry the use of the prophet's vision beyond the people of Israel. The state of the population of the whole unconverted world may be seen in that valley of bones. Converted unto God it is all to be. The heathen are already given to the Lord, our Saviour, "for an inheritance, and the uttermost parts of the earth for a possession;" and a day is fast coming, when the possession and inheritance shall be, not only given, but received and entered on. But what immeasurable difficulties oppose such a conversion and regeneration: such impossibilities! What! shall this little stone ever fill the whole earth? Can all these nations, so long dead and buried under vices, and superstitions, and idolatries, and all darkness, and perversions of mind for so many centuries — can they be made all to turn unto Christ, and live as his people? Make the hopelessness of such an event, to human power, as great as you please. The reality can not be exaggerated. Hopeless it is, indeed, if the power of the church, without the power of its Lord, or without a far mightier putting forth of his power, than the church has known since her first days, is to be our whole trust. But our assured answer to all difficulties, is, *the resurrection of our Lord Jesus Christ from the dead*. His *word* assures us that such great things are *promised*. His *resurrection* assures us that, because promised, they can and will be *accomplished*. What is there in all of them more hopeless, more impossible, than seemed the resurrection of Christ, during those days in which he lay in the grave? To the heathen, nothing was more impossible than that the dead should be raised. Pliny said, that to bring them back to life (*revocare defunctos*), was one of those things which even God could not do. Festus thought Paul mad, and the Athenians mocked at him, because he preached the resurrection. And are there any bonds holding the Jews in unbelief, stronger than those which held our Lord's body in death? Are there any barriers between the resuscitation of the Jews, as a nation, and their being restored to their own land, more impassable than those between our dead and buried Lord, and the kingdom on high, to which he ascended? Have the powers of darkness a more hopeless dominion over the heathen world, than they seemed to have obtained over the rejected, and cruci-fied, and lifeless Head of the promises of the gospel? Is there anything to discourage the Christian from expecting that the Jews, and the heathen, will ever live unto God as a Christian people and church? Is there any thing to make the unbeliever mock at such an expectation, which had not its perfect equal when Jesus lay in the sepulcher, his disciples scattered and dis-mayed, his enemies scoffing and triumphing? But "the Lord is risen indeed." Those impossibilities were all brought to naught. He rose, the "Lord of all power and might." Death could not hold him from ascending to his Father. The nations could not prevent him from fulfilling his word. All that he hath said shall be done. The greatest is done already. Did he raise himself from death? Then he can, and will, bring Jews and Gentiles to spiritual life, because he has promised. *God hath given assurance unto all men in that he hath raised him from the dead.*

4. Lastly, we must consider the resurrection of Christ in its connection *with that of his people,* who sleep in him. There must be *"the redemption of the body,"* because *man* is already re-deemed. Our Lord will not leave his work unfinished. "Your body is the temple of the Holy Ghost," and he will not leave it in ruin and desolation, polluted and outcast. He will build it again, and in far more than its original beauty. It partook of

the sin, and the condemnation, and penalty. In the case of all believers, it must partake of the justification and the glory. What God joined together in the fall, he will join together in the restoration. "We shall all be changed, in a moment, in the twinkling of an eye, at the last trump." "This corruptible must put on incorruption, and this mortal, immortality." The sign, the pledge, the assurance of all is, that *the Lord is risen*. Believers are members of a mystical body, of which he is head. Because he lives, they shall live also. He can no more permit the gates of hell to prevail over them, to keep them in death, than he would allow them to prevail over him. When he rose, as when he died and was buried, it was in his federal relation as a surety and representative of his people. In him the believer rose also. Our graves were opened when the stone was rolled from his sepulcher. Our victory over death was secured when he burst its bands and came forth free. Beautifully is the argument — from his resurrection to ours — delivered in St. Paul's allusion to the presentation of the sheaf of the first ripe wheat in the temple. "Now is Christ risen from the dead, and become the first-fruits of them that slept." The Jews were prohibited the gathering of the harvest, until the first-fruits were offered to God as an acknowledgment of his goodness in the products of the ground. Till then, the harvest was regarded as unholy — unconsecrated. The great proprietor had not received his tribute. That done, all was considered as acknowledged to be his own, and was received by the people as from him, and the harvest, so consecrated, was secure to be reaped and gathered. Vast is the harvest of the dead, lying ungathered. The people of God of all generations, in the graves or earth and sea, under all skies, dust on dust, an immense community, precious beyond thought to him who died for them; what a field from which the angels may gather for the garner of heaven! It is all ready, only waiting "the voice of the archangel and the trump of God," that the work may begin; for the first-fruits have been already presented. Jesus, "the first-begotten from the dead," hath passed within the vail, and now appears in the presence of God for us. Thus the whole harvest of the dead in

Christ is consecrated and pledged. It must be gathered, for the Lord is its owner. O glorious day, when the trump of God sounding from heaven shall give the signal, and, "in a moment, in the twinkling of an eye," the dead in Christ shall all come forth! O, that jubilee, that year of all years, and end of all times, for which all cycles and dispensations have been preparing; when every bondsman of the Lord's household now in the captivity of death, shall go free, and all debts of God's people to this law shall be finally canceled, and all the true Israel, from their wide dispersions, and separations, and bondage, shall go home, returning "to Sion with songs and everlasting joy on their heads;" when loved ones shall meet again to be no more divided, and the great family, the vast communion, the universal brotherhood of Christ, shall meet in their heavenly Jerusalem, to keep their feast of redemption and blessedness for evermore; every trace of the curse and the death abolished; every risen saint beholding in each brother the likeness of the glory of his Lord! That will be a "holy convocation unto God," indeed. How will they crowd the battlements of Sion, to look down upon the deserted graves, and the whole vanquished and ruined dominion of death, whence they have been ransomed! How will they fill that holy city with their praises, as they cry with one voice, "Thanks be to God which giveth us the victory through our Lord Jesus Christ." Then will it be said, as never before it could be said, "The Lord is risen indeed" — risen in his mystical body, the church; for which, in his natural body, he died and rose again. Then his work is done — redemption is complete; the fullness of his glory, as the Savior of sinners, is consummated, and the year of his redeemed is come. O, may our eyes see that endless year! May our feet stand in thy gates, O Jerusalem; to have part with them that shall keep that feast!

Brethren, what shall we do that we may rise to that resurrection of life, and belong to that blessed company? I have time but for one brief answer, "Seek those things which are above, where Christ sitteth on the right hand of God. Set your *affections* on things above, not on things on the earth." Make Christ your heart's treasure and hope, and he will make you, and keep you as his own dear treasure; and at last will receive you unto himself, as the crown-jewels of his kingdom.

BIBLIOGRAPHY

C. P. McIlvaine, in Henry C. Fish: *Pulpit Eloquence.* pp. 442-456
Alexander Maclaren: *Exposition of Holy Scripture. St. Luke XIII-XXIV.* 362-372. Also, in his *After the Resurrection,* pp. 15-27
A. G. Mortimer: *Jesus and the Resurrection.* Philadelphia, 1898. pp. 153-159
Canon Newboldt, in *Christian World Pulpit* Vol. 43. April 19, 1893. pp. 245-248
Charles H. Spurgeon: *Metropolitan Tabernacle Pulpit.* Vol. 41. No. 2408. 1895.

CHARLES PETTIT McILVAINE
(1799-1873)

Charles P. McIlvaine was the son of a distinguished merchant who served in the United States Senate from 1823 to 1826. The future bishop was educated at the college of New Jersey, now Princeton University; at the very early age of twenty-three, served as Chaplain of the United States Senate, and at the same time was the Professor of Geography, History, and Ethics at the West Point Military Academy, 1825-1827. After various ministries, he was appointed the Professor of the Evidences of Christianity in the University of the City of New York 1831, which led to his publishing one of the outstanding works of Christian Apologetics of that time, *Evidences of Christianity in Their External Division.* (Incidentally what has happened to these various Chairs or Professorships of Christian Evidences that could be found in so many of our great institutions a century ago?) When he was only thirty-three years of age, 1832, he was appointed Bishop in the Protestant Episcopal Church for the State of Ohio, and carried on a mighty, often strongly opposed, work of encouraging the clergy, defending the faith, establishing new churches and in every way adorning the doctrine of God. Increasing ill health led him to take frequent trips abroad, and on the last one, death overcame him while he was in Florence, Italy. Unique for an American clergyman, his funeral service was held in Westminster Abbey.

THE STONE ROLLED AWAY
by
C. H. Spurgeon

"The angel of the Lord descended from heaven, and came and rolled back the stone from the door, and sat upon it."
— Matthew 28:2

As the holy women went towards the sepulchre in the twilight of the morning, desirous to embalm the body of Jesus, they recollected that the huge stone at the door of the tomb would be a great impediment in their way, and they said one to another, "Who shall roll us away the stone?" That question gathers up the mournful enquiry of the whole universe. They seem to have put into language the great sigh of universal manhood, "Who shall roll us away the stone?" In man's path of happiness lies a huge rock, which completely blocks up the road. Who among the mighty shall remove the barrier? Philosophy attempted the task, but miserably failed. In the ascent to immortality the stone of doubt, uncertainty, and unbelief, stopped all progress. Who could upheave the awful mass, and bring life and immortality to light? Men, generation after generation, buried their fellows; the all-devouring sepulchre swallowed its myriads. Who could stay the daily slaughter, or give a hope beyond the grave? There was a whisper of resurrection, but men could not believe in it. Some dreamed of a future state, and talked of it in mysterious poetry, as though it were all imagination and nothing more. In darkness and in twilight, with many fears and few guesses at the truth, men continued to enquire, "Who shall roll us away the stone?" Men had an indistinct feeling that this world could not be all, that there must be another life, that intelligent creatures could not all have come into this world that they might perish; it was hoped, at any rate, that there was something beyond the fatal river. It scarce could be that none returned from Avernus: there surely must be a way out of the sepulchre. Difficult as the pathway might be, men hoped that surely there must be some return from the land of death-shade; and the question was therefore ever rising to the heart, if not to the lips, Where is the coming man? Where is the predestined deliverer? Where is he, and who is he, that shall roll us away the stone?

To the women there were three difficulties. The stone of itself was huge; it was stamped with the seal of the law; it was guarded by the representatives of power. To mankind there were the same three difficulties. Death itself was a huge stone not to be moved by any strength known to mortals: that death was evidently sent of God as a penalty for offences against his law — how could it therefore be averted, how removed? The red seal of God's vengeance was set upon that sepulchre's mouth — how should that seal be broken? Who could roll the stone away? Moreover, demon forces, and powers of hell, were watching the sepulchre to prevent escape — who could encounter these and bear departed souls like a prey from between the lion's teeth? It was a dreary question, "Who shall roll us away the stone from the sepulchre? Can these dry bones live? Shall our departed ones be restored to us? Can the multitudes of our race who have gone down to Hades ever return from the land of midnight and confusion?" So asked all heathendom, "Who?" and echo answered, "Who?" No answer was given to sages and kings, but the women who loved the Saviour found an answer. They came to the tomb of Christ, but it was empty, for Jesus had risen. Here is the answer to the world's enquiry — there is another life; bodies will live again, for Jesus lives. O mourning Rachel, refusing to be comforted, "Refrain thy voice from weeping, and thine eyes from tears: for thy work shall be rewarded, and they shall come again from the land of the enemy." Sorrow no longer, ye mourners, around the grave, as those that are without hope; for since Jesus Christ is risen, the dead in Christ shall rise also. Wipe away those tears, for the believer's grave is no longer the place for lamentations, it is but the passage to immortality; it is but the robing-room in which the spirit shall put aside for awhile her garments, travel-worn with her earthly journey, to put them on again on a brighter morrow, when they shall be fair and white as no fuller on earth could make them.

I purpose, this morning, to talk a little concerning the resurrection of our exalted Lord Jesus; and that the subject may the more readily interest you, I shall, first of all, *bid this stone which was rolled away, preach to you;* and then shall invite you *to hear the angel's homily from his pulpit of stone.*

I. FIRST, LET THE STONE PREACH.

It is not at all an uncommon thing to find in Scriptures stones bidden to speak. Great stones have been rolled as witnesses against the people; stones and beams out of the wall have been called upon to testify to sin. I shall call this stone as a witness to valuable truths of which it was the symbol. The river of our thought divides into six streams.

1. First, the stone rolled must evidently be regarded as *the door of the sepulchre removed.* Death's house was firmly secured by a huge stone; the angel removed it, and the living Christ came forth. The massive door, you will observe, was taken away from the grave — not merely opened, but unhinged, flung aside, rolled away; and henceforth death's ancient prison-house is without a door. The saints shall pass in, but they shall not be shut in. They shall tarry there as in an open cavern, but there is nothing to prevent their coming forth from it in due time. As Samson, when he slept in Gaza, and was beset by foes, arose early in the morning, and took up upon his shoulders the gates of Gaza — post, and bar, and all — and carried all away, and left the Philistine stronghold open and exposed, so has it been done unto the grave by our Master, who, having slept out his three days and nights, according to the divine decree, arose in the greatness of his strength, and bore away the iron gates of the sepulchre, tearing every bar from its place. The removal of the imprisoning stone was the outward type of our Lord's having plucked up the gates

of the grave — post, bar, and all — thus exposing that old fortress of death and hell, and leaving it as a city stormed and taken, and henceforth bereft of power. Remember that our Lord was committed to the grave as a hostage. "He died for our sins." Like a debt they were imputed to him. He discharged the debt of obligation due from us to God, on the tree; he suffered to the full, the great substitutionary equivalent for our suffering, and then he was confined in the tomb as a hostage until his work should be fully accepted. That acceptance would be notified by his coming forth from durance vile; and that coming forth would become our justification — "He rose again for our justification." If he had not fully paid the debt he would have remained in the grave. If Jesus had not made effectual, total, final atonement, he must have continued a captive. But he had done it all. The "It is finished," which came from his own lips, was established by the verdict of Jehovah, and Jesus was set free. Mark him as he rises, not breaking prison like a felon who escapes from justice, but coming leisurely forth like one whose time of gaol-delivery is come; rising, it is true, by his own power, but not leaving the tomb without a sacred permit — the heavenly officer from the court of heaven is deputed to open the door to him, by rolling away the stone, and Jesus Christ, completely justified, rises to prove that all his people are, in him, completely justified, and the work of salvation is for ever perfect. The stone is rolled from the door of the sepulchre, as if to show that Jesus has so effectually done the work that nothing can shut us up in the grave again. The grave has changed its character; it has been altogether anni-hilated, and put away as a prison-house, so that death to the saints is no longer a punishment for sin, but an entrance into rest. Come, brethren, let us rejoice in this. In the empty tomb of Christ, we see sin for ever put away: we see, therefore, death most effectually destroyed. Our sins were the great stone which shut the mouth of the sepulchre, and held us captives in death, and darkness, and despair. Our sins are now for ever rolled away, and hence death is no longer a dungeon dark and drear, the ante-chamber of hell, but the rather it is a perfumed bed-chamber, a withdrawing room, the vestibule of heaven. For as surely as Jesus rose, so must his people leave the dead: there is nothing to prevent the resurrection of the saints. The stone which could keep us in the prison has been rolled away. Who can bar us in when the door itself is gone? Who can confine us when every barricade is taken away?

> "Who shall rebuild for the tyrant his prison?
> The sceptre lies broken that fell from his hands;
> The stone is removed; the Lord is arisen:
> The helpless shall soon be released from their bands."

2. In the second place, regard the stone as *a trophy set up.* As men of old set up memorial stones, and as at this day we erect columns to tell of great deeds of prowess, so that stone rolled away was, as it were, before the eyes of our faith consecrated that day as a memorial of Christ's eternal victory over the powers of death and hell. They thought that they had vanquished him; they deemed that the Crucified was overcome. Grimly did they smile as they saw his motionless body wrapped in the winding-sheet and put away in Joseph's new tomb; but their joy was fleeting; their boastings were but brief, for at the appointed moment he who could not see corruption rose and came forth from beneath their power. His heel was bruised by the old serpent, but on the resurrection morning he crushed the dragon's head.

> "Vain the stone, the watch, the seal,
> Christ has burst the gates of hell;
> Death in vain forbids his rise,
> Christ hath open'd Paradise.
>
> Lives again our glorious King!
> 'Where, O death, is now thy sting?'
> Once he died our souls to save;
> 'Where's thy victory, boasting grave?'"

Brethren beloved in Christ, as we look at yonder stone, with the angel seated upon it, it rises before us as a monument of Christ's victory over death and hell, and it becomes us to remember that his victory was achieved for us, and the fruits of it are all ours. We have to fight with sin, but Christ has overcome it. We are tempted by Satan: Christ has given Satan a defeat. We by-and-by shall leave this body; unless the Lord come speedily, we may expect to gather up our feet like our fathers, and go to meet our God; but death is vanquished for us, and we can have no cause to fear. Courage, Christian soldiers, you are encountering a vanquished enemy: remember that the Lord's victory is a guarantee for yours. If the Head conquers, the members shall not be defeated. Let not sorrow dim your eyes; let no fears trouble your spirit; you must conquer, for Christ has conquered. Awaken all your powers to the conflict, and nerve them with the hope of victory. Had you seen your Master defeated, you might expect yourself to be blown like chaff before the wind; but the power by which he overcame he lends to you. The Holy Ghost is in you; Jesus Himself has promised to be with you always, even to the end of the world, and the mighty God is your refuge. You shall surely overcome through the blood of the Lamb. Set up that stone before your faith's eye this morning, and say, "Here my Master conquered hell and death, and in his name and by his strength I shall be crowned, too, when the last enemy is destroyed."

3. For a third use of this stone, observe that here is *a foundation laid*. That stone rolled away from the sepulchre, typifying and certifying as it does the resurrection of Jesus Christ, is a foundation-stone for Christian faith. The fact of the resurrection is the key-stone of Christianity. Disprove the resurrection of our Lord, and our holy faith would be a mere fable; there would be nothing for faith to rest upon if he who died upon the tree did not also rise again from the tomb; then "your faith is vain;" said the apostle, "ye are yet in your sins," while "they also which are fallen asleep in Christ are perished." All the great doctrines of our divine religion fall asunder like the stones of an arch when the key-stone is dislodged, in a common ruin they are all overthrown, for all our hope hinges upon that great fact. If Jesus

rose, then is this gospel what it professes to be; if he rose not from the dead, then is it all deceit and delusion. But, brethren, that Jesus rose from the dead is a fact better established than almost any other in history. The witnesses were many: they were men of all classes and conditions. None of them ever confessed himself mistaken or deceptive. They were so persuaded that it was the fact, that the most of them suffered death for bearing witness to it. They had nothing to gain by such a witnessing; they did not rise in power, nor gain honour or wealth; they were truthful, simple-minded men who testified what they had seen and bore witness to that which they had beheld. The resurrection is a fact better attested than any event recorded in any history whether ancient or modern. Here is the confidence of the saints; our Lord Jesus Christ, who witnessed a good confession before Pontius Pilate, and was crucified, dead, and buried, rose again from the dead, and after forty days ascended to the throne of God. We rest in him; we believe in him. If he had not risen, we had been of all men most miserable to have been his followers. If he had not risen, his atonement would not have been proved sufficient. If he had not risen, his blood would not have been to us proven to be efficacious for the taking away of sin; but as he has risen, we build upon this truth; all our confidence we rest upon it, and we are persuaded that —

> "Raised from the dead, he goes before;
> He opens heaven's eternal door;
> To give his saints a blest abode,
> Near their Redeemer and their God."

My dear hearers, are you resting your everlasting hopes upon the resurrection of Jesus Christ from the dead? Do you trust in him, believing that he both died and rose again for you? Do you place your entire dependence upon the merit of his blood certified by the fact of his rising again? If so, you have a foundation of fact and truth, a foundation against which the gates of hell shall not prevail; but if you are building upon anything that you have done, or anything that priestly hands can do for you, you are building upon the sands which shall be swept away by the all-devouring flood, and you and your hopes too shall go down into the fathomless abyss wrapped in the darkness of despair. Oh, to build upon the living stone of Christ Jesus! Oh, to rest on him who is a tried corner-stone, elect, precious! This is to build safely, eternally, and blessedly.

4. A fourth voice from the stone is this: here is *rest provided*. The angel seemed to teach us that as he sat down upon the stone. How leisurely the whole resurrection was effected! How noiselessly, too! What an absence of pomp and parade! The angel descended, the stone was rolled away, Christ rose, and then the angel sat down on the stone. He sat there silently and gracefully, breathing defiance to the Jews and to their seal, to the Roman legionaries and their spears, to death, to earth, to hell. He did as good as say, "Come and roll that stone back again, ye enemies of the risen One. All ye infernal powers, who thought to prevail against our ever-living Prince, roll back that stone again, if so ye dare or can!" The angel said not this in words, but his stately and quiet sitting upon the stone meant all that and more. The Master's work is done, and done for ever, and this stone, no more to be used, this unhinged door, no more employed to shut in the charnel house, is the type that "it is finished" — finished so as never to be undone, finished so as to last eternally. Yon resting angel softly whispers to us, "Come hither, and rest also." There is no fuller, better, surer, safer rest for the soul than in the fact that the Saviour in whom we trust has risen from the dead. Do you mourn departed friends today? O come and sit upon this stone, which tells you they shall rise again. Do you soon expect to die? Is the worm at the root? Have you the flush of consumption on your cheek? O come and sit you down upon this stone, and bethink you that death has lost its terror now, for Jesus has risen from the tomb. Come you, too, ye feeble and trembling ones, and breathe defiance to death and hell. The angel will vacate his seat for you, and let you sit down in the face of the enemy. Though you be but a humble woman, or a man broken down, and wan, and languid with long years of weary sickness,

yet may you well defy all the hosts of hell, while resting down upon this precious truth, "He is not here, but he is risen: he has left the dead, no more to die." I was minded, as I thought over this passage of my discourse, of that time when Jacob journeyed to the house of Laban. It is said he came to a place where there was a well, and a great stone lay upon it, and the flocks and herds were gathered round it, but they had no water till one came and rolled away the great stone from the well's mouth, and then they watered the flocks. Even so the tomb of Jesus is like a great well springing up with the purest and most divine refreshment, but until this stone was rolled away, none of the flocks redeemed by blood sould be watered there; but now, every Sabbath day, on the resurrection morning, the first day of the week, we gather round our Lord's open sepulchre, and draw living waters from that sacred well. O ye weary sheep of the fold, O ye who are faint and ready to die, come ye hither; here is sweet refreshment; Jesus Christ is risen: let your comforts be multiplied.

> "Every note with wonders swell,
> Sin o'erthrown, and captived hell;
> Where is hell's once dreaded king?
> Where, O death, thy mortal sting?
> Hallelujah."

5. In the fifth place, that stone was *a boundary appointed*. Do you not see it so? Behold it then, there it lies, and the angel sits upon it. On that side what see you? The guards affrighted, stiffened with fear, like dead men. On this side what see you? The timid trembling women, to whom the angel softly speaks, "Fear not ye: for I know that ye seek Jesus." You see, then, that stone became the boundary between the living and the dead, between the seekers and the haters, between the friends and the foes of Christ. To his enemies his resurrection is "a stone of stumbling, and a rock of offence;" as of old on Mar's Hill, when the sages heard of the resurrection, they mocked. But to his own people, the resurrection is the head-stone of the corner. Our Lord's resurrection is our triumph and delight. The resurrection acts much in

the same manner as the pillar which Jehovah placed between Israel and Egypt: it was darkness to Egypt, but it gave light to Israel. All was dark amidst Egypt's hosts, but all was brightness and comfort amongst Israel's tribes. So the resurrection is a doctrine full of horror to those who know not Christ, and trust him not. What have they to gain by resurrection? Happy were they could they sleep in everlasting annihilation. What have they to gain by Christ's resurrection? Shall he come whom they have despised? Is he living whom they have hated and abhorred? Will he bid them rise, will they have to meet him as a Judge upon the throne? The very thought of this is enough to smite through the loins of kings today; but what will the fact of it be when the clarion trumpet startles all the sons of Adam from their last beds of dust! Oh, the horrors of that tremendous morning, when every sinner shall rise, and the risen Saviour shall come in the clouds of heaven, and all the holy angels with him! Truly there is nothing but dismay for those who are on the evil side of that resurrection stone. But how great the joy which the resurrection brings to those who are on the right side of that stone! How they look for his appearing with daily growing transport! How they build upon the sweet truth that they shall arise, and with these eyes their Saviour see! I would have you ask yourselves, this morning, on which side you are of that boundary stone now. Have you life in Christ? Are you risen with Christ? Do you trust alone in him who rose from the dead? If so, fear not ye: the angel comforts you, and Jesus cheers you; but oh! if you have no life in Christ, but are dead while you live, let the very thought that Jesus is risen, strike you with fear, and make you tremble, for tremble well you may at that which awaits you.

6. Sixthly, I conceive that this stone may be used, and properly too, as *foreshadowing ruin*. Our Lord came into this world to destroy all the works of the devil. Behold before you the works of the devil pictured as a grim and horrible castle, massive and terrible, overgrown with the moss of ages, colossal, stupendous, cemented with blood of men, ramparted by mischief and craft, surrounded with deep trenches, and garrisoned with fiends. A

structure dread enough to cause despair to every one who goeth round about it to count its towers and mark its bulwarks. In the fulness of time our Champion came into the world to destroy the works of the devil. During his life he sounded an alarm at the great castle, and dislodged here and there a stone, for the sick were healed, the dead were raised, and the poor had the gospel preached unto them. But on the resurrection morning the huge fortress trembled from top to bottom; huge rifts were in its walls; and tottering were all its strongholds. A stronger than the master of that citadel had evidently entered it and was beginning to overturn, overturn, overturn, from pinnacle to basement. One huge stone, upon which the building much depended, a corner-stone which knit the whole fabric together, was lifted bodily from its bed and hurled to the ground. Jesus tore the huge granite stone of death from its position, and so gave a sure token that every other would follow. When that stone was rolled away from Jesus' sepulchre, it was a prophecy that every stone of Satan's building should come down, and not one should rest upon another of all that the powers of darkness had ever piled up, from the days of their first apostacy even unto the end. Brethren, that stone rolled away from the door of the sepulchre gives me glorious hope. Evil is still mighty, but evil will come down. Spiritual wickedness reigns in high places; the multitude still clamor after evil; the nations still sit in thick darkness; many worship the scarlet woman of Babylon, others bow before the crescent of Mohammed, and millions bend themselves before blocks of wood and stone; the dark places and habitations of the earth are full of cruelty still; but Christ has given such a shiver to the whole fabric of evil that, depend upon it, every stone will be certain to fall. We have but to work on, use the battering-ram of the gospel, continue each one to keep in his place, and like the hosts around Jericho, to sound the trumpet still, and the day must come when every hoary evil, every colossal superstition, shall be laid low, even with the ground, and the prophecy shall be fulfilled, "Overturn, overturn, overturn it; and it shall be no more, until he come whose right it is; and I will give it him." That loosened stone on which the angel sits is the sure prognostic of the coming doom of everything that is base and vile. Rejoice, ye sons of God, for Babylon's fall draweth near. Sing, O heavens, and rejoice, O earth, for there shall not an evil be spared. Verily, I say unto you, there shall not be one stone left upon another, which shall not be cast down.

Thus has the stone preached to us; we will pause awhile and hear what the angel has to say.

II. THE ANGEL PREACHED two ways: he preached in symbol, and he preached in words.

Preaching *in symbol* is very popular with a certain party nowadays. The gospel is to be seen by the eye, they tell us, and the people are to learn from the change of colours, at various seasons, such as blue, and green, and violet, exhibited on the priest and the altar, and by lace and by candles, and by banners, and by cruets, and shells full of water; they are even to be taught or led by the nose, which is to be indulged with smoke of incense; and drawn by the ears, which are to listen to hideous intonings or to dainty canticles. Now, mark well that the angel was a symbolical preacher, with his brow of lightning and his robe of snow; but you will please to notice for whom the symbols were reserved. He did not say a word to the keepers — not a word. He gave them the symbolical gospel, that is to say, he looked upon them — and his glance was lightning; he revealed himself to them in his snow-white garments, and no more. Mark how they quake and tremble! That is the gospel of symbols; and wherever it comes it condemns. It can do no other. Why, the old Mosaic law of symbols, where did it end? How few ever reached its inner meaning! The mass of Israel fell into idolatry, and the symbolic system became death to them. You who delight in symbols, you who think it is Christian to make the whole year a kind of practical charade upon the life of Christ, you who think that all Christianity is to be taught in semi-dramas, as men perform in theatres and puppet-shows, go your way, for ye shall meet no heaven in that road, no Christ, no life. You shall meet with priests, and formalists, and hypocrites, and into the thick woods, and among the dark mountains of destruction shall ye stumble to your utter ruin. The gospel message is, "Hear, and your soul shall live;" "Incline your ear, and come unto me." This is the life-giving message, "Believe in the Lord Jesus Christ, and thou shalt be saved.' But, O perverse generation, if ye look for symbols and signs, ye shall be deluded with the devil's gospel, and fall a prey to the destroyer.

Now we will listen to the angel's sermon *in words*. Thus only is a true gospel to be delivered. Christ is the Word, and the gospel is a gospel of words and thoughts. It does not appeal to the eye; it appeals to the ear, and to the intellect, and to the heart. It is a spiritual thing, and can only be learned by those whose spirits are awakened to grasp at spiritual truth. The first thing the angel said was, "Fear not ye." Oh! this is the very genius of our risen Saviour's gospel — "Fear not ye." Ye who would be saved, ye who would follow Christ, ye need not fear. Did the earth quake? Fear not ye: God can preserve you though the earth be burned with fire. Did the angel descend in terrors? Fear not ye: there are no terrors in heaven for the child of God who comes to Jesus' cross, and trusts his soul to him who bled thereon. Poor women, is it the dark that alarms you? Fear not ye: God sees and loves you in the dark, and there is nothing in the dark or in the light beyond his control. Are you afraid to come to a tomb? Does a sepulchre alarm you? Fear not ye: you cannot die. Since Christ has risen, though you were dead yet should you live. Oh, the comfort of the gospel! Permit me to say there is nothing in the Bible to make any man fear who puts his trust in Jesus. Nothing in the Bible, did I say? There is nothing in heaven, nothing on earth, nothing in hell, that need make you fear who trust in Jesus. "Fear not ye." The past you need not fear, it is forgiven you; the present you need not fear, it is provided for; the future also is secured by the living power of Jesus. "Because I live," saith he, "ye shall live also." Fear! Why that were comely and seemly when Christ was dead, but now that he lives there remains no space for it? Do you fear your sins? They are all gone, for Christ had not risen if he had not put them all away. What is it you fear? If an angel bids you "Fear not," why will you fear? If every wound of the risen Saviour, and every act of your reigning Lord consoles you, why are you still dismayed? To be doubting, and fearing, and trembling, now that Jesus has risen, is an inconsistent thing in any believer. Jesus is able to succour you in all your temptations; seeing he ever liveth to make intercession for you, he is able to save you to the uttermost: therefore, do not fear.

Notice the next word, "Fear not ye: for I know." What! does an angel know the women's hearts? Did the angel know what Magdalen was about! Do spirits read our spirits? 'Tis well. But oh! 'tis better to remember that our heavenly Father knows. Fear not ye, for God knows what is in your heart. You have never made an avowal of anxiety about your soul, you are too bashful even for that; you have not even proceeded so far as to dare to say that you hope you love Jesus; but God knows your desires. Poor heart, you feel as if you could not trust, and could not do anything that is good; but you do at least desire, you do at least seek. All this God knows; with pleasure he spies out your desires. Does not this comfort you — this great fact of the knowledge of God? I could not read what is in your spirit, and perhaps you could not tell me what is there. If you tried, you would say after you had done, "Well, I did not tell him exactly what I felt. I have missed the comfort I might have had, for I did not explain my case." But there is one who deals with you, and knows exactly where your difficulty is, and what is the cause of your present sorrow. "Fear not ye," for your heavenly Father knows. Lie still, poor patient, for the surgeon knows where the wound is, and what is is that ails thee. Hush, my child, be still upon thy great Parent's bosom, for he knows all; and ought not that content thee, for his care is as infinite as his knowledge?

Then the angel went on to say, "Fear not ye: for I know that ye seek Jesus, which was crucified." There was room for comfort here. They were seeking Jesus, though the world had crucified him. Though the many had turned aside and left him, they were clinging to him in loving loyalty. Now, is there any one here who can say, "Though I am unworthy to be a follower of Christ, and often think that he will reject me, yet there is one thing I am sure of — I would not be afraid of the fear of man for his sake. My sins make me fear, but no man could do it. I would stand at his side if all the world were against him. I would count it my highest honour that the crucified One of the world should be the adored One of my heart. Let all the world cast him out, if he would but take me in, poor unworthy worm as I am, I would never be ashamed to own his blessed and gracious name"? Ah! then, do not fear, for if that is how you feel towards Christ, he will own you in the last great day. If you are willing to own him now, "Fear not ye." I am sure I sometimes feel, when I am looking into my own heart, as if I had neither part nor lot in the matter, and could claim no interest in the Beloved at all; but, then, I do know this, I am not shamed to be put to shame for him; and if I should be charged with being a fanatic and an enthusiast in his cause, I would count it the highest honour to plead guilty to so blessed an impeachment for his dear sake. If this be truly the language of our hearts, we may take courage. "Fear not ye: for I know that ye seek Jesus, which was crucified."

Then he adds, "He is not here: for he is risen." Here is the instruction which the angel gives. After giving comfort, he gives instruction. Your great ground and reason for consolation, seeker, is that you do not seek a dead Christ, and you do not pray to a buried Saviour; he is really alive. Today he is as able to relieve you, if you go to your closet and pray to him, as he was to help the poor blind man when he was on earth. He is as willing today to accept and bless you as he was to bless the leper, or to heal the paralytic. Go to him then at once, poor seeker; go to him with holy confidence, for he is not here, he would be dead if he were — he is risen, living, and reigning, to answer your request.

The angel bade the holy women investigate the empty tomb, but, almost immediately after, he gave them a commission to perform on their Lord's behalf. Now, if any seeker here has been comforted by the thought that Christ lives to save, let him do as the angel said, let him go and tell to others of the good news that he has heard. It is the great means for propagating our holy faith, that all who have learned it should teach it. We have not some ministers set apart, to whom is reserved the sole right of teaching in the Christian church; we have no belief in a clergy and a laity. Believers, ye are all God's *cleros* — all of you. As many of you as believe in Christ are God's clergy, and bound to serve him according to your abilities. Many members there are in the body, but every member has its office; and there is no member in the body of Christ which is to be idle, because forsooth, it cannot do what the Head can do. The foot has its place, and the hand its duty, as well as the tongue and the eye. O you who have learned of Jesus, keep not the blessed secret to yourselves. Today, in some way or other, I pray you make known that Jesus Christ is risen. Pass the watchword round, as the ancient Christtians did. On the first day of the week they said to one another, "The Lord is risen indeed." If any ask you what you mean by it, you will then be able to tell them the whole of the gospel, for this is the essence of the gospel, that Jesus Christ died for our sins, and rose again the third day, according to the Scriptures — died the substitute for us criminals, rose the representative of us pardoned sinners — died that our sins might die, and lives again that our souls may live. Diligently invite others to come and trust Jesus. Tell them that there is life for the dead in a look at Jesus crucified; tell them that the look is a matter of the soul, it is a simple confidence; tell them that none ever did confide in Christ and were cast away; tell them what you have felt as the result of your trusting Jesus, and who can tell, many disciples will be added to his church, a risen Saviour will be glorified, and you will be comforted by what you have seen! The Lord follow these feeble words with his own blessing, for Christ's sake. Amen.

BIBLIOGRAPHY

Charles H. Spurgeon: *Metropolitan Tabernacle Pulpit.* 1869. Vol. 15. No. 863, pp. 181-192
David G. Burrell: *The Wondrous Cross.* New York. 1898. pp. 269-278
Alfred G. Mortimer: *Jesus and the Resurrection.* New York. 1898. pp. 82-91
W. Robertson Nicoll: *Sunday Evening,* n.d. pp. 163-169

CHARLES HADDON SPURGEON
(1834-1892)

Of all the noted preachers whose sermons are gathered together in this volume, everyone would grant that Charles Haddon Spurgeon stands preeminent above the others in two matters: he regularly preached to more people Sunday after Sunday in his own pulpit, year after year, than any other minister in Great Britain or America. In the second place, the printed sermons of Charles Spurgeon have had a wider circulation than those of any other preacher of modern times, and still continue to enjoy an extensive public.

Charles Haddon Spurgeon was born June 19, 1834, in Kelvedon, Essex, but spent most of his early years with his grandfather, a clergyman, James Spurgeon, of Stambourne. His early schooling was scattered, but included Greek and Latin, and enabled him to teach school for awhile. His thorough conversion in a primitive Methodist Chapel at Colchester, on a winter Sunday morning, upon hearing a very poor sermon on Isaiah 45:22 (January 6, 1850), is too well-known to require repeating here. Spurgeon began preaching as early as October, 1851, under the compulsion that he must preach the Gospel. In fact, in the first twelve months of this early ministry, in Waterbeach, he preached three hundred times in twelve months! As with Joseph Parker, Campbell Morgan, and many others, so with this young man, his fame spread rapidly, and soon even reached to London. When he was but nineteen years of age, November 1853, he was asked to preach at the New Park Street Chapel, London, to which he was soon called, April 19, 1854. This is where the famous author of a great book on Types, Benjamin Keach, was once pastor, followed, somewhat later, by the distinguished theologian and commentator, John Gill, who was minister from 1720-1771, and John Rippon, who was the pastor for sixty-three years. Here, shortly before Spurgeon came, the minister was Dr. Joseph Angus, later to become the well-known head of a theological seminary. The congregation had tragically dwindled, but with the advent of Spurgeon the building soon was crowded again, so much so it was decided that a new structure must be erected. While the new church edifice was under construction, Spurgeon preached in Exeter Hall every Sunday morning and evening, with such success that the *London Globe* reported that "A traveller along the Strand, about six o'clock on a Sunday evening, would wonder what could be the meaning of a crowd which literally stopped the progress of public vehicles and sent unhappy pedestrians round the by-streets in utter hopelessness of getting along the wider thoroughfare. Since the days of Wesley and Whitfield — whose honoured names seem to be in danger of being thrown into the shade by this new candidate for public honours — so thoroughly a religious furor has never existed. Mr. Spurgeon is likely to become a great preacher; at present his fervid and impassioned eloquence sometimes leads him a little astray, and sometimes there is a want of solemnity which mars the beauty of his singularly happy style."

The enlarged chapel, however, at New Park Street was still not able to accommodate the crowds that wanted to hear Mr. Spurgeon, so it was decided to move to another part of London, where was erected the great Metropolitan Tabernacle seating 5,000 people, the largest non-conformist place of worship in Great Britain.

Spurgeon not only felt the divine call to be continually preaching the Gospel upon every possible occasion, but while yet in his twenties he became convinced that his ministry could be enlarged through the printed page, and as early as 1855 began publishing a weekly sermon in the *New Park Street Pulpit,* later becoming the *Metropolitan Tabernacle Pulpit,* extending to over forty volumes, some of them of 600 pages in length. Thousands of these sermons were separately printed, and then republished in series, such as Christmas Sermons, Sermons on the Second Advent of Christ, etc. Upon everything that Mr. Spurgeon touched, the blessing of God seemed to rest in an unusual degree. During his ministry at the Metropolitan Tabernacle, he received 14,691 members.

Soon Mr. Spurgeon felt the call to establish a training school for ministers, which became Spurgeon's College, and so successful was this work that before he died, over 900 Baptist ministers in Great Britain had had their training there. There is no need to enumerate his numerous other activities, the Colportage work, the orphanages, the great band of visitors which went out from his church constantly, etc. Still Spurgeon had energy for one more extensive undertaking, the publishing of a magazine, *Sword and Trowel,* most of which was written by himself, a magazine that continued for twenty-six years under his editorship.

I wonder if I might add a personal word here. There are probably more biographies of Mr. Spurgeon, including the great four-volume autobiography finished by Mrs. Spurgeon, than there are for any other minister of modern times, with the possible exception of Mr. D. L. Moody, and even then I would not be surprised if there are more pages of biographical material in the books about Mr. Spurgeon than in the volumes gathering around the great evangelist Mr. Moody. In spite of all this, my own conviction is that the great definitive life of Mr. Spurgeon has not yet been written. There are untapped resources available for someone willing to dedicate himself to this task. There are scores of personal anecdotes in Mr. Spurgeon's sermons that have never been incorporated in any biography of him, and the rich pages of the *Sword and Trowel* have practically been untouched by his biographers.

Dr. Dinsdale T. Young in his delightful autobiography, has a paragraph regarding Spurgeon worth quoting here. "Full forty times I heard the incomparable Puritan. What a scene was the Tabernacle whenever he appeared! At his week-evening service, when repeatedly I heard him, three thousand people would frequently gather. I have lectured on C. H. Spurgeon some hundreds of times, and have written considerably of him. But I increasingly feel that it is impossible to say too much of this prophet of God. I deem him, for all the apostolic elements of the pulpit, the greatest of English preachers. Was there ever such abandon in a speaker? Was ever great preaching delivered with such selfless ease? Was ever a minister of Christ more entirely lost in his work? You felt that this man cared not a jot for anything but the honour of his Lord and the salvation of his hearers. And how that matchless voice did its work! It was the grandest voice I ever listened to. It was sonorous and sweet. Its power and its gentleness combined to evoke one's wonder and delight. How expository C. H. Spurgeon was! How always evangelical! How experimental! What a master of the precious art of homiletics! What command of multifarious illustration! What loveliness of phrase! What flashes of poetry! What proverbial sayings! What grace and power of pulpit-prayer!"

THE RESURRECTION APPEARANCES OF CHRIST
by
Doremus A. Hayes

We have come to the end of the list of the appearances of the Lord from the resurrection to the ascension. At this point we would like to make six general observations concerning these appearances. First, we have found them to be ten in number. We name them now in order. First, the appearance to Mary Magdalene in the garden. Second, the appearance to the women on the public road. Third, the appearance to Peter and the private interview in his room. Fourth, the manifestation to the two disciples on the way to Emmaus and in their home. Fifth, the first meeting with the apostolic company and others on the evening of that first Easter day. Sixth, the second meeting with the entire apostolic band of eleven and others with them in the same place on the next Sunday evening. Seventh, the manifestation on the shore of the sea of Tiberias. Eighth, the appointed meeting on the mountain top giving the great commission to more than five hundred brethren at once. Ninth, the appearance to James. Tenth, the final meeting with the eleven at Bethany and the ascension from the ridge over against Bethany, marking the end of his personal instructions to to the leaders of the church and the close of his physical manifestations to believers.

When Paul parted from the elders at Miletus, they sorrowed most of all that they should see his face no more. They clung to him and kissed him and hardly could bear to let him go. When Jesus ascended until the clouds received him from the apostles' sight they looked steadfastly into heaven until he had disappeared, and then they fell on their knees and worshipped this Ascended

Lord; and then they returned to Jerusalem with great joy and were continually blessing God. No sorrow here that they should see his face no more; but great joy he had ascended to his Father and their Father and was preparing for them a home.

They realized that the gospel of the resurrection was a gospel of great joy. It was the greatest reason for rejoicing ever given to the race. In the eighth century John of Damascus put their faith into his verse,

> "Now let the heavens be joyful,
>   Let earth her song begin;
> Let the round world keep triumph,
>   And all that is therein;
> Invisible and visible,
>   Their notes let all things blend,
> *For Christ the Lord* is risen
> *Our Joy that hath no end.*"

Second, while ten of these appearances are recorded in our New Testament, we cannot be sure that this list is complete. No one of our authorities gives the entire list of ten. Mark records only three of them. Matthew gives only two. We think that Luke has the account of four. Paul tells us of another appearance, not recorded anywhere in our Gospels, the appearance to James. Paul's entire list for this period includes five appearances. He mentions more than any one of our Evangelists. If there were these ten appearances and no one of our authorities gives them all but on the contrary each of them omits one half or more than one half of the list, may not each of the authorities have omitted to mention other appearances of which they knew as well as these?

If Matthew records only two appearances and Luke records four entirely different ones and John adds to this list of six, three other appearances of which neither Matthew nor Luke have made any mention and then Paul tells us about another not mentioned in any of our Gospels, if any new writer in the apostolic times had chosen to take this theme, might we not have expected that he would have told us about still other appearances well known at that time but unrecorded by any other? We are not told at any place in our narratives that Mary the mother ever saw the Risen Lord. Surely if he had appeared to Mary Magdalene he would have appeared to her. Surely if he appeared to other women he would appear to his mother too. The private interviews with Peter and with James are merely mentioned in our Scriptures. We are told nothing in detail about them. Possibly the interview with the mother was felt to be too sacred to be made public at all.

Enough appearances have been recorded to settle the fact of the resurrection. That was all which each of our writers was interested to do. No one of them suggests that he is making a complete statement of the facts in the forty days. What he states is a sufficient foundation for the faith. We might have thought that any one of our writers had made a complete statement of the case, if his narrative had stood alone. As it is we find that all the other writers have supplemented his facts. We have no compelling reason to think that when we have put all our narratives together and have made up from all of them our list of ten appearances we thereby have exhausted the number granted at this time. There may have been still others which were of such a private character or which were of such comparatively minor importance to the general church that none of our writers cared to mention them.

We also should remember in this connection that the earliest of our gospel narratives is an unfinished one. The close of the Gospel according to Mark has been lost. We do not know how much of the original manuscript has disappeared. Zahn, Voight, and Burkitt have suggested that possibly as much has been lost as we have now remaining, or at least that a considerable portion of the narrative is lacking at the present time. We may not be sure of that, and yet we may regret exceedingly that even a fragment or a page is missing at just the point which Mark had reached in our manuscripts. It would seem almost certain that he would have given us added information concerning the resurrection appearances. It may be that he would have added to their number considerably. It may be that he would have given us a full account of the appearance to Peter, since he is reproducing the reminiscences of Peter in his book. Streeter, Harnack, and others have suggested that John 21 represents the missing end of Mark. We never shall know how much information concerning the resurrection we have lost with this lost portion of Mark's narrative. Whether he recorded them or not we hope there were other appearances.

We hope that there was the personal appearance to Mary the mother. Surely the sword had pierced through her soul as through no other at the crucifixion. There was no sorrow like unto her sorrow when her son was laid in the grave. Would the risen Jesus appear to Mary Magdalene and Mary the mother of James and Salome and the wife of Cleopas and other women who were much less closely bound to him by natural ties and leave his own mother alone?

We suggested that John hastened away to tell Mary the good news as soon as the resurrection hope had been born within him at the sight of the undisturbed graveclothes, and that Peter thus had been left alone at the time of the Lord's appearance to him. Jesus had entrusted Mary to the keeping of John, but would he be any less interested in her comforting and restoration to hope and to faith than was John? Surely if anyone had been inventing the story of these resurrection appearances, he would have put among them an appearance to Mary the mother, the most highly favored among women, the bride of the Most High, whose son was called the Son of the Most High. No account of any such appearances is given, but we think that her son would not forget her now. She would be given a share in the joy which his resurrection brought.

We hope that there was some private conversation between Lazarus and his Lord. What a privilege it would have been to listen as those two talked, Lazarus raised from the dead and Jesus risen from the dead! What mysteries of the unseen world they may have meditated upon together. Lazarus had been called back into the earthly and fleshly life. Jesus had risen into the life immortal. Lazarus still faced toward death and Hades. Jesus held the keys of death and Hades in his hand. Lazarus had been snatched back out of the grasp of death. Jesus had triumphed gloriously over death.

All other resurrections so-called had been merely reanimations and resuscitations. Those raised from the dead by Elijah and Elisha, like the daughter of Jairus, and the son of the widow of Nain, and Lazarus the brother of Martha and Mary and the friend of Jesus, simply had resumed the conditions of their former life. They were called back from the dead only to live awhile and then again to die. The resurrection of Jesus was of a different sort and of a higher order. They were raised to physical life in a physical body. He was raised in a spiritual body to the enjoyment of life eternal. He was raised never to die. He was in a true sense the firstborn from the dead, the first begotten from the dead, the first fruits of them who slept. The resurrection of Jesus was a veritable resurrection, the first in the history of the race. He could say, not only, "I have been raised from the dead," but also, "I am the resurrection and the life." No other resurrected man could say that.

Every other resurrected man still was under death's power and had to face the possibility and the certainty of death again. Every other resurrected man still was liable to suffering and sin, still was in bondage to mortality and pain. Jesus was the first resurrected man to be released from the dominion of death into a life free from pain and infirmity and filled with glorious immortality. He is Death's conqueror. He has the keys of death and of Hades. He has power over the whole realm of death. He can unlock the doors of the tomb and set free whom he will. We can imagine how in private conversation with Lazarus these things would be made plain to him, and his faith in the power of the resurrection of Jesus would be his hope of immortal life for himself in heaven.

Then, how about John? Jesus loved John as he loved no other. Were there not personal conferences between these two in which John saw more deeply into the plan of salvation and into the heart of God than any other apostle ever did? Was he not trained to be the greatest theologian of the Christian church? In view of the fact that all our accounts of the resurrection are so fragmentary and that every new account gives us the story of some new appearance or appearances we may at least suspect and hope that there were these or other appearances unrecorded by any of our authorities.

We note, in the third place, that Luke tells us that all the post-resurrection and pre-ascension appearances occurred within the space of forty days. This interval of time always is a noteworthy one in our Bible. Westcott says: "The space of forty days is always in Scripture a period of solemn waiting followed by issues of momentous interest. When the hope of the world was sheltered by the ark there was rain on the earth for forty days and forty nights. When the people had been rescued from Egypt Moses was forty days on the Mount before he received the Law. For forty days the spies examined the land of Canaan, the image of our heavenly country. For forty days Elijah tarried in Horeb before he obtained the revelation of God. For so long repentance was offered to the Ninevites; for so long Ezekiel announced the typical punishment of God's people. Only once again the same period is mentioned in the Bible, where it is written that the Lord fasted in the wilderness for forty days before he began to proclaim glad tidings to the world. So it was that Christ's ministry ended as it began. The same mysterious measured space in each case separated and united the old and the new."

Forty days of temptation at the beginning of the ministry; forty days of triumph at the close. At the beginning forty days with the Fiend and the desert beasts. At the close forty days with the Father and the disciples of the new faith. In the forty days in the wilderness Jesus completed his preparation for his life ministry. In the forty days of the resurrection appearances the disciples were prepared for the preaching of their life ministry, the proclamation of their message of the conquering Christ. Jesus was full of the Holy Spirit when he went into the wilderness temptation; the disciples were all filled with the Holy Spirit in the Pentacostal baptism ten days after the Ascension.

If the resurrection took place on Easter Sunday, April 9, A.D.

30, the ascension took place on Friday, May 19. Pentecost would then come on Sunday, May 28. Between the resurrection and the ascension there were five weeks and five days, or forty days in all, "a period of solemn waiting followed by issues of momentous interest." The next ten days must have been days of still more solemn waiting, and yet we are told that they were days of great joy.

We note in the fourth place that the resurrection appearances of the Lord may be divided into two groups geographically, those in Judea and those in Galilee. Seven of the ten recorded appearances were in Judea and three were in Galilee. The three in Galilee were the appearance by the sea, the appearance to James, and the appearance on the mount of the Great Commission. Of these the last was of the greatest importance to the general church.

Chronologically, all the recorded appearances might be divided into three groups, a first group of six appearances in Judea, a second group of three appearances in Galilee, followed by the final appearance to the eleven in Judea again. Of the seven appearances in Judea, the first five were on the first Easter Sunday, the sixth on the Sunday following, and the tenth and final one, forty days after the first; and we cannot definitely date the seventh, eighth, and ninth. The seventh was separated from the sixth by an interval of at least one week and possibly two. The eighth probably was separated from the seventh by an interval of several days and possibly a week or more.

Four of these appearances were to large companies of people, in one case to more than five hundred at one time, and in all of the four cases including either all or a majority of the apostolic band. One appearance was to seven of the disciples together. One was to a group of women. One was to two disciples, and three were to individuals, Mary Magdalene, Peter, and James.

We notice in the fifth place that all of the resurrection appearances, including the Ascension, were granted to believers or disciples, with the possible exception of that to James, who was more than half convinced. As far as we can gather from our records no unbeliever and no enemy of the faith ever had a glimpse of the resurrected Lord up to this time. The appearances to Mary Magdalene, to Peter, and to James doubtless were altogether private manifestations. The two appearances to the disciples at Jerusalem were within closed doors, the Jews being excluded because of fear. There were seven disciples at the sea of Tiberias. There were above five hundred disciples at the appointed mount of meeting; but we have seen that they probably were very carefully selected and that the meeting was in a secluded place where they might be free from any intrusion. Only the eleven and a few other faithful disciples were with the Master on that last night at Bethany, and only this chosen company saw his ascension in the early morning on Olivet.

Now if the appearance to the women on their way from the tomb to the city was on the public road there might have been other passers-by who saw the figure of the resurrected Lord. This appearance, however, may have been on some private path rather than on the public highway, and at any rate it was in the very early morning and before many people would be astir. We have no hint in the narratives that any others than the women recognized the Resurrected One. On the way to Emmaus we suppose that the three pilgrims must have passed many people, but as the two disciples did not recognize the Master as they walked on the road, we may be sure that no one of the multitude did. To everyone who glanced at him he was a pedestrian rabbi and nothing more. So that we conclude that the manifestations of the Risen Lord were to loving friends alone.

We can see at least five reasons for this fact. In the first place, in all probability it would have been of no benefit to his enemies if he had appeared to them. Did not Abraham say to the rich man in the parable, "If they hear not Moses and the prophets, neither will they be persuaded, though one rose from the dead"? Had not the raising of Lazarus from the dead led only to more bitter hostility on their part? It had not helped them to faith. It had made them more determined to make an end of Jesus. Suppose now that Jesus had appeared in the temple courts or on the Jerusalem streets or in a session of the Sanhedrin. Would they not have cried out at once that he was an imposter? Would they not all the more obstinately have clung to their unbelief? Their condemnation would have been the greater if the Risen One had appeared to them and they had rejected him, and there was no reason to think that since they had refused the truth concerning him already given them they would be persuaded though he showed himself to them risen from the dead.

Therefore, in the second place, it was in mercy to them that this revelation of the Resurrected One was not made to their blinded eyes and hardened hearts. It would have been spiritually injurious to them, and therefore it was mercifully withheld.

"Let us for a moment imagine the spiritual and glorified body of the Redeemer exposed to the irreverent or malignant scrutiny of those who had just before been shouting, Crucify him! Crucify him! What would they have said or done? Probably they would have declared that he had never really died. Impossible as it would be for any human being to survive the long torture of the cross, superadded to the preparatory scourging with rods, and to the stab of the soldier's spear, much less to move about in perfect health and strength after all this, as Jesus did, the majority of the nation were so abstinately set against the man who had balked them of the Messiah they wanted (a great earthly conqueror), that they would have accepted any lie that might serve as a pretext for not believing the actual facts.

"As they gave out that his trembling, terror-struck disciples, in their despair, stole away his body, removing for that purpose a huge stone with which the tomb was closed, while sixty Roman legionaries, in spite of the penalty of death for sleeping at their post, all slept so profoundly that not one of them perceived the long and laborious transaction so as to give the alarm that would at once have prevented it; so they would not have scrupled to give out that he had never been really crucified, or that his body had been saved from the torture of the cross by the aid of the demon which they said pessessed him. Or if all these pretexts had broken down, if they were forced to acknowledge that he had really been crucified and had really died, they would have said that the body with which he now appeared was not a real body, but only a specter or apparition.

"And as it would have been inconsistent with the plan of redemption that the Redeemer should suffer a second time, and as it would, therefore, have been necessary to preserve his sacred person inviolate, should they again attempt to seize him, his immunity from insult and injury would have been, no doubt, wrested by those inveterate unbelievers into a proof that the body they were no longer allowed to desecrate must be unreal. So that any possible display of the Risen Savior to the unbelieving nation, made in such a way as not to be absolutely incompatible with the dignity and glory of his new existence, would have been literally a difficulty in the way of their being brought to accept his claims, rather than a recommendation of those claims to their acceptance. It would have been a derogation from the Savior's majesty, without any adequate counterbalancing result." (Reichel).

Then, in the third place, it would have been inconsistent with the whole method of the incarnation if the Lord had granted to the doubting Jews any manifestation of celestial splendor or heavenly being or power which would have compelled their reluctant faith in him. He had refused to give them any sign from heaven again and again in his ministry. He had told them that no sign would be vouchsafed to that evil and adulterous generation. He had refused to call twelve legions of angels to his help. He had refused to come down from the cross at their suggestion. He would compel no man's faith by any gross material manifestations of his Messianic power. Miracle faith was not a substantial or enduring faith. The Christ would build his church not upon wonder or astonishment or fear. He would build his church upon nothing but love. Miracles might strengthen love, but they would not create it. Even this crowning miracle of the resurrection could not be used to create a personal bond of affection between Jesus and any followers. It must simply strengthen such bonds of affection as already had been established.

Let that be a fourth reason why the resurrection appearances were granted to believers alone. They could be of profit only to those who were spiritually susceptible of the truths the resurrection was to teach. Jesus had said to the eleven in that last discourse in the upper room before the crucifixion, "Yet a little while, and the world seeth me no more; but ye see me: because I live, ye shall live also." Judas, not Iscariot, said unto him, "Lord how is it that thou wilt manifest thyself unto us, and not unto the world?" Jesus answered and said unto him, "If a man love me, he will keep my words: and my Father will love him, and we will come unto him, and make our abode wth him." During the whole period of the earthly incarnation Jesus had been manifested to the world. Men might see him, hear him, handle him as they would; but he had told them that after the resurrection it no longer would be so. No longer would he be subject to the malice of men. He would come only to those who loved him. He would be manifest henceforth not to the world but to his lovers alone. He had said it beforehand, "He that loveth me shall be loved of my Father, and I will love him, and *will manifest myself unto him.*"

Peter preached to Cornelius and his family, "Him God raised up the third day, and showed him openly, not to all the people, but unto witnesses chosen before of God, even to us, who did eat and drink with him after he rose from the dead." Jesus said that those who would be chosen of God for this manifestation were the ones who through all their doubt and their despair yet loved him. He rose from the dead to manifest himself to their love. He would appear, not to Pilate but to Peter; not to Caiaphas but to Cleopas, not to the Jewish rulers or the Roman authorities but to the humble men and women who loved him and had been true to his memory and his teaching.

In the fifth place:

"In withdrawing his sacred and glorified body from the rude gaze and the irreverent attempts of determined unbelievers, our Lord acted on the very maxim which he himself enunciated as the rule of all God's providential dealings, and which the experience of mankind declares to be that rule, To him that hath shall be given, and he shall have more abundantly; while from him that hath not, shall be taken away even that which he seemeth to have. Apply this to the case before us. Obstinate refusal to listen to evidence already given disqualifies for the reception of further evidence. When men show that they will not accept and weigh proofs they already have, it is not God's method to give them more. And this holds good just as much in the concerns of this life as in those of the life to come; just as much in secular as in religious history.

"Is truth attained by contemptuously rejecting all evidence which does not fall in with our prejudices? Do men, who set out with a preconceived theory of what the course of history ought to have been, succeed in throwing light upon its dark places? Are they the authorities to whom the intelligence of our race will bow, and by whom it will be lessoned in the future? I trow not. Those who refuse instruction, no matter on what subject, so far as it is at the time accessible, disqualify themselves for additional instruction, supposing additional instruction to become available. By their own act they limit their own powers, and must not complain of this limitation if their powers lessen or destroy their future possibilities of knowledge or of action." (Reichel)

What end was served by these resurrection appearances? They are so few, only ten of them in all recorded. Of these five occurred on one day. There are only six days in the forty on which any appearances are mentioned. The greater part of the forty days Jesus was invisible. Only at intervals of time did he manifest himself to anyone. What was the purpose of the occasional manifestations? (1) They established the faith of the disciples in the fact that Jesus had been declared to be the Son of God with power by the resurrection from the dead. (2) They gave opportunity for a final interpretation of the Scriptures in the light of their fulfillment in the life and death and resurrection of the Lord. (3) The disciples thus were prepared by personal conviction of the truth of the resurrection and by their personal instruction in the exegesis of the Scriptures to be efficient and successful witnesses and preachers of the new gospel of the crucified and resurrected Savior of the world.

We cannot conceive of any better method of establishing the disciples in the faith upon which the Christian church has been founded. Had Jesus appeared among his followers and lived with them continuously in the old habits of life, sleeping in their homes, walking along their highways, talking with everyone in the old familiarity, resuming in every respect the experiences of the former days, would not the disciples have been tempted to think that there was a real and genuine humanity in Jesus, but there was no more of divinity in him than there was in the resurrected Lazarus? On the other hand, if all the appearances of the Resurrected One had been with divine splendors and manifestations of superhuman powers, would not the disciples have been likely to conclude that Jesus had become the Son of God with power but he had lost his humanity in the transformation?

There was a sufficient variety in these appearances through the forty days to convince them of the real humanity of Jesus and at the same time to make it clear that he was in a spiritual body and belonged to a higher order of existence than Lazarus or any other resurrected one ever had known. As we study these appearances in turn we cannot see any better way than that which they furnished of superinducing upon the old faith in Jesus the man the new faith in Jesus the Lord and Christ. Henceforth they were assured of the bodily resurrection and of the reality of the eternal life.

Let us notice again that these resurrection narratives do not have the marks of works of fiction or unlicensed imagination or extravagant invention. An ingenius fiction writer might have had the risen Lord appear to Caiaphas and curse him as the direct instrument of the crucifixion death and send him out as the Wandering Jew to bear his obloquy through all the coming years. He might have pictured an appearance to Pilate, reproaching him for his cowardice and prophesying his future misfortunes and his final death in disgrace. He surely would have had the Lord appear to the Sanhedrin, sitting on the right hand of power, and coming in the clouds of heaven, making good the promise at the time of his trial and proving that he was indeed the Messiah he had claimed to be. Why do we not read such things in these narratives? Because they did not happen.

The resurrection stories we find in our Gospels have an air of soberness and reality about them. There is nothing ecstatic or incoherent in these accounts. They are not the records made by unbalanced minds. These are plain matter-of-fact people telling just what happened to themselves. They tell how impossible it was for them to believe in the possibility of the resurrection at first. They tell of how some of them doubted the evidence of their own senses until they were forced into their final faith. They tell how Jesus was not immediately recognized by many to whom he appeared, and even by some of his most intimate friends. These are damaging facts, but they are not glossed over. Taken as a whole, these narratives do not seem like the products of partisan prejudice or like unbridled flights of fancy. They have all the artlessness of simple honesty. They furnish just such testimony as the facts would warrant, and such as plain people convinced beyond any question or doubt would give. They have all the signs of veracity.

DOREMUS A. HAYES
(1863-1936)

Doremus Hayes was born in Russellville, Ohio, in 1863. His undergraduate work was done at Ohio Wesleyan, from which he received the A.M. degree in 1884. Proceeding at once to graduate study, he received the Th.D. degree from Boston University in 1887, which school in 1901 honored him with the degree of S.T.D. He was the first member of his family to become attached to the Methodist Church and in that denomination he served throughout the remaining years of his life. He began his teaching in the University of the Pacific and then in the Greek Department of San Jose College, and after further graduate study in Leipsig and Berlin, he became the Professor of Biblical Theology at Iliff Seminary in Colorado in 1895. The following year he was named Professor of English Bible at Garrett Biblical Institute in Evanston, Illinois, where he remained for forty years. From 1912 until his death, he was the Professor of New Testament Interpretation, and for many years also was the Librarian of that institution. Among many other notable preachers of this country, he made an indelible impression upon Dr. Charles E. Jefferson of the Broadway Church, New York, and Dr. Charles R. Brown of Yale. Dr. Hayes was the author of some fifteen volumes, among which are the following: *Paul and His Epistles,* 1915; *John and His Writings,* 1917; *Greek Culture and the Greek New Testament,* 1925; *The Heights of Christian Love* (on I Cor. 15), 1926; *The Heights of Christian Blessedness* (on the Beatitudes), 1928; *The Heights of Christian Devotion* (on the Lord's Prayer), 1930; *The Resurrection Fact,* 1932. I cannot recommend these volumes too highly.

"ALL HAIL"

by
C. H. Spurgeon

"And as they went to tell his disciples, behold, Jesus met them, saying, All hail. And they came and held him by the feet, and worshipped him. Then said Jesus unto them, Be not afraid: go tell my brethren that they go into Galilee, and there shall they see me." — Matthew 28:9, 10

On Sabbath mornings, lately, we have been meditating upon the sorrows of our Lord Jesus Christ. We have been, in thought, travelling with him from dark Gethsemane to still darker Golgotha. We have pictured him under accusation before Caiaphas, Herod, and Pilate; we have, in imagination, heard the cruel shouts of the Jews, "Away with him! Crucify him!" These solemn events have been full of pain to us; even the bliss that comes to us through the cross of Christ has been toned down with intense sorrowfulness as we have thought of the agonies our Saviour there endured. But as soon as we get to the other side of the cross, and realize that Christ has risen from the dead, everything is calm, and quiet, and peaceful. There are none of those rough winds and stormy blasts that come sweeping around us as we stand outside Pilate's palace and Herod's judgment hall. All is spring-like, — summerlike, if you will, — ay, and autumnlike, for there are most luscious fruits to be gathered in the garden wherein was a new sepulchre out of which the living Christ arose in all the glory of his resurrection from the dead.

There was just one painful memory during the interview which Christ had with his disciples, when he said to Peter the third time, "Simon, son of Jonas, lovest thou me?" And "Peter was grieved because he said unto him the third time, Lovest thou me?" But all the rest of the manifestations of our Lord to his disciples were singularly placid, joyful, restful.

So, dear friends, I want it to be with you now as you enter into the spirit of the scene described in our text. I pray that the Master may set you on the other side of the sepulchre, and make you feel as if he breathed upon you as he breathed upon his disciples, and said to you as he said to them, "Peace be unto you!" We need this experience, at least sometimes; for while the lessons to be learned at Calvary are inestimably precious, and it is beyond all things necessary to sorrow over our sin as we see how we are reconciled to God by the death of his Son, yet we must ardently desire to gather all the fruit that grows even on the accursed tree, and part of that fruit will give us the sweet rest of reconciliation through our Lord and Saviour Jesus Christ.

This is the time for fellowship with your Lord, beloved. You cannot tread the winepress with him; you cannot pour out your blood to mingle with him, for the atonement is complete, and needs no suffering on your part; anything added to it would spoil it. But now, on the other side of the tomb, you can stand beside your risen Saviour. He can come into our midst, and say, as he has often done, "Peace be unto you!" As we journey to our homes after this service, we can walk and talk with him as they did who went to Emmaus in company with him. We can take him with us into our daily labours, on the morrow, even as he went to the sea where his disciples were fishing, and taught them how to catch a multitude of fish. Familiar acquaintance with Christ should spring out of the fact that he is no longer dead, that he is not now in the grave, but that he has risen in fulness of life, and that, most wonderful truth of all, that life is in all his people.

I. Our meditation upon this text will, I trust, help us to enjoy fellowship with Christ. Read the beginning of it, and learn from it this first lesson. THE LORD JESUS OFTEN MEETS WITH HIS PEOPLE IN THE WAY OF HOLY SERVICE: "As they went to tell his disciples, behold, Jesus met them."

My brother said, just now in prayer, that we do not expect

actually to meet Jesus in flesh and blood, but we know that there is a great blessedness in store for those who have not seen him with their mortal eyes, and yet have believed in him; and we do expect to meet him, after a spiritual fashion, so that faith can recognize him; nay, more, we know that he is here in his real though invisible presence. We may expect this blessed experience when we are in the way of holy service. I grant you that our Lord Jesus comes to us at other times as well.

> "Sometimes a light surprises
> The Christian while he sings:
> It is the Lord who rises
> With healing in his wings."

Ay; and, sometimes, the light of the Sun of righteousness surprises the Christian when he cannot sing. "Or ever I was aware," says the sweet singer of the blessed Canticle, — "Or ever I was aware, my soul made me like the chariots of Ammi-nadib," for the presence of Christ may be suddenly manifested to his people, and they may be as though they were caught away altogether from earthly scenes, and were with Christ in the heavenly places. We have known this to happen, sometimes, in the lonely night watches; and we have said with David, "When I awake, I am still with thee," even in the darkness of the night. We have known it to happen in the very midst of the hurry and worry of business. On a sudden, everything has been calm and quiet. We could not make it out; it seemed like a Sabbath in the middle of the week, — a very oasis in the wilderness. The Lord Jesus Christ has come to some of us when we have been amidst the busy throng in Cheapside. In fact, there is nothing but sin that can keep him away from us, since he is not dependent upon the ordinary rules that regulate the movement of earthly bodies. He was not so on earth after he had risen from the dead, for though I doubt not that he often came and went just as others did, yet, at other times, he came like an apparition, "the doors being shut," and he could be here and there at his own sweet will, passing from place to place, holding the eyes of those to whom he was nearest, or opening their eyes just when he pleased to do so. That is how he acts toward us now. Do not some of you recollect when Christ first appeared to you? Ah! it is years ago with some of us, but we mind the place, the spot of ground where Jesus first manifested himself to us. The joy of marriage, — the joy of harvest, — these were as nothing compared with the joy that came to us from the vision of his face. Many days have passed since then, and we have had fresh visitations from him. He has come to us, and come again, and yet again. He has not been strange to us; and, now, some of us can say that we are not strangers to him, for he is our dear familiar Friend. Yet are there times, even with those who dwell with him, when the light is clearer, and the voice is nearer, and the sense of his presence is more delightful than usual.

These times, I say, come by Christ's own appointment whenever he pleases; yet I again remind you of the lesson we learn from our text, which is, that we may expect these visits from Christ when we are going about his business. These devoted women had been to the sepulchre, and had there seen "the angel of the Lord," who had bidden them go quickly, and tell his disciples that he had risen from the dead, and would meet them in Galilee. So they hastened with all their might to tell the cheering tidings to the sorrowing followers of Jesus; "and as they went to tell his disciples, behold, Jesus met them." It is better to be actively working for Christ than to sit still, and read, and study, and hope to enjoy his company so. There must be alternations between the contemplative and the active life of a Christian. Sometimes, it is best to sit quietly with Mary, and leave Martha and the dishes alone; but, at another time, it is better to bestir yourself, and to run hither and thither with all the diligence of a Martha, for then Jesus will be most likely to meet with you. I notice — and I think that my observation is correct, — that my brethren and sisters who do most for Christ, know most about him, and have most fellowship with him. The Sabbath-school teacher, diligent in his class, and weary, perhaps, now that the Sabbath is well-night spent, yet rejoicing that he has set forth

Christ before his class, is the one to whom the Lord will come and manifest himself. The man who has been in the street preaching, or going from door to door trying to speak for Christ by a tract or by his own voice, and all of you, indeed, who have done anything for your Lord and Master, are the most likely persons for him to meet with at this time.

I have known some, who have been for years members of churches, but who have never done anything for the Saviour; they are the kind of people who do not get on with my ministry long, they say that they are not able to feed upon it. They are generally wanderers who go about from one place to another looking for new light, and they never get to be very happy or very useful; nor do they often have much communion with Christ. No; our Lord is very choice in his company, and he does not frequent the house of the sluggard; but wherever there is one who spends and is spent for Jesus, there we may expect that Jesus will be. If we heartily serve him, the state of mind into which we shall be brought will be congenial to his own; fellowship will be likely between the labouring Saviour and his labouring servant. Follow the example of him who went about doing good, and you will thus be in sympathy with him, and you will find that he will come and walk with you because you two are agreed.

That is certainly one reason why Christ comes to those who are busy about his errands, because he is in agreement with them, and they are therefore travelling in the right road to meet with him. "If any man will not work, neither shall he eat," is a rule that Christ observes; and those who will not work for him get but scant morsels from him. Few of the bits my brother spoke of, that are dipped in the dish with Christ, come to those who never lift a hand to do him any service; but if he brings us into loving obedience, into joyful alacrity and sacred earnestness in doing his will, then it is that he will in all probability meet with us by the way, and manifest himself to us. Sit ye down, then, ye who have come to the end of another day of holy service; and just pray, "Jesus, Master, come and meet us now." Oh, that you might feel as though he stood behind you, and looked over your shoulder, — as if the shadow of the Christ fell upon you, and you felt even now his pierced hand touching you; and that prostrate at his feet your spirit might lie, holding him by the feet and worshipping him!

I do not feel as if I needed to preach upon this subject; I want only to set you longing for larger and deeper communion with Christ, and aspiring after it, especially you to whom this Sabbath has been a day of service, from which service, perhaps, you have not as yet seen any good come. You have come from that field weary, — not weary of it, though weary in it, — for you are ready still to serve your Lord. Now, I want you to feel that Christ is here, and that he comes to commune with you.

II. So we advance a step to our second remark. WHEN JESUS MEETS US, HE HAS EVER A GOOD WORD FOR US: "Jesus met them, saying, All hail."

That is, first, *a word of salutation,* as if he had said, "Welcome, friends! Glad to see you, friends! All hail, my friends!" There is nothing cold and formal about that word; it seems full of the warmth of brotherly kindness and affectionate condescension. "All hail!" says our Lord to the women. "You are glad to see me, and I am glad to see you. 'All hail!'" How much more sweet that sounds than that bitter sarcasm of the soldiers, "Hail, King of the Jews!" And yet it seems almost like an echo of it, as though Christ caught up the cruel word, crushed the bitterness out of it, and then gave it back to the holy women before him full of delicious sweetness. "All hail!" says he. "All hail!"

My dear Christian brother or sister, would you be glad to see the Saviour if he could be made visible to you? Yet you would not be so glad to see him as he would be to see you. He is very dear to you; but he is not so dear to you as you are to him. Out of two friends, the greater affection is always found in the one who has conferred the most favours upon the other. I will not dare to compare for a moment the love which exists between you and Christ, for what have you ever done for him compared with what he has done for you? He loves you more than you can ever love him. Well, then, he says, "All hail! I am glad, my son, — I am glad, my brother, — I am glad, my friend, that thou hast come up to this place where my people meet. All hail! I welcome you."

Besides being a word of salutation, it is *a word of benediction*. Our Lord, by this expression, seems to say, "All health to you, — everything that can do you good! I wish for you every good thing." He speaks it to you, believer. "May you have the haleness, the wholeness, that makes holiness; and, so, may it be all well with you, — all hale with you!"

Then it is also *a word of gratulation,* for some render it, "Rejoice," and, indeed, that is the meaning of the term, "Let us joy and rejoice together." Jesus gives to you, beloved, this watchword as he meets you, "Rejoice." The children in your class are not yet all converted; nevertheless, rejoice in Christ. All in the congregation, about whom some of us are concerned, are not saved; nevertheless, let us rejoice in Christ. You yourself cannot run as quickly on your Lord's errands as you wish you could; nevertheless, rejoice in Christ Jesus, though you can have no confidence in the flesh. It is a blessed thing when it becomes a sacred duty to be glad. What man, to whom our Lord Jesus Christ says, "Rejoice," can have an excuse for misery? So, "All hail!" is a word of gratulation.

And according to some versions, it may be read, "Peace be unto you!" That is *a word of pacification,* — as though our Lord had said, "Ah! you women did not run away from me, as the men did; but, still, you were afraid and very timid; and though you were at the sepulchre, you went there trembling. You did not believe my word, or you scarcely believed it, — that I would rise from the dead, but I am not going to have any back reckonings with you. 'Peace be to you!' " Now, dear friends, have you heard your Lord and Saviour say to you, "It is all forgiven — every omission and every commission, every slip and every fault, — all the lukewarmness, and all the coldness; it is all gone"? That is the meaning of the greeting, "All hail!" from the lips of Christ. "There is nothing between me and thee, dear heart, but perfect peace and unbroken love. I rejoice to see thee; and I would have thee rejoice, and rest, and be quiet, for I have come near unto thee, to bless and cheer thee."

That is the second lesson I learn from the text. First, that, when we are runing on our Master's errands, we may hope that he will meet us; and, next, when he does meet us, we may expect that he will always have a good word for us.

III. Thirdly, WHEN JESUS MEETS US, IT BEHOVES US TO GET AS NEAR TO HIM AS WE CAN: "And they came and held him by the feet."

Note that they first stood still. They had been running quickly to carry the angel's message to the disciples, but at the sound of their Lord's voice they stopped, half out of breath, and they seemed to say by their looks, "It is indeed our blessed Master. It is the very same Lord whom we saw laid in the tomb, the best-beloved of our soul." Then, next, they approached him. They did not flee away backward at all, but they came right up to him, "and held him by the feet." Now, dear friends, if Jesus is near to you, come closer still to him. If you feel that he is passing by, come near to him by an act of your will. Be all-alive and wide-awake; do not be half-asleep in your pew; but say, "If he is here, I will get to him. If he is anywhere about, I will speak with him, and beg him to speak to me." If ever our heart was active in all our lives, it ought to be active in the presence of Christ. And let us try to be all aglow with joy, for so were these women. They were delighted to behold their risen Lord, so they drew nearer to him; and, all intent with earnest, burning, all-conquering love, they came so close to him that they could grasp him, for they felt that they must adore him.

Now, beloved, let it be so with you and with me. Do not let us lose a single word that our Lord is ready to speak to us. If this be the time of his appearing to us, let him not come and find us asleep. If he be knocking at the door, if he be saying to us, "Open to me, my sister, my love, my dove, my undefiled," let us not reply that we cannot leave the bed of sloth to let him in; but now, if ever in our lives, let us breathe a mighty prayer, "Come, O thou blessed One whose voice I know full well, and commune with me." If Jacob held the angel whom he did not know, — if, as our hymn puts it, he said, —

> "Come, O thou Traveller unknown,
>   Whom still I hold, but cannot see!
> My company before is gone,
>   And I am left alone with thee;" —

let us much more say, —

> "Come, O thou Traveller well-known,
>   Whom still I hold, but cannot see;" —

"I must have thy company. My spirit craves it, sighs for it, pines for it; I must have thee. I will hold thee. Leave me not, but reveal thyself to me now."

That is the third lesson we may learn from our text.

IV. And the fourth I have almost touched upon; I could not help it. It is this, WHEN JESUS MEETS US, WE SHOULD RETAIN HIM, AND WORSHIP HIM: "They came and held him by the feet, and worshipped him."

When Mary Magdalene first sought to hold her Lord, Jesus said to her, "Touch me not; for I am not yet ascended to my Father;" but now he permits what he had formerly forbidden: "They came and *held him by the feet,*" — those blessed feet that the nails had held but three days before. He had risen from the grave, and therefore a wondrous change had taken place in him, — but the wounds were there, still visible, and these women "held him by the feet." And, beloved, whenever you get your Lord Jesus near to you, do not let him go for any little trifle, — nay, nor yet even for a great thing; but say, with the spouse in the Canticles, "I found him whom my soul loveth: I held him, and would not let him go." The saints themselves will sometimes drive Christ away from those who love him; therefore the spouse said, "I charge you, O ye daughters of Jerusalem, by the roes, and by the hinds of the field, that ye stir not up, nor awake my love, till he please." Be jealous lest you lose him, when you have realized the joy, the rich delight, of having him in your soul! You feel, at such a time as that, as if you scarcely dared to breathe; and you are so particular about your conduct that you would not venture to put one foot before the other without consulting him, lest even inadvertently you should cause him grief. Bow thus at his feet; be humble. Hold him by the feet; be bold, be affectionate. Grasp him, for though he is your God, he is also your Brother, bone of your bone, and flesh of your flesh.

But take care that, in it all, you worship him: "They came and held him by the feet, *and worshipped him.*" This is not the Socinians' christ; they cannot worship their saviour, for he is but a mere man. This is our Christ, "the Son of the Highest," "very God of very God," "God over all, blessed for ever." As we hold him by the feet, we feel a holy awe stealing over us, for the place whereon we stand is holy ground when he is there. We hold him, but still we reverently bow before him, and feel like John in Patmos when he wrote, "When I saw him, I fell at his feet as dead." Well spoke one of old, to whom it was said, "Thou canst not see Christ, and live." "Then," replied the saint, "let me see him, and die." And we would say the same; for, whatever happens to us, we wish for a sight of him. I have read of one who cried, under the overpowering weight of divine manifestations, "Hold, Lord! Hold! I am but an earthen vessel, and if thou dost fill me fuller, I must perish." Had I been in his place, I think I would not have spoken quite as he did, but I would have said, "Go on, Lord, with the blessed manifestation of thyself. Let the earthen vessel be broken if need be; it cannot possibly come to a better end then by being crushed and even annihilated by the majesty of thy glorious presence." At any rate, we will hold him, and worship him; the Lord help us to do so more and more!

V. The last remark I have to make is a practical one, which also comes out of our text. FROM SUCH A MEETING WITH CHRIST, WE SHOULD GO ON A FURTHER ERRAND FOR HIM: "Then said Jesus unto them, Be not afraid: go tell my brethren that they go into Galilee; and there shall they see me."

When we have such a meeting with Christ as these women had, let us go on some further errand for him, as soon as he permits us to do so. It is a very blessed thing to have fellowship with Christ, but it would be a very ill result of our communion with him if it led any one of us to say, "Now I shall not go back to my service any more. I shall not go to my class again. I might be provoked by the scholars; I might be careless there, and so I might lose the fellowship I am now enjoying with Jesus. I shall not go and preach again; I shall stop at home, and have communion with Christ all the day." I knew one brother, who got into such a condition that he really thought that, to see the face of his people on the Lord's-day, robbed him of fellowship with Christ. All the week long, he never saw anybody, for his fellowship with Christ, he said, was so intense that he could not bear to look upon mankind; and when the Sabbath came, and he had to meet with his people, he would, if he could, have preached out of a box so that they might hear his voice, and he might never see them. Now, I do not think that such a spirit as that is at all right. Who is the man who can best bear witness for Christ, but the man who has been with him in secret and sacred fellowship? And what is a better return for Christ's wondrous grace to us than that we should consecrate ourselves to the holy task of showing forth his glory amongst our fellow-men?

There is a striking legend illustrating the blessedness of performing our duty at whatever cost to our own inclination. A monk had seen a beautiful vision of our Saviour, and in silent bliss he was gazing upon it. The hour arrived at which it was his duty to feed the poor at the convent-gate. He would fain have lingered in his cell to enjoy the vision; but under a sense of duty, he tore himself away from it to perform his humble service. When he returned, he found the blessed vision still waiting for him, and heard a voice saying, "Hadst thou stayed, I would have gone. As thou hast gone, I have remained." So, dear friend, ask thyself, "Since Jesus is very precious to me, what more can I do for him? I was running to his disciples when he met me; so when he bids me go to them, I will run the faster that no time may be lost to the disciples before they also share the enjoyment with which my Master has indulged me. And when I get to them, I shall have more to tell them than I had before. I was going to tell them that I had seen the angel of the Lord; but I shall be able to tell them that I have seen the Lord himself, and I shall tell the message so much more brightly and powerfully now that I have had it confirmed from his own lips."

Those holy women were full of fear and joy, strangely mingled emotions, before; but now, surely fear must have taken to flight, for Jesus had said to them, "Be not afraid;" and it must have been joy, and joy alone, with which these blessed women would break in upon the eleven, and say, "We have seen what is far better than a vision of angels, for we have seen the Master himself. We held him by the feet till we knew that it was really our Lord, we held him till we had worshipped him, and heard him say, 'Be not afraid;' and then he gave us a message from his own dear lips, and this is what he said to us, 'Tell my brethren that they go into Galilee; and there shall they see me.' "

Happy preacher, who, on his way to his pulpit, is interrupted by meeting his Master! Happy preacher, who has lost the thread of his discourse, for few discourses are worth much that have too much thread in them, but who has found something infinitely better than thread, — some links of sacred fire, — some chains of heavenly love, that go from end to end of the discourse, so that he tells what he knows, and testifies what he has seen, for men must give heed to such a witness. His countenance is all aglow with the light that shines from the face of Jesus; it is bright with the joy that fills the preacher's own soul, and those who listen to him say, "Would God we knew that joy!" and those that do share it say, "Yes, we know it," and they respond to it till hearts leap up to speak with hearts, and they sing together a chorus of praise unto him whom they unitedly love. I wish it were so at this moment. I should like, dear friends, to be able to tell my message the better because of having met my Master; and I should like you to go out to the work and service of another week strengthened, and rendered mighty and wise for all you have to do, because

Jesus has met you, and has said to you, "All hail," and you have held him by the feet, and worshipped him.

There I leave the subject with you. Perhaps some of you are saying, "We wish we could hold him by the feet." Ay, but in this blessed supper, which is spread upon the table, you have an outward emblem of how to hold him better than by the feet, for, in the eating of bread and the drinking of wine in memory of him, he sets forth to us how his whole self can be spiritually received into the innermost chambers of our being, — how he can come unto us, and sup with us, and we with him, — how he can dwell in us, and we can dwell in him. Not only the peace of God, but his very self, can now come, and abide in your very self, and there can be a union between you and him that never shall be broken. God grant that you may enjoy it even now!

But I know that some here present cannot understand what I have been talking about; it must have seemed like an idle tale to them. Ah, dear friends! and if we were to go into a stable, and were to talk to horses about the ordinary concerns of our home life, what would they know about it all? They understand about oats, and beans, and hay, and straw; but what can they know of the themes that interest intelligent human beings? So, there are some men in this world, of whom Dr. Watts truly says, —

"Like brutes they live, like brutes they die."

They have no spiritual nature, even as the horse has no immortal soul, and they cannot therefore comprehend spiritual things. And as I might pity the horse because it is a stranger to mental enjoyments, so I would pity the unregenerate man who is a stranger to spiritual enjoyments. For, as much as the mind of man is above the living something that is within the brute, so much is the spirit of the believer above the ordinary mind of the unregenerate man. We have joys, the sweetness of which is such that honey is not to be compared with them; we have bliss, the like of which Solomon's wealth could not have purchased; and we have been introduced into a world which is as much fairer than this material universe as the sunlight is better than the darkest midnight of a dungeon. Oh, that you did all know it! May God, of his grace, give you his Spirit, create you anew, and breathe faith in Jesus into your soul! Then will you know the bliss of meeting with him, and of serving him.

God bless the Word, for Jesus' sake! Amen.

BIBLIOGRAPHY

Charles H. Spurgeon: *Metropolitan Tabernacle Pulpit.* Vol. 39 (1873), No. 23323, pp. 409-420; and Vol. 45 (1882), No. 2628, pp. 301-309
Joseph Parker: *City Temple Pulpit.* London. 1899. Vol. I. pp. 142-148
Philip Bennett Power: *The Feet of Jesus.* London. 1872. pp. 243-256

THREE PHASES OF THE RISEN CHRIST
by
Dinsdale T. Young

"And they said one to another, Did not our heart burn within us, while He talked with us by the way, and while He opened to us the Scriptures?" — Luke 24:32

In this glowing testimony three phases of the Risen Christ are set forth. Each aspect of the Lord of Eastertide is delectable. I know not which is the most charmful.

Bishop Moule has a note on the story of which these words are a grateful reminiscence: 'The charm of this immortal story lies largely in the strange facility with which, in it, the supernatural comes upon us in all its mystery and majesty, literally walking and talking with the natural. To depict such a converse has been the attempt not seldom of literary genius, but where has it succeeded? Shakespeare has assuredly failed in *Hamlet*. Scott himself admits that he has failed in *The Monastery*. But St. Luke succeeds.'

And why does St. Luke succeed? Because he records a real experience: he tells a true story. Godet speaks of the 'intimate' character of these words, and well he may. Here the supernatural walks and talks with men. The Risen Lord holds converse with His disciples.

They sometimes tell us that no one has ever come back from the other world to give us assurance of it. But that is not so. Christ came back. He authenticated the unseen universe. And now amid all the proofs of immortality no evidence is so decisive as the Resurrection of our Lord.

The Risen Master is here portrayed as the companionable Christ, the expository Christ, and the enkindling Christ. Let us seek to catch the triple glory of this manifestation.

I. THE COMPANIONABLE CHRIST.

'He talked with us by the way,' cry these glad-hearted men. 'He spake to us in the way' is the rendering of the R.V.

This is one of the surprises of the Resurrection. I should not have dreamed that the Risen Lord would be companionable. My fear would be that resurrection might have involved remoteness. He has been 'declared to be the Son of God with power, according to the Spirit of holiness, by the resurrection from the dead.' Will He henceforth be accessible as aforetime? I should not have dared to expect it. With this new and wonderful accession of deity surely He can scarcely be as human as before! Yet He is. More divine than ever, He is more human than ever. The Lord of all is a brother still. 'He talked with us by the way.'

Resurrection has not quenched His sympathy. Exalted, He is tender as He was on His humiliation. He is the friendly Lord. He is the companion of His people. His heart yearns with His ancient love. Although bedewed with new glory, He comes close as ever to those His heart approves and pities.

The Emmaus story is a perennial parable of Christian experience. Still the Risen Christ is the companionable Christ. This is very practical mysticism. This is factual poetry. I have known many who were little of mystics and less of poets, but they emphatically declared 'the Saviour walks and talks with me.'

'He spoke to us in the way.' We ever need the Christ of 'the way.' We must have the Christ of heaven; we cannot do without the Christ of the sanctuary; but the Christ of 'the way' is a deep necessity of our daily toilful life.

How wonderful that 'He' should have joined His followers 'in the way'! He seemed as one of themselves, but they speedily discerned that He was not one of themselves. He appeared as a common traveller, but they early found that He was Lord of 'the way.' He talked to them till the eight miles of country road seemed as a golden street, and the journey had more appropriately ended in the city of light than in an Oriental village.

Will He talk to *us* 'in the way'? Is He still the companionable Christ? Assuredly so! In the common ways of life He joins us. He floods prosaic streets with His peerless glory. His companionship destroys the monotony of the most monotonous way, and the steepness of the most uphill way, and the peril of the most declivitous way. He causes a vulgar road to be crowded with the angels of God.

But is His companionship the prerogative of every one? Not so. Mark that 'us.' These men were disciples of Christ. Only such can say 'He spake to *us* in the way.' Discipleship alone has the privilege of Divine Companionship. If any of Christ's depressed disciples hereupon exclaim, 'We are such poor unworthy disciples,' I would reply that you cannot be less promising disciples than these men were at that time. They had almost made the great renunciation. Their discipleship was at the lowest ebb. I should not wonder but they had left Jerusalem that morning all but determined to quite the discipleship-band for ever. Yet it is with such the Saviour walks and talks! Divine fellowship does not depend upon the merit of the disciples, but upon the grace of the Master. You, therefore, O poor dispirited and sin-plagued disciples, may be included in this happy 'us.'

They were sorely troubled disciples with whom Christ companied. They were all but heartbroken. Sorrow had overwhelmed them. All their hopes were buried in their Master's grave, and they knew not yet of His resurrection. They could scarcely speak: they could only sob. Their golden days were all in the past. But these sorrowing ones presently testify, 'He spake to us in the way.' Christ is most companionable to His troubled children. When we tread the way of grief, oh, how He speaks to us in the way! And if His words do not arrest our tears they alleviate them. There are roads we could not tread were it not for our loving Lord's companionship. Reckon on His presence with thee when thou dost tread a darkened way! He will conquer the darkness with the light of His countenance.

Of Wisdom we read that his delights are with the sons of men. Verily this is true of the Christ. He rejoices in the habitable parts of the earth. On life's various ways He loves to walk with His disciples.

And how He talks with us in the way! His words are rest and comfort. They soothe and they invigorate. 'Never man spake like this man.' Blessed souls that know the sweetly companionable Christ!

2. THE EXPOSITORY CHRIST.

'He opened to us the Scriptures.' I cannot overstate the significance of the fact that our Lord's primary solicitude when he rose from the dead was the Bible. Too great attention cannot be called to our Saviour's holy enthusiasm for the Word of God. He lived and died devoted to it with peerless devotion.

I should have imagined that the Risen Lord would be independent of the Bible. But no! He cleaves to it with all the old affection. He came up from the grave and hastened to the Holy Book. He flooded it with the glory of His countenance, and the precious pages retain the lustre. Nothing reveals to me so clearly the indispensability of the Bible. This is of a truth the token of its authority.

Was not our Lord in this a prophet? He surely foresaw that the great necessity was to set His people in a right relation to the Bible. Did He not realize that the battle of faith and unbelief would rage around the Bible? And to ensure its safety was His first endeavour when He was risen from the dead. 'He opened to us the Scriptures.' Evidently then our Lord regarded the Bible as no mere fortuitous collection of documents more or less inspired. It was no 'dogma' to Him. Nor to Him was it simply 'literature.' He treated it as of supreme spiritual authority. He appealed to it as such. He expounded it as such.

More and more must Christians emulate Christ's attitude towards the Bible. There is too often a marked and deplorable disparity between the Lord's relation to the Book and the relation of His servants. Never shall we be a conquering Church till we recover the Saviour's standpoint. What is the Bible to you? Are you its critic or its humble and believing expositor? Is it your final court of appeal? Do you look upon its holy pages with the loving gratitude with which our Lord regarded it?

The Bible requires opening. 'He *opened* to us the Scriptures.' It is full of intellectual and spiritual mystery. It is a sealed Book till Jesus opens it. Its mystery is a sign of its divinity. A divine book is sure to be mysterious. Its Author is the Author of Nature, and the element of mystery is in all His works. You would not believe in a Bible which had no mystery, any more than you would believe in a God who was easily understood. The mystery of the Bible need be no stumbling-block to us, for it evidences its heavenly origin. And such a one as Huxley said that the mysteries of the Bible are child's play to the mysteries of nature.

But however mysterious be the Bible, Christ can open it. And He alone can do this. Yes, how wonderfully He does it for His children! Have we not often heard this testimony, 'He opened to us the Scriptures'? The secret of the exposition is not cleverness, but the illuminating presence of Christ. If He shine upon your Bible it will be a book of light to you. When we sit alone with our Bible and invoke the companionship of Jesus, how He gives us to understand the wonderful words of life! Unlettered men who have the Divine Expositor near see wondrous things in God's law.

Is Christ always opening to you the Scriptures? Are you always seeing new things in the old Book? O blest Expositor, be ever near us and reveal the hidden wealth of the Word of God!

This is what the Church needs — the presence of Christ as the expository Christ. We need the Author of the Book to give us the infallible interpretation of the Book. Then the Bible will regain its old authoritative position in the Church; then the power of the holy people shall prevail in the earth.

It is not my present task to show the expository method of our Lord, but I cannot refrain from alluding to one feature of it as disclosed in this story. 'And beginning at Moses and all the prophets, He expounded unto them in all the scriptures the things concerning Himself' (ver. 27). Mark that recurring 'all.' According to the expository Christ the whole of the Old Testament is full of 'things concerning Himself.' There are those who have driven Him out of the Old Testament. How opposed to His teaching is such a course! It is sheer blasphemy, though it may pose as scholarship. Either Christ was wrong or these present-day teachers are in error. I believe they are absolutely in error. No valid reason can ever be assigned for contradicting the teaching of the Incarnate God. And He declares that 'all' the Old Testament holds 'things concerning Himself.'

This is the clue to the true exposition of the Old Testament. There are some who discuss the question, 'How can we preach the Old Testament to the present age?' They reply that the best way, the only way, is to deduce from it ethical instruction. That was not our Lord's method. Nor is it the true method. To reveal the Saviour everywhere concealed therein is the inspired way of interpreting the Old Testament. Preaching which follows the Lord's expository example must be crowned with the Lord's benediction.

Is your Bible fuller and fuller to you of 'things concerning Himself'? It will be if He opens to you the Scriptures. Abide with us, Thou Expositor Divine, and give the gift of life to the Word of God!

3. THE ENKINDLING CHRIST.

What a witness these men bear! 'They said one to another, Did not our heart burn within us?' The Companion-Expositor set their hearts aglow. Oh how He always enkindles the heart! 'He that is near Me is near the fire' is reputed to be a saying of the Christ's It is assuredly true. He, like the Jehovah of the Old Testament, answered by fire. The Spirit He imparted was a spirit of burning.

He loves to set the heart aflame. And none can come under His influence without realizing the secret mystery of the burning heart. The glow He leaves attests His supernal influence. You cannot know His dear companionship and His irradiating exposition without also knowing what it is to have a heart white-hot with holy fervour.

John Wesley, in his invaluable *Notes,* says it was 'warmth of love.' So it was. He ever enkindles with love. He inflames the heart with love to God and to Himself, and to all disciples, and to the Word of God, and to everything that is divine. John Wesley knew in his own wonderful experience that Christ is the enkindling Christ. How ideally he formulated his conversion! 'I felt my heart strangely warmed.' And the great Evangelical Revival began and continued in an enkindled heart. Have we such a heart?

Christ enkindled these hearts with comfort. It is the fine comment of Professor Bruce in the Expositor's Greek Testament that 'it is the heart that has been dried by trouble that burns so.' Well and truly said. Each of these men had a heart that had dried by trouble, but the Lord makes it glow with strong consolation. Christ uplifts us oft-times above our troubles by the burning comfort He imparts. He enkindled their hearts with joy and with hope till they knew nothing of all their former sadness. The flame of gladness enfolded their soul; the flame of hope enwrapped their spirit.

The tense of the verb indicates that the enkindling was permanent. The fire was burning still. The episode was over, but not the influence. The Master has departed, but has left His glorious traces in their heart.

Do we all know Christ as the enkindling Christ? Has He really set our hearts on fire? And is the fire still burning? The modern Church greatly needs the burning heart. Is not the fire quenched in many a Church? Where is the old-time ardour? Is not the sacred passion spent? It is a serious thing if we know not Christ as the enkindling Christ. The world will never be greatly impressed with a Church which has not a burning heart. Jesus, set our hearts on fire and keep them flaming even whilst the love of many waxes cold!

Matthew Henry sees here a lesson for preachers and for hearers. He says that is the right style of preaching which makes the heart

94

of the hearer burn. He was himself a great preacher and the son of a great preacher, and all preachers will do well to ponder his words. If we bring Christ to men and treat the Bible as Christ treated it, we shall be of that enkindling school of preachers.

The great commentator says they are the best hearers who listen with a burning heart. Are you such hearers? With enkindling preachers and enkindled hearers may God fill our pulpits and our pews!

BIBLIOGRAPHY

R. M. Benson: *Life Beyond the Grave,* 3rd ed., London, n.d., pp. 104-114, 387-397

J. D. Jones: *The Unfettered Word,* London, 1912, pp. 170-175

F. W. Krummacher: *The Risen Redeemer,* Eng. tr., New York, 1863, pp. 69-75

H. P. Liddon: *Easter in St. Paul's,* pp. 180-191, 192-202

Alexander Maclaren: *Expositions of Holy Scripture, St. Luke XIII-XXIV,* pp. 335-342; also in his *After the Resurrection,* pp. 28-39

G. Campbell Morgan: *Westminster Pulpit,* Vol. VI (1911) pp. 49-55

George H. Morrison: *The Weaving of Glory,* London, n.d., pp. 107-120

L. R. Scarborough: *How Jesus Won Men,* New York, 1926, pp. 168-176, 179-185

Alexander Whyte: *Bible Characters,* Vol. II, pp. 103-107, Grand Rapids, Mich., 1952

Dinsdale T. Young: *The Travels of the Heart,* pp. 221-233

DINSDALE T. YOUNG
(1861-1937)

Dinsdale T. Young was born November 20, 1861 at Corbridge-on-Tyne, a few miles from Hexham, the birthplace of Joseph Parker, the son of a physician, William Young. His father was brought up in the Church of England, but felt led to leave it to join the Wesleyan group, and the love for Methodism was born in the son's heart at that time, never to be quenched. After a brief ministry in Edinburgh, he was called to the great Queen Street Chapel, Holborn, in London, the same area in which was located Dr. Joseph Parker's City Temple. The Queen Street Chapel was the largest Wesleyan Chapel in London, but had "fallen upon pathetically evil days." The chapel subsequently being given over to the West London Mission, Young served as pastor at Wesley's Chapel, City Road, of which he himself says, "I preached oftener in Wesley's Chapel than any man has ever done — not excepting John Wesley himself."

In 1914, a double responsibility came to Dinsdale Young: he was elected President of the Methodist Conference and he was appointed Minister of Central Hall, Westminster, the largest Methodist auditorium in that part of England. Here he ministered for twenty years, the church being crowded morning and evening. I remember the night, in 1924, when five of us men went down to Westminster to hear the famous, then white-haired minister, and arriving only five minutes late, we found the auditorium so crowded that we had to sit on the cement steps leading up to the choir. He was beginning that night a series of sermons on the Apostles' Creed, and preached from the opening declaration, "I believe." He read extensively from Pearson's profound work on the Creed, and because of nearsightedness, he had to hold these slips of paper up very close to his eyes. But not a person moved; the attention remained undivided and one could sense an attitude of reverence toward this mighty prophet of God.

Frequently he bore vigorous testimony to the sufficiency of the Scriptures and the need of constant Biblical preaching. In his delightful autobiography, *Stars of Retrospect,* he affirmed, "With

all movements for the circulation and defence of the Bible I have
had and have intensest sympathy. My faith in the power of
Scripture when brought under the most evil eyes grows stronger
and stronger. The evangelistic influence of the printed Word
can never be exaggerated. I have had no richer service than such
as I have been enabled to render in London, especially of late
years, to the cause of the Bible. We want far more assertion of
what the Bible is, and far less assertion of what it is not. The
lack of positiveness concerning Holy Scripture is one of the most
tragical weaknesses of the present-day churches and pulpits. . . .
I testify that God never fails to supply one's pulpit needs as one
searches the Scriptures. Make the Bible your text-book, preacher,
and it will be to you a book of texts! . . . I have found the Bible
an ever more delightful companion. I humbly think I have sur-
mounted the fearful danger of treating it as a professional instrument. To read it anywhere and everywhere has been my
increasing joy. Never was it so sweet to my taste as it is today. It
abases me into the dust. It makes me smart with self-condem-
nation. But it cheers, it interests, it inspires me more and more.
It flings the light of the morning star upon my darkest hours of
night. That my ministry has brought me into constant contact
with God's written Word is a mercy of mercies in my experience."

THE REKINDLED FIRE
by
G. Campbell Morgan

"And they said one to another, Was not our heart burning within us, while He spake to us in the way, while He opened to us the Scriptures." — Luke 24:32

During this week in conversation with an eminent scholarly, and devout professor of our Theology Colleges, he told me that he had been now for some years preaching Sunday after Sunday in different parts of the country, seeing Church life at the normal; and he declared that the impression upon his mind as to the condition of affairs is that there is everywhere an appalling *flatness* — I use his own word — and at the same time wherever ministers, office-bearers, or church members are led into conversation on this condition of affairs they earnestly express a desire for better things; a consciousness of deadness and a desire for life.

It is because I share this conviction that I bring you this evening the message of the incident in connection with which the words of my text occur. It is one of the post-resurrection stories. Here Christ is seen; no longer in the limited, straitened, circumstances in which, according to His own confession as recorded by Luke, He exercised His ministry of three or three and a half years; but in all the glory and power which came to Him by resurrection. He was the same as He had been during the days of His sojourning with men; yet entirely different in very many ways. The appositeness of the story to ourselves is born of this fact. The forty days of our Lord's sojourning on this earth after resurrection were characterized by appearance and vanishing; and I personally should be inclined to say that the main purpose of His tarry-

97

ing was not that of appearing, but that of vanishing. He appeared to Peter, and vanished! He presenced Himself, without the opening of a door or the shooting of a bolt, in the midst of His disciples in the upper room; and vanished! He walked with disciples on the road to Emmaus, sat with them at the board; and suddenly vanished! He hailed the fishermen after the night of fruitless work, Himself standing in bodily presence upon the shore of the lake, "Children, have ye any meat?"; and they came and partook of the breakfast which He had prepared; He talked to Peter across the flicker of the fire, in the early morning, while the light of the sun was shimmering upon the sea, about past failure, challenged his love, called forth his confession, gave him his commission, and then vanished!

The chief value in each case was not in the appearing, but in the vanishing. He was teaching those disciples, not for their sakes alone, but for the sakes of all who should follow them, that even though they could not see Him with the eyes of sense He was always nigh at hand. He was training them to be independent of the senses, and dependent upon the spirit, in the matter of their fellowship with Him; accustoming them not to see Him, and yet to know that He was at hand; training them so that presently, one of the number of the disciples, not of those who saw Him in the days of His flesh, but of those who were brought to Him afterwards, Saul of Tarsus, could write, "Henceforth we know no man after the flesh: even though we have known Christ after the flesh, yet we know Him so no more." He was training men to know that absence of the bodily presence was not absence of the Lord; that the fact that He could not be touched by the hand, or handled as John said, or looked upon with the eyes of sense, did not for a single moment matter; He was ever close at hand.

Today we are living in post-resurrection days in the fullest sense; in days when we no longer have the presence of our Lord as to the physical fact, but when we know He is nigh at hand, in the midst of every assembly of His people, the close, personal companion of every pilgrim of faith, the constant comrade of every trusting soul.

We come back then to this picture of the transition period, when He was preparing men to do without His bodily presence, and we feel there is in it great value for us.

After He had vanished; they knew that although they could not see Him, He was with them. Talking over their experience they said: When He talked to us by the way the old fire burned, the old enthusiasm returned, the vision which had faded from the glowing sky was restored; "Was not our heart burning within us, while He spake to us in the way."

Let us then examine the story; looking at the disciples; their possession and their lack; then carefully observing the Christ; His quest; His method and His victory.

What then did these disciples possess? They still loved Him; they still believed in Him. Their journey was not one of forgetfulness. He was the theme of their conversation. So far as He personally was concerned they were absolutely loyal to Him still; they would have suffered no one to traduce the name of their loved and lost leader. They still believed that His intention had been of the highest, that His purpose had been of the noblest, that the passion of His heart had been the redemption of Israel. They had not lost their love and their faith. Amid the bitterness of disappointment and darkness, and disgrace, they still spoke kindly of Him, and in terms which manifested their confidence in Him.

What then did they lack? They had lost their confidence, not in Him, but in His ability to do what they thought He was going to do. They had come to the conviction in the presence of the tragedy of the Cross that He had failed. They had hoped he would redeem Israel, break the yoke of the oppressor, restore the people of the ancient economy, bring in that day of which prophets had spoken and psalmists had sung through the long ages; but He had failed. That was their outlook, and in consequence there had been a cooling of their enthusiasm. They loved Him still, and believed in His high and holy intention, and in His endeavour, but they had lost hope. Not in forgetfulness did they walk to Emmaus, but in keen disappointment; with a great sense

100

oppressing them that their Master, however noble in Himself, however high and holy in His ambition, had failed. Therefore they lacked the burning, the enthusiasm, which is the dynamic of service.

I believe that at the present moment, that is the condition of the Christian Church to a large extent. I am perfectly convinced that there was never more personal, individual loyalty to the Lord than there is today; a loyalty which is undoubted if we think of the individual, in personal relationship to Christ. There are not tens, hundreds, thousands, but tens of thousands of those who believe in Him for themselves; believe in Him as the true Lord of their life, having perfect, abiding, abounding confidence in Him; those who, even in the hour of doubt and difficulty, almost of despair, yield to Him a great personal allegiance and loyalty. But there are thousands of persons of whom all that is true, who are nevertheless suffering from a lack of certainty as to His ability to do what they thought He was going to do. They are inwardly, if not confessedly, pessimistic as to the issue of our Lord's work in the world. They are not quite sure.

Let me give you some of the symptoms of this lack of assurance. You find Christian people are content to give attention to men who are putting Him into comparison with human teachers. I find among my brethren in the ministry as I travel through the country that the articles they are reading are those which question Him. The Hibbert Journal is the most popular magazine, I find, among ministers today; and in so far as it is a medium for those who criticise Him adversely its influence is pernicious. We are questioning Him, asking whether after all He is the One we thought He was; admitting some kind of supremacy to Him, professing loyalty to Him, but putting Him into comparison with others, asking the question that came out of Herod's prison long ago, asked then by a man perfectly loyal but perplexed, "Art Thou He that cometh, or look we for another?"

Another symptom is that we are modifying our conception of His victories. We are not sure that the victories won were won in and by that Name alone. We are willing to discuss the possibility of some other form of religion being more suited to certain races than that of the Lord Christ. We are not quite sure whether it is final. Therefore we are a little uncertain of the possibility of His ultimate triumph.

There is consequently a marked cooling of enthusiasm, a lack of passion, an absence of fire; until today, the Church of God, taking it as a whole, making every allowance for exceptions, is a little afraid of enthusiasm. If I may quote again the words of my professor friend, there is everywhere an appalling *flatness*.

Now let us go back to our story. How did Christ deal with these men? First I pray you notice the fact of His quest. As I look at it, I am going to say a thing which perhaps reveals my own failure to understand my Lord. If I am surprised at these men — and I do not know that I am, I think I understand their mental mood — I am more surprised at my Lord. I am surprised that He thought it worth while to take that walk to Emmaus with two disciples who, while still loyal to Him in heart, had abandoned their confidence in His ability to accomplish the purpose of God in the world. When I listen to His estimate of them, "O foolish men, and slow of heart to believe," I am still the more surprised that He should care to walk with them and talk with them.

What a revelation this is of the Christ. If we want to know what Christ is, as revealed in that story, let us put Him into contrast with ourselves. We seek for confidence in ourselves, even before we care about love of ourselves. If a man believes in us, and in our ability to do things, we are willing to be His comrade even if he do not love us. If a man love us and have lost his confidence in our ability, we are not careful for his comradeship.

That leads us to the discovery of what Christ was really seeking. He was seeking love, and the bursting of it into a flame, into passion, the rekindling of it into a fire! He knew it was there, overshadowed; He knew there was faith in Him, loyalty to Him, and that is but another way of saying that love for Him still remained. They had lost their confidence in His ability. They were disappointed. They felt He had been defeated, but in their heart there was love, and He was seeking that; to bring it again from underneath the shadow, and to fan it into the flame of a great devotion.

Now mark His method. He did not make Himself known in order to kindle that love. He brought them back to the things they knew full well, to the old, familiar things. He brought them nothing new, but He turned the old into the new, by His interpretation. Have you ever dreamed dreams as you have read that story? Have you ever wished you could have listened to His interpretation of Moses and the prophets? I often have. They listened to this Stranger as He took their own sacred writings, and interpreted to them their deepest meaning. They listened to Him as He revealed to them the profoundest depths in the suggestive ritual of the Mosaic economy, as He breathed in their ears the secret of the love which lay at the heart of the ancient law. They listened to Him as He traced the Messianic note in the music of all the prophets; showing that He was David's King, "fairer than the children of men," and in the days of Solomon's well-doing He it was that was "altogether lovely." He was Isaiah's child-king with a shoulder strong to bear the government, and a name Emanuel, gathering within itself all excellencies; Jeremiah's "Branch of righteousness; executing judgment and righteousness in the land"; Ezekiel's "Plant of renown," giving shade, and shedding fragrance; Daniel's stone cut without hands, smiting the image, becoming a mountain, and filling the whole earth; the ideal of Hosea, "growing as a lily," casting out his roots as Lebanon"; to Joel, "the hope of His people and the strength of the children of Israel"; the usherer in of the fulfilment of the vision of Amos, "the plowman overtaking the reaper, and the treader of grapes him that soweth seed"; of Obadiah "deliverance upon Mount Zion and holiness"; the fulfilment of that of which Jonah was but a sign; the "turning again" of God, of which Micah spoke; the One Whom Nahum saw upon the mountains "publishing peace"; the Anointed, of Whom Habakkuk sang as "going forth for salvation"; He Who brought to the people the pure language of Zephaniah's message; the true Zerubbabel of Haggai's word, rebuilding for ever the house and the city of God; Himself the Dawn of the day when "Holiness unto the Lord shall be upon the bells of the horses" as Zechariah foretold; and He the refiner's fire," "the fuller's sope," "the Sun of righteousness" of Malachi's dream.

What was the result? He won the victory. They came to new possession of Jesus, while as yet they did not know the One interpreting the Scriptures was Jesus in very deed. They looked back to the Cross, and saw it set in the light of the ancient symbolism, of the ancient prophecy; and the inglorious tree gleamed with glory of which they had never dreamed.

They listened in astonishment, and as they listened, to employ their own word, their hearts burned within them. Coolness gave way to heat, despair to hope, disappointment to certainty; and there flamed within them the fire, not merely of the old and lost enthusiasm, but of a new passion for this very Christ in Whom they believed and Whom they loved, as they learned by interpretation of their own Scriptures at the lips of the Stranger, that all the things which had filled them most with fear, were according to the predictions of those Scriptures.

Thus their burning of heart was the thrill of a new discovery of the old things. It was the shame of past failure. It was the passion of a new endeavour. And this was created by Christ's interpretation of the ancient Scriptures which they knew, with which they were perfectly familiar: the Scriptures which they thought they had understood. They were so familiar with them that they had ceased to make themselves familiar with them.

I pray you mark this carefully; my insistence upon it is repeated because it is the key to the situation. They did not know Who this was Who talked to them; He was quite a stranger; but listening to the old words, giving new attention to them under His guidance they found new meaning, new value, and new power.

What then does the Church need today in order to kindle again the fire, to renew the enthusiasm, to set upon the faces of her members the flaming glory of the morning, and to create again the fervour. She needs that the things she possesses should become real to her. The word of our Lord spoken to one of the Asian churches, is what the Church needs to hear and obey today; "Strengthen the things that remain." I might speak of the necessity for strengthening the doctrine — not of adding to or taking from the doctrine — but of coming to the realization of the essential truth within the doctrine, and of believing in very deed and with all the heart and soul the very things we think we do believe. I might speak of the ordinances of the Church, of the things we think we do believe. I might speak of the ordinances of the Church, of the things that are still with us, call them if you will, the sacraments of the Church, call them if you please more inclusively, the means of grace; we need to see these things renewed in power, to go back again to the simple meaning of them, and to abandon ourselves to their suggestiveness, and to take out of the letter the heart and spirit and obey it and follow it.

But supremely we need exactly what happened to these men on the way to Emmaus, a new understanding of the Scriptures of truth, a new discovery of them as the Scriptures that set forth the things concerning Christ, a new test of the Scriptures by the study of them; and the abandonment of the life to the law which flames forth from them; and the putting of them to the test in all our work and all our living.

Yet, I have not touched the deepest note of all! The Bible we have, and there is a sense in which it is being studied today as it has never been studied. There were more Bibles published last year than in any prior year in the history of the world; there were more Bibles printed than any other book in all the wide world; they are everywhere, and men are turning back to the study of the Bible with a keen and remarkable interest, as I know full well. Yet we lack the fire, the fervour, the enthusiasm. What then do we supremely need? To gather together around the Bible which we have, recognising that we never can know it, never can understand it, save as we take time to listen to the Lord's interpretation of it to our own souls.

It is possible for a man to analyse the Bible and lose it in the process; to prepare a synthesis of the Bible and lose his soul at the work; to make himself perfectly familiar with the letter, and to find out that the letter killeth because he has lost touch with the spirit!

The Church supremely needs to learn the secret of listening to the voice of the Master. Oh, but we cannot hear it today as those disciples heard it! If only He would come to the Bible School, or to the Conference, we would gladly sit down and listen while He opened to us the Scriptures! If anyone shall say such a thing as that, it is because they have not yet learned the lesson His vanishing was intended to teach. It is not not a question as to whether He will come; He does come; He is always present to teach; but we do not take time to listen. It is true of our personal life and study of the Word; it is true of the assemblies of the saints; we do not listen for Him.

These men did not say, "Was not our heart burning within us" while we talked about Him, or talked to Him. It is not an evil thing to talk about Him; for in the ancient days when the saints talked together about Jehovah, He hearkened and heard, and the book of remembrance was written. It is not an evil thing to talk to Him; He has bidden us bring words and speak in His presence. But neither of these things will bring us into right relation with the truth and values of Christianity. Not by the things we say to each other about Him; nor by the words we speak to Him in praise or prayer; but by the word He speaks to us about His Word is the fire kindled.

Am I not touching the very centre of our need today? Is not this the thing we are not sure about? Are we not inclined to say: Yes, but if God ever did so speak to men, the day of such speaking is past. Is not that the widespread opinion of the Church? The loss of the mystic sense of the actual presence of the Lord and of His willingness to speak immediately directly to the soul; is not that the secret of the killing of our love, the deadening of our emotion, the turning to ashes of our fires?

All this is very general, and perhaps in that sense quite useless; certainly it is if we only hear it as a generality. Therefore come back to the individual and the particular. How much time have we given, not to prayer, not to fellowship with each other, not even to technical study of the Bible; but to listening for His voice? Is it not almost a lost art of Christian experience, this ability to sit still and wait?

In amazement someone is saying, Does the preacher mean that if I sit still and listen I shall hear His voice? Not with the ears of sense, but with the spirit life, yes! Shall I see the form? Not with the eyes of sense, but with the inner spiritual vision assuredly!

If in the life of the Church today we could call a halt to half our endeavour, and consecrate the redeemed time to quietness and waiting, to listening; we should gather again to the next service of the sabbath, men and women with hearts on fire with a burning enthusiasm, and the hymn would not be a song languishing on our tongues, and the reading of Scripture would not be something to which a man may listen or not as he pleases. There would be a great burning enthusiasm, a flaming new fire, a day of new activity and new dynamic.

Thus the one word of application of the evening meditation, a word of application intended for the preacher as well as the hearer, is this: Let us practice the presence of our Lord. Let us take time to listen, waiting at His gates, shutting out the babel of other voices.

I speak now by way of personal conviction. If we will do so, all our doubt about Him will vanish, all our uncertainty as to whether or not He is the Christ will pass away; for not finally by the letter even of this sacred Scripture; but finally, by direct immediate impartation of Himself to the soul will He satisfy the soul and fill it with light and hope and enthusiasm. May He teach us how to listen while He talks to us in the way.

BIBLIOGRAPHY

David James Burrell: *God and the People*. New York. 1899. pp. 252-263
Russell H. Conwell: *Sermons for the Great Days*. New York. 1922. pp. 89-106
John A. Hutton, in *Record of Christian Work*. 1910. Vol. 29. pp. 855 ff.
H. P. Liddon: *Easter in St. Paul's*, new ed., London. 1892, pp. 192-202
G. Campbell Morgan: *Westminster Pulpit*. Vol. I. 1906. No. 16; Vol. VI. 1911. pp. 49-55
George H. Morrison: *The Unlighted Lustre*. New York. 1905. pp. 133-143
W. R. Nicoll: *The Garden of Nuts*. pp. 123-130
D. T. Young: *Travels of the Heart*. London, n.d. pp. 221-233

G. CAMPBELL MORGAN
(1864-1945)

The greatest Biblical expositor in the early part of the twentieth century was G. Campbell Morgan, most of whose ministry was carried on at Westminster Chapel, London. Morgan was born in Tetbury, Gloucestershire, Dec. 9, 1863. Even at the age of thirteen, at his request, a little group of men and women and boys and girls, gathered together in a Methodist church to hear him *preach,* August 27, 1876. The hearing of Mr. Moody in 1883 left a deep impression on the young man's life. It is hardly believable, but nevertheless true, that when Morgan, one among one hundred fifty young men, sought entrance into the Wesleyan ministry in 1888, he was refused ordination, along with 105 others. But he knew he was called to preach, and ultimately, he began his ministry in 1891 at Rugely, in Staffordshire, at a salary of 160 pounds a year. The episode of his receiving a letter from the deacons of this church, complaining of the pastor's oft repeated absence because of the many invitations he was receiving to speak in other churches, is vividly set forth in Mrs. Jill Morgan's fascinating life of Dr. Morgan, *A Man of the Word.* So well known was Mr. Morgan before he was forty years of age, that he was requested by Mr. Moody to come up to Northfield for an interview with him, which was the beginning of a long and intimate friendship with the great evangelist. Dr. Morgan probably in the years that followed contributed more to the fame and value of the summer conferences at Northfield than anyone else, except Mr. Moody, and Morgan kept coming, long after Moody's death.

With Campbell Morgan's ministry at Tollington from 1897-1904, we need not tarry here. Already he was so famous throughout Britain, that more invitations poured in upon him than he was able to accept, but the schedule he kept would have exhausted an ordinary person. "The man who had achieved national prominence at the age of thirty-five, and who found it impossible to fulfill all the demands made upon his time, had, to all appearances, reached the summit of his career. It was not unusual for

Campbell Morgan to preach at New Court on Sunday, or deliver
a Bible lecture on Wednesday evening,and go straight from the
church to the station, to board a train for the West of England
or the South of Scotland, the Isle of Man or the Welsh coast,
where he would speak three or four times, and go back to London
for the next scheduled service in his own pulpit. Many of these
engagements were important Bible conferences, or services in
city churches, but he liked to return, whenever possible, to the
little towns of the Potteries where so much of his earlier work
was done.''

Like Lancelot Andrewes and Joseph Parker and Canon Liddon,
Morgan gave himself every day to long hours of study. He rose
early and retired late. I have been told by those who knew him at
Northfield, that he could be seen at a small table behind the cot-
tage he occupied, at six o'clock in the morning, carefully going
over the message of the eleven o'clock hour, which had already
appeared in print some years before. At the age of thirty-five he
was invited to become the pastor of the great Fifth Avenue Presbyterian Church of New York City, but declined. In fact, he
once wrote to a friend that during that particular year, he had
received invitations to become the minister of six different
churches and the head of three theological colleges.

It was at Westminster Chapel, Buckingham Gate, London,
however, that Morgan did his greatest work, first for thirteen
years from 1904-1917, beginning when he was forty-one years of
age, and for the second time, from 1933-1943. Just to look at
these dates will remind us that Morgan was at Westminster
Chapel during both the First and Second World Wars. Here he
preached those great sermons which go to make up the eleven
volumes of the *Westminster Pulpit,* in my opinion the greatest
eleven volumes of sermons by any preacher in the English language of our century. He also established and was the living force
in the Mundesley Bible Conference, and probably even more
significant, he established the Bible Teachers Association in London. I have in my files a prospectus for one of the years of this
period, for the Bible Teachers Association, in which announce-

ments were made concerning Bible courses being taught in thirty different centers in London and Greater London, all inspired by Dr. Morgan.

It is just impossible to communicate to paper the tremendous force that radiated from Morgan in the years when he was at his very best, "the intangible atmosphere of union between teacher and taught," as Mrs. Morgan calls it. It has been my privilege ever since I was a boy, to hear practically all the great biblical expositors of the last fifty years and I must say that Dr. Morgan had something beyond what all others had.

I often recall those lectures in Baltimore, about 1923 or 1925, when, whether it was raining or the sun was shining, fifteen hundred people would crowd into a suburban church in the *afternoon,* day after day, and hear this man expound the Gospel of Luke. There was a tenseness there, a magnetic pull, a lift, an atmosphere saturated with terrific intensity, our souls confronted with these eternal and transforming truths that sent us out of that sanctuary cleansed, ennobled, determined to go back to the Book. I have been moved by others, in one way or another, but no Bible teacher in the world, in the twentieth century, could cast over his audience, without effort, without flash, without show, that mystic spell that Campbell Morgan cast when he was at his best.

One must say a word about Dr. Morgan's writings. Morgan began to write for publication before he was forty years of age, in fact, he was only thirty-nine when one of his greatest books, *The Crises of the Christ,* was published. I have been reading again for the nth time for a Bible class I have been teaching, Morgan's large volume on the book of Acts, and though I had read it often before, I still marvel at the truths he brings forth from the text which no other writer seems to have apprehended. He wrote, of course, ten volumes of the *Analysed Bible,* volumes on each of the Gospels, and on Jeremiah and the Corinthian Letters, a great volume on *The Parables and Metaphors of Our Lord,* with another similarly large volume, *The Great Physician,* a series of brilliant studies of our Lord's interviews with the men and women of the Gospels. Three of his smaller books are to me priceless, incomparably better than any other volumes of the same size on these subjects, *The Ten Commandments, Hosea,* the sub-title significantly expressing the very essence of the book, The Heart and Holiness of God, and *A First Century Message to Twentieth Century Christians,* on the Seven Letters of the Risen Lord to the churches of Asia. As far as I know, no full bibliography of Morgan's works has ever been compiled. Above all the other great preachers from whom sermons have been drawn for this volume, Morgan, though well-read, could preeminently be said to be a man of one book. He lived in and for the exposition of the Word of God. He perfectly illustrated what St. Paul meant when he said to Timothy, "Give thyself utterly to these things."

JESUS ON THE EVENING OF EASTER DAY

by

H. P. Liddon

"Behold My Hands and My Feet, that it is I Myself: handle Me, and see; for a spirit hath not flesh and bones, as ye see Me have."
— Luke 24:39

It was on the evening of the day of His Resurrection, and on the occasion described by St. John in today's Gospel, that our Lord uttered these words. Of the Eleven, in St. Thomas's absence, only ten were present. They were assembled in a secret chamber for fear of the Jews; and with them were other friends and disciples. They were discussing the report of our Lord's appearance to Peter, when they were joined by the two disciples who had met our Lord, as St. Mark says, in a different form or guise, on the Emmaus road during the afternoon, and who had known Him in the Breaking of Bread. Not to mention what must have reached them from St. Mary Magdalene and the other women, these two reports from the two disciples and from St. Peter thus combined, may well have made the hearts of those present beat more quickly than they did before. Where was He? Would He show Himself? Would they too see Him? Would He most resemble the Jesus of the Transfiguration or the Jesus of Calvary? Would He be as He was before He suffered? or would His visage be still so marred that only a few would know Him? or would He be so changed into an unimagined form of glory and beauty, that the Sacred Face would be hardly recognized, except by very intimate friends, like Simon Peter? Or was all this purely speculation? Might not Peter — some may have reasoned thus at that time, — might not Peter have been himself deceived? Might the two disciples have mistaken some one else for their Master; could they have read His well-remembered Features into the countenance of some other Rabbi? It was in the midst of some such a turmoil of hopes and fears, of speculations and doubts, of bold anticipations and despairing conjectures, that Jesus Himself appeared. He gave no sign of His approach. Angels were guarding His empty tomb; but no angel visibly announced Him. There was no sound that rent the air; no blaze of brilliant light, as on the Holy Mount, illumined the chamber; no wall fell, as before the conqueror of Jericho; no door was opened. All had been fastened up for safety's sake against the Jewish enemy; all remained as it had been. But they looked; and behold He was there; He was in the very midst of them. How they knew not, but so it was; the thin air had yielded to their sight that Form, that Countenance Which they could not but recognize. And then, a second sense was summoned to support the evidence of sight. The Form which they beheld spoke; He spoke in a Voice with whose every intonation they were so familiar; "Jesus saith unto them, Peace be unto you."

The Evangelist describes the immediate effect. They were terrified and affrighted. They had seen, as they thought, an inhabitant of another world. Not an appearance without essence, as some have conjectured; not an angel, since an angel is a specifically distinct being from a man; still less, as it has been imagined, an evil spirit self-changed into a form of light; but the disembodied spirit of ther dead Master making itself visible; this was what the disciples supposed that they saw. The language of the Evangelist leaves no real room for question on this head. They thought that the Body of Jesus was still resting in the grave in the rich man's garden; their incredulity, which was proof against the remembered predictions of their Master, was also proof against the report of Peter and the two disciples. But, as they could not mistake either the Form before them or the Voice to which they listened, they supposed that Jesus, being dead, had appeared to them as spirit without a body. It was, they believed,

His ghost that they saw. My brethren, however we may account for it, man has a secret terror at the thought of contact with pure spirit, unclothed by a bodily form; this dread, I say, is part of our human nature. Perhaps it is due to an apprehension that a disembodied spirit, with its superior freedom and subtlety of movement, may easily take beings such as we are, weighted with a body of sense, at a fearful disadvantage. Perhaps it is to be referred to a dim sense of the truth that our nature is really mutilated, when, during the interval between death and the resurrection, the soul exists for a time apart from the body; it is difficult else to account for the dread of such appearances among those who look forward to a time in which they themselves will be bodiless spirits. St. Paul betrays something of the feeling in question, when he writes to the Corinthians of the spirit after death as "unclothed;" as though death inflicted an outrage upon our poor humanity, and the state of the dead until the resurrection had about it inevitably a touch of the unnatural. Certain, at any rate, it is that the feeling expressed by Eliphaz the Temanite holds good for all time: —

> "In the visions of the night,
> When deep sleep falleth on men,
> Fear came upon me, and trembling,
> Which made all my bones to shake.
> Then a spirit passed before my face;
> The hair of my flesh stood up:
> It stood still, but I could not discern the form thereof:
> An image was before mine eyes;
> There was silence. . . ."

This instinct of our nature, which shrinks from contact with the spirits of the dead, is by no means confined to, or chiefly exhibited in, fervent believers in Divine Revelation. On the contrary, doubt as to Revealed Truth is the natural soil for all unreasoning fears: men ever feel that any horror from beneath is possible, when no blessing is certain from above. Saul is naturally drawn towards the witch of Endor; and the spiritualism, so called, of our day, weird and even grotesque as it often is, gains its most distinguished adherents from among the advocates of pure materialism. Had the disciples looked forward to the fulfilment of their Master's word, as a simple matter of course, they would have welcomed Him with reverent love; and this love would have cast out tormenting fear. As it was, they fell back upon the surmise that He was a ghost; and they shivered at perceiving how near this unearthly being was to each of them.

They said nothing. But He, as always, knew what they felt, what they thought. He did not conjecture their thoughts and feelings; He read them with that penetrating inward glance, which makes Him, in time and in eternity, the Master and Judge of souls; and He was ready with His consolations. "Why are ye troubled? and why do reasonings arise in your hearts? Behold My Hands and My Feet, that it is I Myself: handle Me, and see; for a spirit hath not flesh and bones, as ye see Me have."

This scene is suggestive of so many considerations that a choice is difficult. But there are three which, as it appears to me, claim especial attention just at present.

I.

Here we note first of all our Lord's indulgent treatment of mistakes and imperfections in religious belief. We may venture to say that the disciples, seeing our Lord in the midst of them, ought to have recognized Him at once. They know, from long companionship with Him, that there were no discoverable limits to His power over life and nature. They knew that He had been transfigured on the mountain, and had walked upon the sea. They knew that He had formally claimed to be Messiah, by assuming the distinctive title of Messiahship, — the "Son of Man." They knew that He had shown to them from the Old Testament that the Messiah must suffer, and rise again the third day, in virtue of a prophetic necessity. They knew indeed that to remove all doubt He had, on more occasions than one, and very solemnly, stated that this would happen to

Himself; so that, when they saw Him led forth to death, and expiring in agony, and laid in a tomb, they might have known what would follow. The earlier part of His prediction had been fulfilled to the letter; were they not sure enough of His power to be certain that what remained would be fulfilled as well?

That our Lord held His disciples responsible for such knowledge as this is plain from the words which He had used, earlier in the afternoon, when addressing the two on the Emmaus road: "O fools, and slow of heart to believe all that the prophets have spoken: ought not the Christ to have suffered these things, and to enter into His glory?" And then, continues the Evangelist, "beginning at Moses and all the prophets, He expounded unto them in all the scriptures the things concerning Himself." The reproach addressed to the two disciples seems to imply that, in their case, the responsibility may have been enhanced by the enjoyment of certain opportunities which we cannot accurately measure. But St. Mark refers to the very scene we are now considering by saying that Jesus appeared to the Eleven as they sat at meat, and upbraided them for their unbelief and hardness of heart, because they believed not them that had seen Him after He rose from the dead. Yet, looking to St. Luke's report, what tender censure it is! Here certainly is no expression which betrays grief or anger. He meets their excitement with the mildest rebuke; if it be a rebuke. "Why are ye disquieted? and why do critical reasonings arise in your hearts?" He traces their trouble of heart to its true source; the delusion which possessed their understandings, about His being only a "spirit." In His tenderness He terms their unworthy dread a mere disquietude of the heart; they are on a false track, and He will set them right. They doubt whether what seems to be the Body which hung upon the Cross is really before them; let them look hard at His Hands and at His Feet which had been pierced by the nails. They doubt their sense of sight; very well, let them handle Him; they will find that it is not an ethereal form, which melts away at the experiment of actual contact. He does not peremptorily condemn their notion that a bodiless spirit had appeared to them, as if it were a mere superstition; He even seems to sanction it, when He observed that such spirits have not flesh and bones which answer to the sense of touch. He appeals, let us observe, not merely to hearing and to sight, but to touch. "Handle Me," He says, "and discern." Remember St. John's language at the beginning of his First Epistle; "That Which we have heard, That Which we have seen with our eyes, Which we have looked upon, and our hands have handled, of the Word of Life;" it may well show that they took Him at His word. Touch indeed is the least intellectual, the bluntest, the most material of the five senses. In the order of spiritual precedence, it is below taste and smell, just as sight, and still more hearing, are above them. Touch may be deceived at least as easily as sight. But in certain depressed mental states touch affords a sense of confidence which sight cannot command; it supplies a kind of evidence which, united with other and higher testimony, removes a last obstacle to faith.

Our Lord knows that all this might have been, that it ought to have been unnecessary. But He also measures human weakness. He knows how the tyranny of sense, and of the mental habits which are governed by the senses, holds down the aspirations of faith and love. He, the True Parent and Deliverer of men, "knoweth of what we are made; He remembereth that we are but dust." . . .

II.

Here, too, we see our Lord's sanction of the principle of inquiry into the foundations of our religious belief. Certainly He said to St. Thomas a week afterwards, that they were blessed who had not seen His open Wounds, and yet had believed His Resurrection. But in St. Thomas's case, as a week earlier in that of the Ten and their friends, He sanctions, nay He invites, inquiry, observation, reflection. He does not say, 'If after the testimony of My prophets, after My Own assurances, after the report of My disciples, you cannot believe that I am risen from My grave, and that you see Me before you; then continue in your unbelief; be gone.' He does say, 'Use the means of inquiry which

God has given you: behold My pierced Hands and Feet; see for yourselves that I am He Who hung upon the Cross: nay, touch Me, if thus only you can escape from your illusion, and can discover for yourselves that a Body of flesh and bones is before you, endowed indeed with new and glorious properties, but with Its substantial identity unimpaired.'

Certainly, my brethren, inquiry into the grounds of faith is not the noblest department of religious activity. Our highest duty towards religious truth is to act on it; to expend the strongest and choicest forces of our souls in paying the rightful tribute of love, adoration, obedience, joyful and constant devotion to Him Whose glory and beauty, and mercy and strength, are thus made known to us. And undoubtedly there are souls who, from childhood until death, thus offer to God a continuous service of the affections and of the will. They see truth intuitively as did St. John; they sit and gaze on it as did Mary of Bethany; to them one prayer beyond all others is dear: "Behold, my delight is in Thy commandments; O quicken me in Thy righteousness." And thus, though they live in an age of cold indifference to, or of insolent rebellion against, Revealed Truth, they are "not afraid for any terror by night, nor for the arrow that flieth by day; for the pestilence that walketh in darkness, nor for the sickness that destroyeth at the noonday." Happy and privileged souls! some of whom are to be recognized in every generation, and not least in our own; happy souls whose eyes are ever directed upwards, whose feet are ever pressing forwards, upon whom the burning fiery furnace of human struggle and passion has had no power; as though they had been all along "hidden privily in God's Own Presence from the provoking of all men, and kept secretly in His Tabernacle from the strife of tongues." Some such there were in that upper room. They needed not to gaze curiously at the glorious Wounds, or reverently to handle the very Limbs of the Redeemer; they knew that He was there; that He had risen indeed; that He had appeared unto Simon.

With most of us, it is different; God knows how different. We are of our age; acting perhaps feebly upon it; acted upon by it, we may be sure, most powerfully; sharing its great privileges, its inspiriting hopes and efforts; sharing too its prejudices, its errors, its illusions. On most of us it leaves many a scar; if it does no worse. We, after our fashion, meet Stoics and Epicureans at Athens; we, too, after the manner of men, fight, or ought to fight with beasts at Ephesus. And this means that the life of affection and obedience is necessarily traversed by another life; the life of the critical understanding. If in our day the understanding cannot but survey religious truth, seriously, eagerly, keenly; it need not forget the duties of reverence; it may enable us the better to do the Apostle's bidding, and "be ready to give to every man a reason of the hope that is in us."

Undoubtedly the understanding has great and exacting duties towards Revealed Truth. If God speaks, the least that His rational creatures can do is to try to understand Him. And therefore, as the powers of the mind gradually unfold themselves, the truths of religion ought to engage an increasing share of each of them, and not least of the understanding. What too often happens is, that while a young man's intelligence is interesting itself more and more in a widening circle of subjects, it takes no account of religion. The old childish thoughts about religion lie shrivelled up in some out-of-the-way corner of a powerful and accomplished mind, the living and governing powers of which are engaged in other matters. Then, the man for the first time in his life meets with some sceptical book; and he brings to bear on it the habits of thought and judgment which have been trained in the study of widely different matters. He forms, he can form, no true estimate of a subject, so unlike any he has really taken in hand before: he is at the mercy of his new instructor, since he knows nothing that will enable him to weigh the worth or the worthlessness of startling assertions. He makes up his mind that science has at length spoken on the subject of religion; and he turns his back, with a mingled feeling of irritation and contempt, on the truths which he learned at his mother's knee. . . .

Depend on it, a time comes to many thoughtful young men and women, when they are tempted to think that what they have learnt in childhood about life and death, and God and Jesus Christ, and all that bears on our place in the eternal world, is uncertain; the shadow of an old creed which still haunts the earth; the echo of voices which ought wholly to have died away at the close of the Middle Ages. To many a young man, the first visit to his mind of this terrible suspicion, has brought real and keen agony, in this our own day and country. But in every such trial, to every sincere soul, there is, I dare to say, a voice to be heard which still whispers, "Behold My Hands and My feet, that it is I Myself: handle Me, and see; for a spirit hath not flesh and bones, as ye see Me have." You think, young man, that it is the ghost of a religion which confronts you; handle it, and you will see for yourself that it rests on a basis, at least as sure as any of the ordinary forms of human knowledge. It rests on history. The Life, and Death, and Resurrection of Jesus Christ is not a work of the sanctified imagination of a later age; it is, at least, as much a part of the story of our race as are the life, the victories, the assassination of Julius Caesar. Handle it, searchingly but reverently, and you will discern this for yourself: you will see that there is in it an intrinsic consistency, a solidity, power of resistance to critical solvents, which you have not suspected. But do not suppose that, because it condescends to be thus tested by your understanding, as regards its reality, it is therefore within the compass of your understanding, as regards its scope. It begins with that which you can appraise; it ends in that which is beyond you: because while you are finite and bounded in your range of vision, it is an unveiling of the Infinite, of the Incomprehensible. Yes; Christianity plants its feet firmly on the soil of earth; its hands are seen again and again working in the stirring agencies of human history; but it rears its head towards the sky; it loses itself amidst the clouds of heaven. We see the very feet, the hands, the utter reality of the One Incomparable Life; but we only see enough to know assuredly that there is much more which is necessarily and utterly above us, since it is lost, as the Apostle would say, in the majestic "depths of the riches both of the wisdom and of the knowledge of God."

III.

Once more, note here the direction which our Lord purposely gave to the thoughts of His perplexed disciples. He does not turn them in upon themselves; He does not take their trouble, so to speak, sympathetically to pieces, and deal with its separate elements: He does not refute one by one the false reasonings which arise within them. He does not say to them: 'These disquietudes, these doubts, are mere mental disorders, or interesting experiences, and the mind itself can cure diseases which the mind has produced.' He would, on the contrary, have them escape from themselves; from the thick jungle of their doubts and fears and hopes and surmises; and come to Him. Whatever they may think, or feel; He is there, seated on a throne which enthusiasm did not raise, and which doubt cannot undermine; in His Own calm, assured, unassailable Life. "Behold My hands and My Feet, that it is I Myself: handle Me, and see; for a mere spirit hath not flesh and bones, as ye see Me have."

Religious men, speaking broadly, may be divided into two classes: those who are mainly occupied with themselves, and those who are mainly occupied with God. In modern language, we should call the religion of the first class, subjective; that of the second, objective. Subjective religion makes self the centre of all else; the soul's feelings, thoughts, experiences, are of first account; while Almighty God, His Truth and Grace, are interesting as ministering to or illustrating the varying experiences and moods of the thinking subject, of self. Thus self is the centre of the circle; God is only a point on the circumference. Objective religion, on the contrary, makes God the Being around Whom all else, the soul included, revolves. God, the Perfect and Self-existing, His Almightiness, His Intelligence, His Mercy, His Justice, His matchless Beauty, His unruffled and everlasting Peace; and then, His self-manifestation in the Eternal Son, Incarnate and Crucified, with the resulting Gifts of Grace, ministered by His Spirit, through His Sacraments; all this is of first account. When contemplating this splendid vision of the Truth the soul forgets itself. It forgets the relative, the shifting, the transitory, when it gazes on the Absolute, the Unchanging, the Eternal; it forgets its own petty, narrow, uncertain moods, when it looks out in good earnest on the awful and entrancing magnificence of God. Of objective religion, then, God is the centre; and self, with all its fitful experiences, is a mere point on the circumference.

Not that any religion, to be adequate, can be wholly of the one or of the other description. Objective religion, if unaccompanied by earnest care of the conscience, may easily degenerate into the sort of interest which an intelligent man cannot but take in the highest of all subjects, without its practically changing, moulding, invigorating his life. Doubtless to know God truly we must feel our personal need of Him; the fear of the Lord is the beginning of wisdom. To commune with our own hearts and search out our spirits, till we can say with David, "My sin is ever before me;" to study self in order to be self-distrustful and humble, and for no other purpose whatever; — this is beyond doubt of vital import to our eternal peace. It is in the feebleness of his own resolutions, in the history of his own failures, often in the profound degradations of his own life, that the Christian learns the folly of "going about to establish his own righteousness" instead of submitting himself to the righteousness given by God in Jesus Christ. Not to know self, is to be only a speculative divine, or a heartless formalist.

But the danger of our day lies mainly in the opposite direction. Of modern religion, the greater part is subjective. It is not our Lord Jesus Christ, but our faith in Him, our affections towards Him, our experiences, our assurances, our convictions, about which many of us think chiefly. If it is healthy to dwell on our sins, it is very far from healthy to dwell on our emotions. Man himself, not Christ, is the object of this sort of religious enthusiasm. There is in it no forgetfulness of self, for a single moment; there is nothing of the spirit of St. Paul's saying, "To me to live is Christ;" since self is exalted at the very Feet of the Redeemer. We even hear faith spoken of as a creative faculty. It is said by some to create whatever God gives us through His Sacraments. Others, with fatal consistency, go further, and speak as though faith could create the righteousness which justifies the sinner, or even the Attributes of the Eternal Being. And thus, as the human mind is represented, not as simply receiving, but as originating the strength which is to save it and the objects upon which it dwells, it soon finds out that it can change these objects at will. Idols may be made by the mind just as easily as with the hands; and so it comes to pass that, side by side with the Christ of the Gospels, there are false and imaginary Christs in Christendom, who approve of all that their votaries desire, who condemn only what their votaries dislike, who are crowned, not with thorns, but with roses, and who smile tolerance or recognition upon errors and excesses which the true Christ of Christendom has for ever condemned. And thus is realised the stern irony of the Psalmist: "With the holy Thou shalt be holy: and with a perfect man Thou shalt be perfect. With the clean Thou shalt be clean: and with the froward Thou shalt learn frowardness." This is the ripe product of the subjective spirit in its exaggeration; and you will observe how closely allied it is to the conclusion of a Pantheistic thinker, that the whole object-matter of religion is really reflected into the heavens by the real or supposed necessities of the human soul. The only safeguard against it lies in clinging firmly to the objective character of real Christianity, as based upon assured historical facts. Let us remind ourselves that whether we believe them or not, the facts of the Christian Creed are true; and that faith only receives, but that it cannot possibly create or modify Christ and His gifts. Whether men believe or not in His Eternal Person, in the atoning virtue of His Death, in the sanctyfying influences of His Spirit, in the invigorating grace of His Sacraments; — these are certain truths. They are utterly independent of the hesitations and vacillations of our understandings about them. To ourselves, indeed, it is of great moment whether we have faith or not: to Him, to His truth, to His gifts, it matters not at all. "The Lord sitteth above this waterflood" of our changing and inconstant mental impressions; "the Lord remaineth a King for ever." If we believe not, yet He abideth faithful; He cannot deny Himself."

Let this, then, be our Easter work; to forget ourselves, if we can; to gaze on the Wounds, to clasp the Feet of our Redeemer. Water cannot rise above its level; and if the soul of man is to be restored, it must be from without. It cannot be from within. Left to itself, the soul lacks the light, the strength, the impetus which it needs; it finds them in the Eternal Christ. It can, by faith, gaze on Him even now. It can, by faith, handle Him and discern that He is Man as well as God, God as well as Man, even now. Let us associate ourselves with that company in the upper chamber. Many of us share their trouble; why should we be denied their consolations? To our weakness, to our fears, to our indolent despair, to our barren self-complacency, He says, "Behold My Hands and My Feet, that it is I Myself: handle Me, and discern." Away, brethren, with the illusions which may have kept us from Him! Let us arise, and live.

BIBLIOGRAPHY

Phillips Brooks: *The Candle of the Lord and Other Sermons.* pp. 253-269
G. H. Knight: *The Master's Questions to His Disciples,* 1904, pp. 339-343
H. P. Liddon: *Easter in St. Paul's,* new ed., London, 1892, pp. 203-216
G. H. Morrison: *The Unlighted Lustre.* New York. 1905. pp. 216-225
Charles H. Spurgeon: *Metropolitan Tabernacle Pulpit.* 1895. Vol. 41. No. 2408. pp. 169-178

CANON H. P. LIDDON
(1829-1890)

Of all the gifted preachers from whose works sermons on the Resurrection have been chosen for this collection of messages, H. P. Liddon was preeminently the churchman, though I would not say ecclesiastic, an Anglican of the High Church, but fervently evangelical, with emphasis first upon the Word of God rather than upon ritual or form. Henry Parry Liddon, the son of Captain Liddon, R.N., born August 20, 1829, in his early years was sent up to King's College School in London, from which at the age of seventeen, he proceeded to Oxford, having been nominated to a studentship at Christ Church. Here he devoted himself earnestly to his studies and to the cultivation of his own spiritual life. Strange for a young Englishman, he took no part in games or athletic sports, though watching them with interest. In 1852 he was ordained and began his work as Assistant Curate at Wantage, under the one who was later to become the Dean of Lincoln. In 1854, when only twenty-five years of age, he was appointed by Bishop Wilberforce to the important office of Vice Principal of the newly established Theological College at Cuddeson, where, though he remained only five years, he exercised an enormous influence over a number of young theological students, many of whom were subsequently to obtain fame in the Church of England.

Returning to Oxford, Liddon became Vice Principal of St. Edmund Hall and began that long intimate friendship with the learned Dr. Pusey, which exercised so deep an influence upon the younger man, in spite of his strongly independent nature. In 1868, when Liddon was not yet forty years of age, he delivered his famous Bampton Lectures, "The Divinity of Our Lord and Saviour Jesus Christ," upon a very short notice because of the sudden illness of the one who had previously been appointed for this year. This is without doubt the greatest of all the Bampton Lectures of that generation, and my own opinion would be that it is one of the ten most notable books on the Deity of Christ that appeared in the nineteenth century, full of learning, and fervor, with a glowing love for the Lord Jesus and almost irresistible logic. For twelve years, Liddon continued his position as Ireland Professor of Exegesis at Oxford, but in the midst of this, in 1870, he was called to be a Canon of St. Paul's Cathedral in London. At St. Paul's there now commenced what was without doubt the greatest ministry of Preaching in the Anglican Church of Great Britain for the next twenty years. The cathedral once again became a great national center of worship. In spite of the fact that none of his sermons was less than three-quarters of an hour in length, and some an hour and twenty minutes long, St. Paul's was soon crowded at the Sunday services when Liddon was preaching, with people from every walk of life, many of them leading intellectuals of their day. The verdict of Dean Stanley, himself a notable preacher and a great scholar, would be echoed by thousands of others. "Liddon took us straight up to heaven and kept us there an hour." His sermons were prepared with great care and very thoroughly revised before publication, so that the some twenty volumes of sermons that bear his name are among the most perfect specimens of the homiletic art, some of the most massive and yet inspiring pulpit messages that have appeared in print since the middle of the nineteenth century.

Liddon's love for the Bible and his constant defense of its divine origin gave to his messages an authority which those of weaker convictions could not command. Comparing the Bible to St. Paul's cathedral he called it "the Great Temple of Christ," and then went on to say, "When we take up the Bible, we enter in spirit a far more splendid temple, which it needed some fifteen centuries to build, and the variety and resources of which distances all comparison — a temple built, not out of stone and marble, but with human words, yet enshrining within it, for the comfort and warning, the correction and encouragement of every human soul, no other and no less than the Holy and Eternal Spirit. Of that temple the Old Testament is the nave, with its side-aisles of Psalm and Prophecy; the Gospels are the choir — the last Gospel, perhaps, the very sanctuary; while all around and behind are the Apostolic Epistles and the Apocalypse, each a gem of beauty, each supplying an indispensable feature to the majestic whole. With what joy should we daily enter that temple! With what profound reverence should we cross its threshold! With what care should we mark and note — where nothing is meaningless — each feature, each ornament, that decorates wall, or window, or roof!"

The strain of twenty years of the most intense preaching, the result of constant mental labor and spiritual exercise, together with some years of teaching at Oxford and the publication of many volumes, including the writing of the monumental life of Dr. Pusey, brought on ill health in 1885, and he was persuaded to take an extensive vacation, devoting some months to travel in the Near East. His recognition of declining health led him to refuse with sorrow the offer of the Bishopric of Edinburgh, and later, of St. Alban's. In spite of some months of ill health, his death September 1890, at the age of sixty-one, came as a surprise to his friends, and a shock to the Church of Christ everywhere.

THE CHURCH OF THE RESURRECTION
by
Thomas A. Gurney

"Jesus therefore said to them again, Peace be unto you: as the Father hath sent Me, even so send I you. And when He had said this, He breathed on them, and saith unto them, Receive ye the Holy Ghost: whose soever sins ye forgive, they are forgiven unto them; whose soever sins ye retain, they are retained."

— John 20:21-23

In the great Church of Sancta Sophia at Constantinople, once the glory of all Christendom, but now a Mohammedan mosque, after the eye has gazed with weariness upon the symbols on every hand of Moslem exclusiveness and Moslem superstition, and has yearned, apparently in vain, for some lingering reminder of the glorious Church as it once was in the long-ago, early summer days of its pristine beauty, an imperial witness to the world of devotion to Christ, you may ascend the southern gallery which looks into the great central apse, and, gazing from among the six colonnaded columns towards the vaulted ceiling above its five windows, gradually behold in the dim, half-shadowed sweep of the beautiful roof above, the colossal Figure, wrought in mosaic, of the Glorified and Reigning Christ, with right hand outstretched, as of old, in blessing. The contrast is immediately significant. It is a prophecy which dominates with hope the desecrated Church. The Central Figure, unseen save when earnestly sought for, gathers up into itself all the history of the past and all the promise of the yet more glorious future, and creates the sense in the heart that even still, in hidden but ever present might, the Lord of Glory careth for His own, watching with patience over the chequered life of His people.

This ruling thought of the glorified, reigning Christ, imprinted like that mosaic in His Church's heart, makes the contemplation of the future possible without despair, as it makes the story of the past intelligible. Too often that history of the past, as with Sancta Sophia, seems one long story of human failure to realise the highest and most splendid ideals. The sense of confusion and loss is all the more terrible because of the majesty of that ideal, as when we contemplate how much devotion and enthusiasm lie buried in that dishonoured church. The awful consequences of past unfaithfulness appal the soul with their manifest present results, and draw from us the cry, 'O Lord, how long?'

The story is indeed humiliating, with its weary record of priestly tyranny, of gross materialism and worldliness, of slavish superstition and spiritual lethargy. But in the upward glance lies the solution of all our difficulties. Around us, only too evident, are the marks of the world's scorn, and the Crescent of our foes seems to have overmastered the Cross. But the figure of the Reigning Christ still dominates all, hidden indeed save to the eye of faith. The Hand once pierced on Calvary is still uplifted to give its benediction to her fortunes. The exaltation of the Lord is the pledge of a magnificent future. It suggests hope in the midst of failure, and holds out the certainty of an ever-nearing victory.

The resurrection of Jesus Christ is the assurance of the final triumph of Christianity itself. It is the revelation to the world of a life which must overcome and subdue it. It is the unlocking to the nations of the secret by which alone they can become strong. It is the undying bond of human brotherhood. It is the sole, unfailing inspiration of all true personal hope. 'Christ is risen'; 'He is risen indeed.' Such is the Easter greeting of Greek with Greek on the resurrection morning. The assertion of the fact itself is answered by the reminder of the absolute certainty of conviction which that fact has produced in the heart. And that twofold fact has been the key to all Christian history since. For it means, and must mean to the very end of time, the victory of the Risen Lord. It is the witness to a Life which in its social aspect, as well as its personal, 'overcometh the world.' Wrought into every brick which supports the airy dome of Sancta Sophia are the words in Greek, 'God is in the midst of her; she shall not be moved. God shall help her, and that right early.' It is only an earlier form of the Easter message, 'Lo, I am with you all the days, even unto the end of the age.'

The manifestation by which the Lord Jesus Christ revealed Himself to His Church, though it actually occurred on the evening of Easter Day, yet is reserved by the order of Church teaching until the Gospel for the First Sunday after Easter. Nothing could be plainer than the idea which underlies this arrangement. The thought of the great festival-day itself is the application to the individual of the blessings and responsibilities which derive their reality and meaning from the Resurrection, and this, especially in ancient times, in special relation to the great Baptism of Easter Eve. For much of our Easter teaching has special relation to the newly baptized. It is, therefore, personal — the Resurrection in its bearing upon individual character.

When we come to the last day of the Great Octave we find ourselves confronted with other thoughts. It is no longer the individual, but the Church of which he is a member which forms now our subject. It is the resurrection-life, not in the form which it must take in the character of the individual, but as imparted to, and manifested by, the Christian community. It is the first revelation of Christ to the Christian society in the upper chamber, consequent upon the revelation to Mary, and to the disciples on the roadway to Emmaus. It is that revelation, not as St. Luke regards it, as confirming to the collective disciples the reality of the Lord's resurrection-nature, the correspondence of His resurrection with the prophecies which had gone before. It is, on the other hand, Christ's revelation to His Church as such, with the special accompaniments which convey to us, as they conveyed to them at the time, its absolute significance and uniqueness in relation to the whole of her after-life and history. It is the first bestowment of the collective blessing. It is the first fulfillment of the promise to be hereafter again and again fulfilled, on many a dark evening in the Church's history, 'Where two or three are gathered together in My Name, there am I in the midst of them.' It is the realisation, which must be kept wholly distinct from the promise of the Comforter, not to be fulfilled till Pentecost, of the Saviour's restored presence which He had led them to expect. 'I will not leave you comfortless (or desolate); I come unto you.' It is the collective vision of a Risen Christ, which the world could not have, but which had been promised to them. 'Yet a little while and the world seeth Me no more, but ye see Me.' But it is even more than all this, and the special promise of Life through the Living One which had been attached to that Vision as the property which was to belong to them as a community is the key to its supreme and solemn significance. It was to convey His risen life to His church, or at least to seal them with the pledge of its bestowal, that the manifestation of the Easter evening was granted. It was to unite and to consolidate them into one collective whole, bound together by the sense of a common life, possessed of one inspiration in common, sealed and set apart for one absorbing and victorious mission, charged with the credentials of one world-wide spiritual authority. He stood in their midst and led on their attention at once from the identity yet glory of His risen Being, as they gazed in surprise and awe upon it, to the purpose for which that glory was revealed. That purpose was to thrust forth into the world a living and abiding Representative of His own life, which should break in fragments and consume, overturn and restore, transform and change, yet itself stand for ever — that Church of the Resurrection against which so often the gates of Hell have belched forth their fire and frenzy, yet have not prevailed to overthrow it.

For the Church of Christ is a *Divine* institution, and as such she needs a Divine origin and the enduement with a Divine power. Accordingly the day of Pentecost with its baptism from Heaven, is the commencement of her mission and its manifestation to the world. From that day the Holy Ghost has never ceased to dwell in the hearts of men. But the Church is also intensely *human* in the elements of which she is composed, and it is in the power of her true humanity that in all ages her true mission to men is accomplished. She is, as it were, the Sacrament of the Incarnation ever present to the eyes of men. Accordingly she needs for the human side of her mission the realisation of her unity with the Second Adam risen from the dead. She requires not only the enduement with the Holy Ghost, but also the quickening of the Risen Lord. She needs not only diversities of spiritual gifts for varieties of spiritual function, but also the gift of life itself by which alone they can be received and exercised, and the sense of a mission whereby they can be fulfilled. She must be one with her Lord in all the features of His true humanity, both in suffering and glory. It is here that so often, through the false and unscriptural notion of a priesthood *in* the Church different from her priesthood as a whole, not merely in degree but in quality, the Church Catholic has failed to realise her true mission. But this identity must be a real identity, and can only become so through the impartation of His life from Himself as source. He alone can be the Quickening Spirit to His Church. He alone, Who has passed through the death which we mst share, can say across the grave, 'Because I live, ye shall live also.'

For this reason the manifestation of the first Easter evening is of such supreme importance. It is the gift to the Church of an Overcoming Life. All views of it which regard it as a mere promise of a gift hereafter to follow, and not actually bestowed for fifty days, or as their endowment with a special kind of spiritual charisma consecrated to some special and peculiar purpose, surely miss the evident significance of an act and words so singular in connection with an occasion so unique. The Risen Lord had come back, according to His promise, from the grave. His word was seen to be fulfilled: 'I will see you again, and your heart shall rejoice.' He shows them the reality of His resurrection by offering them proofs of it in His action. At the same time, the very manner of His coming leaves no doubt in their minds as to the reality of the change which His Being has undergone. And immediately, as though He confirmed the thought in their hearts,

He proceeds to demonstrate to them by word and action His power to convey that life to them. He gives them a commission which arises in its majesty and dignity far above any words which they had heard from Him before. 'As My Father hath sent Me, even so send I' (or, am I sending) 'you.' Their hearts would at once question, How could any parallel be established between such a mission as belonged to Him and theirs? How could any such sending be even possible when in their case all those symbols of the Father's special presence, of the unity of nature and of life between the Father and the Son, were wanting? But they were not kept in suspense long. 'And when He had said this, He breathed on them, and saith unto them, Receive ye the Holy Ghost' (or, a gift of the Holy Ghost). 'Whose soever sins ye remit, they are remitted unto them; and whose soever sins ye retain, they are retained.' With the mission, the power to fulfil that mission is given. And that power of fulfilment lies in the unity established now once for all between their life and His. The resurrection-life is given that the Church of Christ may be for all time the witness of the Resurrection endowed with the gift of the Incarnation.

What is this intimate connection between the first moment of the Lord's return after His resurrection and the enduement of His Church with life from above? The answer to the question lies in the fact, so often lost sight of, that Christ rose not merely to manifest but also to convey that life. It is true that by His appearance to His disciples He placed the fact of His resurrection beyond dispute. But the purpose of His return goes far beyond that. His manifestation is the revelation of a new and resurrection-life, and we have seen how much that involves in relation to our Lord's person. But we have now to see how much it involves in relation to His Body, the Church, 'begotten again,' according to His mercy, 'unto a lively hope by His resurrection from the dead.'

Let us try to realise what had been the earthly result of the presence of the Divine Life among men up to this moment. There had been, as the outcome of the witness of word and work, a discrimination made between the hearts of men. A revelation of unwillingness and hostility and unbelief had accompanied the revelation of a growing and deepening faith and love. St. John seems to set this before himself as the great underlying purpose of his gospel; to mark how hostility and devotion deepened side by side, and to point out the inner necessity of things to which this was due. His gospel has been described as the 'vital analysis of faith and unbelief.' A 'judgment' was going on all the time, and that judgment lay in the fact that the coming of the True Light into the world involved a necessary separation between those who 'loved the darkness rather than the light because their deeds were evil,' and those who, 'doing the truth,' 'came to the light that their deeds might be made manifest that they were wrought in God.' The more fully that light shone as it reached the meridian of its earthly day, the more it drew forth out of the winter of the world's sin the heavy clouds of prejudice against which it strove. The gospel is thus a revelation of character brought swiftly to its complete issue. We see the result by a comparison of Pilate and Nicodemus, of Judas and Thomas, of Caiaphas and Peter, of the Pharisees and Mary Magdalene. The potent crucible of Jesus Christ's holy presence resolved character into its true constituents with a swiftness and certainty which were unerring. Up till the present moment, therefore, the creation and disciplining of faith in Himself as their Messiah had been the whole result of His dwelling amongst His own. The fuller revelation of life through His Name which lay beyond was a mystery only as yet dimly foreshadowed and not yet understood. The earlier chapters of the gospel, the questionings of Nicodemus about the New Birth as an absurdity, the scene between Martha and Jesus on His arrival at the home of sorrow, the despairing exclamation of Thomas, all confirm this impression.

We see, therefore, a faith created in Jesus as the Anointed Son of God, which bears in itself the capacity for fuller revelations. We mark a group of disciples gathered in the upper chamber, restored by contact with Him to the true comprehension of the Promised Messiah up to a certain point. We behold in them the lineal descendants and representatives of the whole Old Testament witness which prepared the way for Christ. They are a two-fold product, standing, as it were, between the ages, in the midst of all time, the product of the witness of the Church of Israel under the training of that Prophecy which 'takes off its crown and lays it at the feet of One who is to be,' and the product of the witness of the Incarnate Life. But they are not yet the Christian Church, though the elements and units of that Church are there already. They have as yet no common and corporate life. They are not yet 'His Body, the fulness of Him that filleth all in all.' The teaching and influence of Jesus has made them disciples, learners, but there is no apostleship, no realised collective mission.

But when Christ rose from the dead He came back the Bearer of a Life which He could impart to others. He came back 'the Prince of Life, Who had life in Himself,' and would quicken whom He would. He came back, subject no longer to the old limitations of the flesh, but with a Spiritual Body to become a Quickening Spirit. The Holy Ghost was not to be bestowed independently of the Saviour's previous action, and He would not come to dwell in His fulness in hearts which had not been made ready for His presence. Jesus must first quicken the hearts in which the Comforter was hereafter to dwell. He must first create that which it was the office of the Spirit to sustain. The Life of the Word made flesh must first be bestowed upon His Church. Then the filling up of that life, out of the infinite fullness of God the Holy Ghost, would assuredly follow.

Upon that chosen band of faith this grace of life was bestowed by the Living One on the first Easter evening. Suddenly their eyes beheld Him in the hour of need and perplexity and danger, when the doors were closed for fear of the Jews, and Thomas was absent, and the stories of the apostles and of the women from the sepulchre and the travellers from Emmaus made them astonished. The questions which must have already confronted those who had seen Him would be: How could they remove and overcome the prejudices and hostility of their countrymen? How could they convince those who, like Thomas, had not seen the Risen Lord? The Lord of Life stood in the midst, and all became plain. The words of peace were spoken; the affrighted hearts were reassured; the proofs of the reality of a bodily presence were given. Then the great purpose of the coming was unfolded, and the object which lay behind it. The words of age-long meaning were spoken: 'As My Father hath sent Me, even so send I you; receive ye the Holy Ghost.' The Mission and the Church are one, and spring from the same great moment. The society of the Risen Lord arises with the gift of a resurrection-life and with a mission which is to embrace the whole world. And with that mission and gift goes also the authority which makes both effective and real in the world, before God and before men. 'Whose soever sins ye remit, they are remitted unto them; and whose soever sins ye retain, they are retained.'

Thus the resurrection ushers in *a New Era in Human History*. From the moment of that revelation in the upper chamber the relationships of God and man have undergone an abiding change. Spiritual life is no longer the special and unusual endowment of a privileged few, but the property of a permanent society. The greatness of the change can only be realized by a steady contemplation of the greatness of the results which have followed from it. The history of a large portion of mankind has been marked from that first Easter evening onwards by a new and strengthening current which has been the secret of all its progress and all its life. The Christian society in the midst of the world has leavened that world with the influences of its own victorious life. From depths of degradation, the full measure of which we can never now know, against forces which were tremendous and unparalleled in the power of their common cohesion and common interest, it has uplifted earthly society to the level at which we behold it today. It has achieved this in spite of the fact that it has often been grossly untrue to its own ideals and for whole periods has neglected or ignored its true mission. 'For more than a century,' writes Professor Bryce, 'the chief priest of Christendom was no more than a tool of some ferocious faction among the nobles. Criminal means had raised him to the throne; violence, sometimes going the length of mutilation or murder, deprived him of it. The marvel is a marvel in which Papal historians have not unnaturally discovered a miracle, that, after sinking so low, the Papacy should ever have risen again.' The confession is indeed a terrible one. But it only shows to what lengths a wrong and quasi-heathen conception of the Church can carry us. Yet, though its members have too often been the victims of false hierarchical theories, or dupes of worldly policy and worldly ambition, or the prey, as Christ foretold, of hirelings who cared not for the sheep, such as John Twelfth, Caesar Borgia, or other Popes of the tenth or even later centuries, the Christian society, though human in all its terrible defects, has been also the witness to a Divine Life within. Never has the light been wholly extinguished, though often the windows have been darkened. Never has the Life been wholly lost, though its energies have been paralysed by sin. Never has the Holy Ghost, grieved beyond measure with man's wilfulness and waywardness, withdrawn from the Body which He had filled and returned to the Heaven whence He came down. The record of human unfaithfulness is wonderful when we consider the fact from which we start, but the story of Divine Patience is still more wonderful. The salt has never lost its savour completely; the leaven, however checked in its effects, has carried still some germ of life within. The history of the Church of Christ has been one of progress, though the progress has had many drawbacks. The history of human society as affected by it has been one of gradual but permanent advance. The Risen Christ has confirmed to His Church, by a charter which even Hell cannot annul, the gift of His own victorious life. 'He breathed on them and said unto them, Receive ye the Holy Ghost.' From that moment His continual presence becomes an assured, unalterable fact. The endowment of His own immortal life is made over unto men. The power of His resurrection is given to His Church. The indwelling Spirit of the Risen Christ becomes from that moment her true keynote, and that gift for its fulness only now awaited His return to where He was before.

The Church of the resurrection springs from the first Easter evening. *Certain features* were then impressed upon the Christian society, which that society must retain to the very end of time. One such feature is that (I). It is a *visible society*. The words of our Risen Lord imply this. 'As My Father hath sent Me, even so send I you.' Jesus Christ came in the flesh to men in the flesh, as He preached in the spirit on the first Easter Eve to men in the spirit. He came, therefore, with signs which appealed to human nature as it is and were intelligible by laws of natural reason. His manifestation of Himself to men was not wholly and entirely supernatural. As man, mingling with men, He showed forth the perfect portraiture of the ideal obedience of man to God. As man He drew human nature by the force of human character and human sympathy into fellowship with the Divine. But He 'is gone into Heaven' and has left His Church behind. The Church of the resurrection is, therefore, a Church of visible witness. This is not the transubstantiation of the spiritual into the visible and material, but the continuance of Christ's own plan. Through human channels flow the influences of Heavenly grace. Holy men of God spoke in the Old Testament, 'as they were moved by the Holy Ghost.' Through a life and death set forth before men Christ drew men unto Him. 'As My Father hath sent Me, even so send I you.' The Church is, now that He is 'withdrawn,' the sacrament of Christ's continued presence in the world and the visible witness to the Incarnate and Risen Life. By human agencies and human testimony the Mission of Christ is to be carried forward into the ages yet to come. The appeal for God in the world is couched in language all may understand, and is made by signs which reason herself can test, and rests on facts which form a true historic order. So the society which embraces those who share Christ's Risen Life and have received His commission and authority is a Visible Society, and her work is accomplished by visible members.

A second feature of this society is that (II.) it is a *missionary society*. The Church and the Mission are indeed two aspects of one and the same thing. We speak of 'the Church.' We mean thereby to emphasise unity of Christians in their head and their 'calling out' from the world according to the election of grace into the fellowship of the gospel. Now the 'Mission' is simply the 'Church' in her attitude towards the fulfilment of the Lord's revealed Will, the needs of mankind, and the realisation of His world-wide kingdom. The calling out and the sending, the 'Church' and the 'Mission' were born at one and the same moment. They both alike sprang Athene-like from the same Living Head in the upper chamber on the first Easter evening. One fact is as important as the other, and both facts alike need to be emphasised again and again. 'The Church' failing to realise herself as 'the Mission' is an absurdity, a monstrosity, almost a contradiction in terms. The very gift of life itself was bestowed upon her as the means of fulfilment of a mission already made known. On the other hand, 'the Mission' can only be truly and adequately realised when we realise it not merely as a personal mission, or as 'missions' in which we are specially interested, but also as the Mission of the Church as a whole in her corporate capacity.

We are beginning to realise this aspect of the Church more truly today. But we are only *beginning* to realise it. The utterances of the last Lambeth Conference go far beyond previous pronouncements on the subject, and in comparison with the attitude of other Churches on Foreign Missions they leave little to be desired. Yet they have to confess that in this they go beyond, rather than voice, the actual opinion prevalent in that Church, which at the present moment is the most Missionary Church in the world. 'The duty has not been quite forgotten, but it has been remembered only by individuals and societies; the body as a whole has taken no part. The Book of Common Prayer contains very few prayers for missionary work. It hardly seems to have been present to the minds of our great authorities and leaders in compiling that Book that the matter should be in the thoughts of every one who calls himself a Christian, and that no ordinary service should be considered complete which did not plead amongst other things for the spread of the Gospel. We are beginning, though only beginning, to see what the Lord would have us do. He is opening the whole world to our easy access, and as He opens the way He is opening our eyes to see it, and to see His beckoning hand,'

For the object for which the Life became incarnate was this. 'The Father SENT the Son to be the Saviour of the world.' 'I am come that they might have life, and that they might have it more abundantly.' 'Thou gavest. Him authority over all flesh, that whatsoever Thou hast given Him, to them He should give eternal life.' 'As Thou didst send Me into the world, even so sent I them into the world.' The Life in the flesh of the Son of Man was a life held in trust toful fil a certain mission. In the great sending of the Easter evening our Lord renews this fact in our case and theirs. Upon the fulfilment of that mission to the world not merely the healthfulness, the expansion, the vigor of the Church will depend. It is a deeper fact even than this. The mission realised is not a *Bene Esse,* but the *Esse* of the Church. It is an essential feature, without which you cannot have Christ's conception of the Church at all. When Leonhard Dober, one of the early Moravians, had it laid upon his heart that he must go as first missionary to the negroes of the West Indies in 1732, even though it might involve his selling himself as a slave in order to reach them, it caused him much distress and uncertainty of mind, so entire was the sacrifice, yet so imperious seemed the call. In the course of a sleepless night, he resolved, after true Moravian fashion, to arise and open his Bible and see what message of light it brought him. The Book fell open at Deuteronomy, and the first passage which his eye lighted upon was in the thirty-second chapter, the forty-seventh verse: 'It is not a vain thing for you, because it is your life.' He saw in it the call of God, and became the first missionary sent by Christian Europe to the slaves. He was right. The 'life,' whether of the Church or of the individual, depends on the fulfilment of the mission.

(III.) Another feature of the Christian society is that it is *an Organic Society.* The gift of newness of life is to be realised as the property of the society as a whole, and not merely of one portion of the members who compose it. The gift is not personal merely, but collective, as the authority conveyed with the gift is not an authority conferred upon an order of the Church but upon the whole Christian society. 'The body is one, and hath many members.' The gift of the life is one, and it energises in

every part. The organism possesses a life which transcends the
life of the members, though the life of the members strengthens
and nourishes it, and though each has his all-important function
in relation to the health of the body as a whole. Kant affirmed
that 'the organised being is one in which all is reciprocally means
and ends.' He might have said it of the Church in a higher sense.
The harmonious co-ordination of all individual and personal
life to one great principle of life which governs the whole is one
true keynote of the Church. The whole Body draws its fulness
from the Head, even Christ,' and is, as His body, 'the fulness of
Him That filleth all in all.' The growth of each several part is
dependent upon the realisation of this law of correspondence.
The purpose which underlies all personal gifts is 'the edifying of
the body of Christ.' 'The effectual working in the measure of
every part' is to make increase of the body as a whole. The very
nature of a Body carries with it variety of organs, differentiation
of functions, exercise of control from within, and these ideas
imply a Ministry of Clergy and Laity in their several orders. But
the life is imparted to the whole body, and the Holy Ghost dwells
directly in every member. There are gifts correspondent to the
functions, but to all the mission has been given, upon all the
gift of life is bestowed, and all alike are sharers in the Church's
imperial, authoritative character. It is not the power to fulminate
excommunications, or to grant official indulgence for sin, or to
reign as lords over Christ's heritage, which the Great Head of the
Church granted on that Easter evening. The gathering was general
and representative of the whole Christian society. The Church in
her various elements had drawn together with one accord in one
place. Neither then nor later at Pentecost is there any limitation
of the blessing. It fell on all alike, though the apostles were the
exponents of its results in the second case. Upon the Church as
a whole He breathed then His risen life and sealed it later from
on high. Even the mission of women, which the Church is beginning in these days to realise tentatively and hesitatingly, regarding
it indeed rather from the utilitarian than the Divine standpoint,
springs as directly from the upper chamber as the mission of the

apostles themselves. The vital feature thus impressed upon the Church is one in sympathy with the better thought of our time: her essentially DEMOCRATIC character. No order of sacerdotal privilege creates a barrier between the humblest member of the society and his direct contact with his glorious Head. There are diversities of gifts indeed, but it is the same Lord over all, rich to all alike.

(IV.) From this feature of the Church as a *Democratic Society* arises her social mission. The Church being herself not an order but a society, or rather, *the* society thrust forth into the world, her task is to leaven all human society. She must, therefore, deal with men in their social aspect. Her mission is to empires, to nations, to communities, to man in every aspect of social intercourse. Her splendid task is the 'stewardship of the fulness of times,' the gathering up of all things into one supreme unity in Christ as Head. All which concerns the race and its humblest toilers and breadwinners is her concern. There is certainly ample scope for the fuller realisation of this idea at the present day. For it is an age of social revolution and of social progress full of hope and encouragement to one who regards the social wellbeing of mankind as one great aim of the Church. The powers governed by altruistic ideas through the direct teachings of the Christian faith hold the next age of the world in their hands. The forces working for human improvement are unparalleled in their strength and cohesion.

The actual field of operations is rapidly embracing all mankind. Within the past few years we have seen huge regions hitherto inaccessible in Central and Southern Africa pass within the control of the progressive Christian races, and now we have in addition the Soudan, both east and west, the released Colonies of a decaying power, and probably with them in the near future, the opening out to the same influences of the whole of South America. Besides, we mark the vast upheaval in China, with its inevitable establishment of European and American influence upon a firmer and broader basis. At home, social questions are being dealt with in a spirit of thoroughness and fairness which

142

inspires confidence in the future. The limitations of the scope of the intellect in such matters, unaided by revelation and by conscience, are more and more realised. And the Church herself is beginning to awake to her true responsibility in such questions. Though 'numberless Christians have as yet never thought of applying Christian principles' in such a field, yet of late there has been 'no little improvement in this respect,' and the last pronouncement of the Church through her bishops is that 'Character is influenced at every point by social conditions, and active conscience, in an industrial society, will look for moral guidance on industrial matters.' Great Christian principles are there set forth (in the recognition, inculcation, and application of which Christian social duty will operate), the principle of brotherhood in Christ, the principle of labour, as 'the honourable task and privilege of all,' the principle of justice, recognising that God is no respecter of persons, and the principle of public responsibility, that 'a Christian community is morally responsible for its own economic and social order.'

(V.) One other feature of the Church of the Resurrection yet remains, derived from the Easter evening manifestation. It is her character as an *Imperial Society.* 'Whosesoever sins ye remit, they are remitted unto them; and whosesoever sins ye retain, they are retained.' The power to bind and loose in a certain sense is given with the first moment of her bestowed life. The Church is a spiritual *Kingdom,* and as such exercises authority over all those who come within her pale or within reach of her witness. That authority is not, indeed, the exclusive authority of a spiritual hierarchy; we have marked already how essentially democratic the Church is. It is the authority of the whole organism, an authority in which each humblest member shares. It is not exercised by violent or arbitrary acts, but by faithful, believing, witnessing in the power of the Holy Ghost. That mediaeval picture of the proudest of earthly monarchs, Henry IV., 'in the yard of Countess Matilda's castle, an imperial penitent, standing barefoot and woollen-frocked on the snow three days and nights, till the priest who sat within should admit and absolve him,' may

143

appeal to our imagination as a witness to the growing absolution of the mediaeval papacy, but that very absolution ruined it, and this is not the spirit of the society of Christ, nor does it increase our respect for human nature. The view of the Church of Rome is familiar still, but it is not supported by Holy Scripture, and is at variance now as then with all the essential features of the Church. Yet, nevertheless, there is an Authority above kings and nations and the passing opinions of men. Such authority is ratified in Heaven. The gospel of the Church is the offer of salvation upon certain conditions in the name of the Risen and Exalted Christ. And the simplest way to form a clear idea of what was intended to be bestowed here is to follow out to their logical and practical conclusions the features of the Church upon which we have already dwelt, especially her missionary aspect. It is, indeed, in the awful responsibility arising from this fact that she realises her mission and its tremendous significance to the souls of men. For we see not yet all things put under Christ. But the Imperialism of a world-wide hope brightens her outlook into the future.

'What was good, shall be good, with, for evil, so
        much good more;
On the earth the broken arcs; in the heaven,
    a perfect round.'   (Browning).

BIBLIOGRAPHY

Lancelot Andrewes: *Sermons*, Vol. V, pp. 82-103
G. G. Findlay: *The Things Above*, London, 1901, pp. 119-138
T. A. Gurney: *The Living Lord and the Opened Grave*, London, 1901, pp. 256-278
J. S. Holden: *The Price of Power*, pp. 55-61
Alexander Maclaren: *Expositions of Holy Scripture, St. John XV-XXI*, pp. 308-317; also in his *After the Resurrection*, pp. 40-51
G. Campbell Morgan: *Westminster Pulpit*, Vol. IV (1909), pp. 137-144; Vol. X (1915), pp. 409-416
A. G. Mortimer: *Jesus and the Resurrection*, Philadelphia, 1898, pp. 176-183
B. F. Westcott: *The Revelation of the Risen Lord* (1881), London, 1907, pp. 79-90
D. T. Young: *The Enthusiasm of God*, London, 1905, pp. 62-78

THOMAS ALFRED GURNEY

The author of this sermon was for many years the Vicar of Emmanuel, Clifton, and had a wide reputation for messages of rich devotional content as well as a scholarly undertone. Among his writings are *Nunc Dimittis*, 1906; *The Living Lord and the Open Grave*, 1901; the volume on First Timothy in the Devotional Commentary series, 1905; and *Alive for Evermore; Studies in Manifestations of the Risen Lord*, 1928.

THE DOUBT OF THOMAS
by
A. B. Bruce

John 20:24-29

"Thomas, one of the twelve, called Didymus, was not with them when Jesus came" on that first Christian Sabbath evening, and showed Himself to His disciples. One hopes he had a good reason for his absence; but it is at least possible that he had not. In his melancholy humour he may simply have been indulging himself in the luxury of solitary sadness, just as some whose Christ is dead do now spend their Sabbaths at home or in rural solitudes, shunning the offensive cheerfulness or the drowsy dullness of social worship. Be that as it may, in any case he missed a good sermon; the only one, so far as we know, in the whole course of our Lord's ministry, in which He addressed Himself formally to the task of expounding the Messianic doctrine of the Old Testament. Had he but known that such a discourse was to be delivered that night! But one never knows when the good things will come, and the only way to make sure of getting them is to be always at our post.

The same melancholy humour which probably caused Thomas to be an absentee on the occasion of Christ's first meeting with His disciples after He rose from the dead, made him also sceptical above all the rest concerning the tidings of the resurrection. When the other disciples told him on his return that they had just seen the Lord, he replied with vehemence: "Except I shall see in His hands the print of the nails, and put my finger into the print of the nails, and put my hand into His side, I will not believe." He was not to be satisfied with the testimony of His brethren: he must have palpable evidence for himself. Not that he doubted their veracity; but he could not get rid of the suspicion that what they said they had seen was but a mere ghostly appearance by which their eyes had been deceived.

The scepticism of Thomas was, we think, mainly a matter of temperament, and had little in common with the doubt of men of rationalistic proclivities, who are inveterately incredulous respecting the supernatural, and stumble at everything savouring of the miraculous. It has been customary to call Thomas the Rationalist among the twelve, and it has even been supposed that he had belonged to the sect of the Sadducees before he joined the society of Jesus. On mature consideration, we are constrained to say that we see very little foundation for such a view of this disciple's character, while we certainly do not grudge modern doubters any comfort they may derive from it. We are quite well aware that among the sincere, and even the spiritually-minded, there are men whose minds are so constituted that they find it very difficult to believe in the supernatural and the miraculous: so difficult, that it is a question whether, if they had been in Thomas's place, the freest handling and the minutest inspection of the wounds in the risen Saviour's body would have availed to draw forth from them an expression of *unhesitating* faith in the reality of His resurrection. Nor do we see any reason *à priori* for asserting that no disciple of Jesus *could* have been a person of such a cast of mind. All we say is, there is no evidence that Thomas, as a matter of fact, was a man of this stamp. Nowhere in the gospel history do we discover any unreadiness on his part to believe in the supernatural or the miraculous *as such*. We do not find, e.g., that he was sceptical about the raising of Lazarus: we are only told that, when Jesus proposed to visit the afflicted family in Bethany, he regarded the journey as fraught with danger to his beloved Master and to them all, and said, "Let us also go, that we may die with Him." Then, as now, he showed himself not so much the Rationalist as the man of gloomy temperament, prone to look upon the dark side of things, living in the pensive moonlight rather than in the cheerful sunlight. His doubt did not spring out of his system of thought, but out of the state of his feelings.

Another thing we must say here concerning the doubt of this disciple. It did not proceed from *unwillingness* to believe. It was the doubt of a sad man, whose sadness was due to this, that the event whereof he doubted was one of which he would most gladly be assured. Nothing could give Thomas greater delight than to be certified that his Master was indeed risen. This is evident from the joy he manifested when he was at length satisfied. "My Lord and my God!" that is not the exclamation of one who is forced reluctantly to admit a fact he would rather deny. It is common for men who never had any doubts themselves to trace all doubt to bad motives, and denounce it indiscriminately as a crime. Now, unquestionably, too many doubt from bad motives, because they do not wish and cannot afford to believe. Many deny the resurrection of the dead, because it would be to them a resurrection to shame and everlasting contempt. But this is by no means true of all. Some doubt who desire to believe. Nay, their doubt is due to their excessive anxiety to believe. They are so eager to know the very truth, and feel so keenly the immense importance of the interests at stake, that they cannot take things for granted, and for a time their hand so trembles that they cannot seize firm hold of the great objects of faith — a living God; an incarnate, crucified, risen Saviour; a glorious, eternal future. Theirs is the doubt peculiar to earnest, thoughtful, pure-hearted men, wide as the poles asunder from the doubt of the frivolous, the worldly, the vicious: a holy, noble doubt, not a base and unholy; if not to be praised as positively meritorious, still less to be harshly condemned and excluded from the pale of Christian sympathy — a doubt which at worst is but an infirmity, and which ever ends in strong, unwavering faith.

That Jesus regarded the doubt of the heavy-hearted disciple as of this sort, we infer from His way of dealing with it. Thomas having been absent on the occasion of His first appearing to the disciples, the risen Lord makes a second appearance for the absent one's special benefit, and offers him the proof desiderated. The introductory salutation being over, He turns Himself at once to the doubter, and addresses him in terms fitted to remind him of his own statement to his brethren, saying: "Reach hither thy finger, and behold My hands; and reach hither thy hand, and thrust it into My side; and be not faithless, but believing." There may be somewhat of reproach here, but there is far more of most considerate sympathy. Jesus speaks as to a sincere disciple, whose faith is weak, not as to one who hath an evil heart of unbelief. When demands for evidence were made by men who merely wanted an excuse for unbelief, He met them in a very different manner. "A wicked and adulterous generation," He was wont to say in such a case, "seeketh after a sign, and there shall no sign be given unto it, but the sign of the prophet Jonas."

Having ascertained the character of Thomas's doubt, let us now look at his faith.

The melancholy disciple's doubts were soon removed. But how? Did Thomas avail himself of the offered facilities for ascertaining the reality of his Lord's resurrection? Did he actually put his finger and hand into the nail and spear wounds? Opinions differ on this point, but we think the probability is on the side of those who maintain the negative. Several things incline us to this view. First, the narrative seems to leave no room for the process of investigation. Thomas answers the proposal of Jesus by what appears to be an immediate profession of faith. Then the form in which that profession is made is not such as we should expect the result of a deliberate inquiry to assume. "My Lord and my God!" is the warm, passionate language of a man who has undergone some sudden change of feeling, rather than of one who has just concluded a scientific experiment. Further, we observe there is no allusion to such a process in the remark made by Jesus concerning the faith of Thomas. The disciple is represented as believing because he has seen the wounds shown, not because he has handled them. Finally, the idea of the process proposed being actually gone through is inconsistent with the character of the man to whom the proposal was made. Thomas was not one of your calm, coldblooded men, who conduct inquiries into truth with the passionless impartiality of a judge, and who would have examined the wounds in the risen Saviour's body with all the coolness with which anatomists dissect dead carcases. He was a man of passionate, poetic temperament, vehement alike in his belief and in his unbelief, and moved to faith or doubt by the feelings of his heart rather than by the reasonings of his intellect.

The truth, we imagine, about Thomas was something like this. When, eight days before, he made that threat to his brother disciples, he did not deliberately mean all he said. It was the whimsical utterance of a melancholy man, who was in the humour to be as disconsolate and miserable as possible. "Jesus risen! the thing is impossible, and there's an end of it. I won't believe except I do so and so. I don't know if I shall believe when all's done." But eight days have gone by, and lo, there is Jesus in the midst of them, visible to the disciple who was absent on the former occasion as well as to the rest. Will Thomas still insist in applying his rigorous test? No, no! His doubts vanish at the very sight of Jesus, like morning mists at sunrise. Even *before* the Risen One has laid bare His wounds, and uttered those half-reproachful, yet kind, sympathetic words which evince intimate knowledge of all that has been passing through His doubting disciple's mind, Thomas is virtually a believer; and *after* he has seen the ugly wounds and heard the generous words, he is ashamed of his rash, reckless speech to his brethren, and, overcome with joy and with tears, exclaims, "My Lord and my God!"

It was a noble confession of faith, — the most advanced, in fact, ever made by any of the twelve during the time they were with Jesus. The last is first; the greatest doubter attains to the fullest and firmest belief. So has it often happened in the history of the church. Baxter records it as his experience that nothing is so firmly believed as that which hath once been doubted. Many Thomases have said, or could say, the same thing of themselves. The doubters have eventually become the soundest and even the warmest believers. Doubt in itself is a cold thing, and, as in the case of Thomas, it often utters harsh and heartless sayings. Nor need this surprise us; for when the mind is in doubt the soul is in darkness, and during the chilly night the heart becomes frozen. But when the daylight of faith comes, the frost melts, and hearts which once seemed hard and stony show themselves capable of generous enthusiasm and ardent devotion.

Socinians, whose system is utterly overthrown by Thomas's confession, naturally interpreted, tell us that the words "My Lord and my God" do not refer to Jesus at all, but to the Deity in heaven. They are merely an expression of astonishment on the part of the disciple on finding that what he had doubted was really come to pass. He lifts up his eyes and his hands to heaven, as it were, and exclaims, My Lord and my God! it is a fact: The crucified Jesus is restored to life again. This interpretation is utterly desperate. It disregards the statement of the text, that Thomas, in uttering these words, was answering and speaking to Jesus, and it makes a man bursting with emotion speak frigidly; for while the one expression "My God" might have been an appropriate utterance of astonishment, the two phrases, "My Lord and my God," are for that purpose weak and unnatural.

We have here, therefore, no mere expression of surprise, but a profession of faith most appropriate to the man and the circumstances; as pregnant with meaning as it is pithy and forcible. Thomas declares at once his acceptance of a miraculous fact, and his belief in a momentous doctrine. In the first part of his address to Jesus he recognises that He who was dead is alive: My Lord, my beloved Master! it is even He, — the very same person with whom we enjoyed much blessed fellowship before He was crucified. In the second part of his address he acknowledges Christ's divinity, if not for the first time, at least with an intelligence and an emphasis altogether new. From the fact He rises to the doctrine: My Lord risen, yea, and therefore my God; for He is divine over whom death hath no power. And the doctrine in turn helps to give to the fact of the resurrection additional certainty; for if Christ be God, death *could* have no power over Him, and His resurrection was a matter of course. Thomas having reached the sublime affirmation, "My God," has made the transition from the low platform of faith on which he stood when he demanded sensible evidence, to the higher, on which it is felt that such evidence is superfluous.

We have now to notice, in the last place, the remark made by the Lord concerning the faith just professed by His disciple. "Jesus saith unto him, Thomas, because thou hast seen Me, thou hast believed: blessed are they that have not seen, and yet have believed."

This reflection on the blessedness of those who believe without seeing, though expressed in the past tense, really concerned the future. The case supposed by Jesus was to be the case of all believers after the apostolic age. Since then no one has seen, and no one can believe because he has seen, as the apostles saw. They saw, that we might be able to do without seeing, believing on their testimony.

But what does Jesus mean by pronouncing a beatitude on those who see not, yet believe?

He does not mean to commend those who believe without any inquiry. It is one thing to believe without seeing, another thing to believe without consideration. To believe without seeing is to be capable of being satisfied with something less than absolute demonstration, or to have such an inward illumination as renders us to a certain extent independent of external evidence. Such a faculty of faith is most needful; for if faith were possible only to those who see, belief in Christianity could not extend beyond the apostolic age. But to believe without consideration is a different matter altogether. It is simply not to care whether the thing believed be true or false. There is no merit in doing that. Such faith has its origin in what is base in men, — in their ignorance, sloth, and spiritual indifference; and it can bring no blessing to its possessors. Be the truths credited ever so high, holy, blessed, what good can a faith do which receives them as matters of course without inquiry, or without even so much as knowing what the truths believed mean?

The Lord Jesus, then, does not here bestow a benediction on credulity.

As little does He mean to say that all the felicity falls to the lot of those who have never, like Thomas, doubted. The fact is not so. Those who believe with facility do certainly enjoy a blessedness all their own. They escape the torment of uncertainty, and the current of their spiritual life flows on very smoothly. But the men who have doubted, and now at length believe, have also their peculiar joys, with which no stranger can intermeddle. Theirs is the joy experienced when that which was dead is alive again, and that which was lost is found. Theirs is the rapture of Thomas when he exclaimed, with reference to a Saviour thought to be gone for ever, "My Lord and my God!" Theirs is the bliss of the man who, having dived into a deep sea, brings up a pearl of very great price. Theirs is the comfort of having their very bygone doubts made available for the furtherance of their faith, every doubt becoming a stone in the hidden foundation on which the superstructure of their creed is built, the perturbations of faith being converted into confirmations, just as the perturbations in the planetary motions, at first supposed to throw doubt on Newton's theory of gravitation, were converted by more searching inquiry into the strongest proof of its truth.

What, then, does the Lord Jesus mean by these words? Simply this: He would have those who must believe without seeing, understand that they have no cause to envy those who had an opportunity of seeing, and who believed only after they saw. We who live so far from the events are very apt to imagine that we are placed at a great disadvantage as compared with the disciples of Jesus. So in some respects we are, and especially in this, that faith is more difficult for us than for them. But then we must not forget that, in proportion as faith is difficult, it is meritorious, and precious to the heart. It is a higher attainment to be able to believe without seeing, than to believe because we have seen; and if it cost an effort, the trial of faith but enhances its value. We must remember, further, that we never reach the full blessedness of faith till what we believe shines in the light of its own self-evidence. Think you the disciples were happy men because they had seen their risen Lord and believed? They were far happier

153

when they had attained to such clear insight into the whole mystery of redemption, that proof of this or that particular fact or doctrine was felt to be quite unnecessary.

To that felicity Jesus wished His doubting disciple to aspire; and by contrasting his case with that of those who believe without seeing, He gives us to know that it is attainable for us also. We too may attain the blessedness of a faith raised above all doubt by its own clear insight into divine truth. If we are faithful, we may rise to this from very humble things. We may begin, in our weakness, with being Thomases, clinging eagerly to every spar of external evidence to save ourselves from drowning, and end with a faith amounting almost to sight, rejoicing in Jesus as our Lord and God, with a joy unspeakable and full of glory.

BIBLIOGRAPHY

L. A. Banks: *The Fisherman and His Friends*, New York, 1896, pp. 111-121
A. B. Bruce: *The Training of the Twelve*, 3rd ed., 1883, pp. 492-500
J. M. Gibbon: *Evangelical Heterodoxy*, London, 1909, pp. 106-115
H. Scott Holland, in *Christian World Pulpit*, 1901, Vol. 59, pp. 243-246
John Keble: *Sermons for Easter to Ascension Day*, Oxford, 1876, pp. 230-239
F. W. Krummacher: *The Risen Redeemer*, Eng. tr., New York, 1863, pp. 111-126
Alexander Maclaren: *Expositions of Holy Scripture, St. John XV-XXI*, pp. 317-327; also, his *After the Resurrection*, pp. 52-64
John Macmillan, in *Christian World Pulpit*, Vol. 86 (1914), pp. 37-39
G. Campbell Morgan: *Westminster Pulpit*, Vol. V. (1910), pp. 129-136; Vol. X (1915), pp. 249-256
Hubert L. Simpson: *Nameless Longing*, London, 1930, pp. 280-292
Robert South: *Sermons Preached upon Several Occasions*, Philadelphia, 1844, Vol. II, pp. 348-367
Charles H. Spurgeon: *Metropolitan Tabernacle Pulpit*, 1888, Vol. 34, No. 2061, pp. 713-720
R. C. Trench: *Sermons Preached in Westminster Abbey*, New York, 1866, pp. 35-47
B. F. Westcott: *The Revelation of the Risen Lord* (1881), 6th ed., London, 1907 pp. 95-106

ALEXANDER B. BRUCE
(1831-1899)

Alexander B. Bruce was born in the parish of Abernethy in Perthshire, January 30, 1831. Bruce was educated at Edinburgh University, and then in the Divinity Hall of the Free Church of Scotland, which he entered at the early age of eighteen. His years in New College was a period of intellectual strain and stress, when at times he was greatly troubled with doubts about the Christian faith. Surmounting these, he entered the ministry, preaching in various places, until appointed to the chair of Apologetics and New Testament Exegesis in the Free Church Hall Glasgow in 1875, retaining this position until his death.

Bruce's life might be divided into three major sections — the years of training and overcoming doubt, the years of strong faith and deep insight into the Scriptures, and the last period when his faith in some truths seemed to waver, so that he was once brought before the Assembly and questioned as to his orthodoxy. His greatest works were the earliest. He was just forty years of age when he published his *Training of the Twelve,* which within a few years was on the shelf of almost every minister in Great Britain and thousands in our own country. For what he attempted in this volume, it has never been surpassed. Professor Bruce, in spite of his profound insights, strangely ignored, or rarely considered, the theological teachings of the Old Testament, the subject of the Holy Spirit, and the great areas of Eschatology.

The other epochal work of his was *The Humiliation of Christ,* published in 1876. The comment of the great scholar, Dr. Warfield of Princeton, it seems to me, needs to be remembered. These first two books he affirmed "will assuredly embalm his faith in future generations. As the minimizing spirit of a concessive apologetic grew on him, his theological product decreased in value; and his later works illustrate all too vividly the wrong impression that the Gospel for an age of doubt should preferably be a doubting or even a doubtful Gospel."

Dr. W. M. Clow, also to attain great fame as a writer, remarked in his biographical sketch in the *Expository Times* that "he was not an ecclesiastic and was alien in spirit to the 'body' who finds his delight in a committee. He could not understand the gleam of joy which floods some men's faces as they frame an overture."

THE CHURCH AND THE WORLD
by
Adolph Saphir

"Go ye therefore, and teach all nations, baptizing them in the name of the Father, and of the Son, and of the Holy Ghost; teaching them to observe all things whatsoever I have commanded you." — Matthew 28:19, 20

The ascension of our Lord into heaven is not narrated by the Evangelist Matthew. The last view of our Lord which is given us in this Gospel is Christ on earth, surrounded by His disciples; and the last accents of His blessed voice which are recorded contain the assurance of His presence with us unto the end of this dispensation. The truth which is thus impressed on us is that our Lord, although ascended and seated at the right hand of the Father, is still on earth, that in His disciples He continues His work and mission, that His Church is identified with Him, that through His believers, as the members of His body, He exerts His power and manifests His grace among the nations of the world. The Church is the representative and the continuation of Christ. "And now I am no more in the world, but these are in the world." Apart from Christ the Church has no light or life; unless His presence go with us, we cannot continue our pilgrimage in the wilderness. Christ is with and in the Church. As He promised, so the Church has experienced it. In coming down from heaven He never left the Father, and in going up to heaven He never left the Church. Wherever two or three are gathered in His name, wherever disciples go forth to preach the glad tidings and to teach the counsel of God, wherever the Church of Christ is, there is Immanuel, the real presence of our Divine Lord.

As Christ was sent by the Father, so is the Church sent by Christ. Jesus was sent to be the Revelation and Representative of the Father, to testify of Him, to declare Him, to do His will, and to finish the work. He was a true and faithful witness; He was the perfect Servant, whose meat it was to do the Father's will; He declared the name of God, and finished the work. Now Christ sends us into the world that we may show forth His life, that we may be His witnesses, that His light and love may shine, attract, and bless men through us, that men may behold in us Christ, as they beheld the Father in Him. As Christ was, so are we in the world. The Church is so identified with Christ, that she is called Christ. "As the body is one, and hath many members, and all the members of that one body, being many, are one body; so also is Christ." How clear and wonderful is the position of the Church on earth! She is sent, she is entrusted with a high mission, she has only one aim and object — to represent, imitate, obey Christ; nay, more than this, one with Christ by the Holy Ghost, Christ dwelling in her by faith, it is Christ whose testimony is to be heard through her, whose energy and love saves, gathers, comforts, and builds up the souls of men unto eternal life.

What is the foundation on which the Church of Christ rests? What is the basis, peculiar, distinctive, and all-glorious, on which she is built? What is that marvel and joy which prophets and kings desired to see and hear, but which was reserved for the last days? It is nothing less than the incarnation of the Son of God. . . . The Church is the body of Christ, the Son of God in human nature, exalted after His sufferings to be our Head. We are the sons of God in Christ, the only-begotten of the Father. Our sonship is based on the death of the cross; it springs out of the resurrection of Jesus; it is given unto us by the Holy Ghost, whom the Father sends us through His Son. The peculiar glory of the Church is *sonship*. Her peculiar mission is to show forth the character and life of the sons of God, who, born of the Spirit, are by Him united with the only-begotten of the Father. The Church is in the world, as Jesus was in the world, who in the lowliness of His humanity revealed His divine glory in love and obedience.

The Church is in the world. This position is assigned to her of God, according to the prayer of Christ, "I pray not that Thou shouldest take them out of the world, but that Thou shouldest keep them from the evil."

The reason is threefold. The first reason is, as always, the glory of God. As Jesus was sent by the Father, that in the face of Christ the glory of God might be manifested; so the Church is to reflect the image of her unseen but ever-living Lord, and thus show forth the glory of God. We do not think sufficiently of this first fundamental and central object of the Church's existence. To glorify God is not merely the chief end of man, but it is the great end which God has set before Him in all His acts and revelations. Not merely creation, but redemption has this great end — the manifestation of God. By the Church the manifold wisdom of God is to be made known unto all angelic hosts. Throughout all ages God is glorified in the Church by Christ Jesus. . . .

The second reason why the Church is in the world is, that she may follow Jesus, who through suffering entered into glory. Called unto a heavenly inheritance, chosen to be joint heirs with Christ, and to sit with Him on His throne, the Church is first to learn the wisdom and patience of the saints, to know the fellowship of Christ's sufferings, being made conformable unto His death. In temptation and sorrow, in conflict and trial, in hardship and grief, the disciples of Christ are to grow in grace and knowledge, to become strong in meekness, in love, in faith, and to be conformed to the image of Christ. It is necessary that through much tribulation we should enter into the kingdom of glory.

The third reason why the Church is in the world is, the conversion of sinners. Through her testimony men are to be brought to the knowledge of Christ. God may reveal His grace to the soul directly. Thus Jesus appeared unto Saul of Tarsus: but notice that even Saul, who was converted by the Lord Himself, was, according to Christ's command, linked unto the Church by Ananias, and baptized by him, and thus brought into the congregation of disciples, in which it pleases God to reveal His grace on earth. The Church is to be the witness of God, and mother of the faithful. Herein is the love of God, the Source of all blessedness, who draws into the circle of giving and blessing all His angels and saints. As God is Love, and as mercy and blessing are His delight; so it is His love that all should partake, according to their several position and capacity, in this joy of love, this delight of giving. Angels, therefore, minister unto the heirs of salvation; apostles, evangelists, elders, deacons, all disciples, are called to be workers together with God; to go forth sowing, that they may rejoice with Him who giveth seed to the sower, and share His joy of harvest with the labourers, whom His grace permitted and enabled to work for and with Him. And thus all things are of Him and through Him and to Him, and He is Love. Of the Father as the Source, through Christ as the Mediator, and by the energy of the Holy Ghost, the Church is gathered in, angels and saints obeying His command and fulfilling His will; and the blessings which thus descend, ascend again through the Spirit and by the Son to the Father in thanksgiving and adoring joy.

We read that Messiah shall see of the travail of His soul; and yet Paul the Apostle writes, "My little children, of whom I travail in birth, let Christ be formed in you;" and the beloved disciple writes, "I have no greater joy than to hear that my children walk in the truth." Blessed union! Christ and the Church are one, the Light of the world, the Sent of the Father. Through the Church Christ seeks and saves that which is lost; through her He speaks peace and comfort to the weary and heavy-laden. The sinners whom His grace has redeemed and His Spirit renewed, He sends forth as His ambassadors, and they beseech men in His stead. He makes them fishers of men; they win souls. And when the Chief Shepherd appears, He crowns the under-shepherds with glory and joy, even with the children who through their testimony were born unto eternal life.

. . . To remember both her duty to, and her danger in, the world is difficult; and experience shows that the Church is apt, either to take a narrow view of her mission, and to fail in aggressive courage and breadth of love and sympathy, or to be dazzled by a superficial success, and, conforming herself with this present world, increase her numbers with those who, being dead and unrenewed, are without the Spirit, and therefore without the love of Christ.

The Church and the world form a contrast, and they are also opposed to each other. In one aspect, the Church and the world are a contrast, but not antagonistic. In another, the Church and the world are opposites. The world hates the Church, and the Church, delivered from this present evil world, constantly overcomes it. The world is made for the Church. The Church is sent to the world. The world is loved of God, and Jesus is the world's Light. But world and Church form a contrast. The one is in the sphere of nature, the other is in the sphere of the Spirit. The world's life is based upon the work of God in creation, the Church is founded by the outpouring of the Spirit on Pentecost. The world is of the first Adam, who (even before the fall) was of the earth earthy; the Church is born of the second Adam, the Lord from heaven, the spiritual man. Viewed as creation, the world is good, beloved of God, and made for the Church. It is the mission of the Church to enter into every department of human life. We must remember that all the relationships of the family and the state are instituted by God. They are of the Father, and therefore for Christ and the Church. Jesus changes the water, which is God's creature and good, into wine, which is a better and higher gift. Body, soul, and spirit are to be sanctified to the service of God. Man's intellectual and social life on earth — all that humanity is and possesses — is the territory and sphere upon which the Church should exert her power. Here the Church may not be aggressive enough. She may not enter into the wide range of applications which belong to the Word of her Master — "I am not come to destroy, but to fulfil." She may not possess sufficient insight, patience, and courage of love to go into the world and attract those who are drawn by the Father and seeking after Him, though as yet they are in darkness and in sin. She may mistake an outward and mechanical separation for the true holiness which Jesus manifested. He came eating and drinking, and went to the Pharisees who invited Him to be their guest. It is no doubt much easier to follow the method of John the Baptist than to imitate the example of our blessed Lord, who in the fulness of spiritual power and love lived among men. For we must never forget that wherever Jesus went He was about His Father's business, fulfilling the mission for which He was sent, and testifying of the kingdom. . . .

The Christians are thus prepared and gifted to explain and interpret the world. They are taught by Scripture to praise the Lord in all His works, in all places of His dominion. They can recognize and enjoy beauty in art as well as nature. They can trace the hidden longings after God's salvation and light; they love to find in Athens the altar with the inscription, "To the Unknown God;" they love to quote the testimony "of your own poets." They are called to befriend and cherish whatsoever things are true and venerable, just and pure, lovely and of good report. They are commanded to seek out "them that are worthy," and bring to them the gospel-salvation of peace.

The Church of Christ, in its best and healthiest days, never despised learning and culture, but received it with thanksgiving and diligent care, judging all things by the Word of God, and measuring all things by the standard of revelation.

But the world must be viewed in another light, sad, but equally true. The world lieth in the wicked one. Humanity has fallen; we live in an evil world. And what the evil of the world is in which we are, we may easily know by the evil of the world which is in us; selfishness, pride, lust, covetousness, trust in that which is outward, and unbelief in that which is spiritual, seeking our own glory, in short, all manifestations of departure from God. Against this world the Church must continually fight. She must assert the opposition between nature and grace, flesh and spirit, anti-Christ and Christ, Satan and God; she must assert the great distinction between the best works, and the most beautiful and noble products of man's spirit, and the new creation of the Holy Ghost. She must declare the judgment by which the Prince and the spirit of the world are already condemned, and the wrath which is to come on the enemies of God, and must exhort men to separate themselves from the world, to save themselves from this untoward generation. She must not allow her testimony to be so indistinct, her life and walk so colourless, her discipline so lax, that unrenewed men can fancy themselves to be members of the mystical body of which Christ is the Head, or that they who are strangers to the grace and power of Christ, can presume to take part in the guidance of the Church, or in the ministrations of Christ's heritage.

Much evil has arisen from the indistinct and erroneous views which have prevailed from an early period of the Church, on the character and position of Christ's flock in the present age, the times of Gentiles. The distinction between the Church and the kingdom was forgotten. The Scripture teaches clearly, that until the return of our blessed Lord Jesus the Church is a little flock without outward strength and glory, hated and persecuted by the world; and her hope is in the Father's counsel and power, her eye is directed to the future, when by divine interference the kingdom will be given to her. Christ has delivered us from this present evil world, of which Satan is the Prince. The wisdom of this world is not able to recognise the truth as it is in Jesus. When we become enamoured of this world, we forsake the apostle and his Master. The world, as our Saviour has foretold, shall hate us. The more we show forth Christ's image, the more closely we follow Him, and testify for Him in word and truth, the more shall the enmity and persecution of the world among all nations rest on us; for the world loveth its own, and hateth what is not of the world, but from above. And as the hatred of the world to Christ on earth increased in bitterness, cruelty, and self-consciousness, till at last they nailed Him to the cross; so the word of prophecy reveals to us that the history of the Church, the Bride, will resemble that of her Divine Lord, that the world in the latter days will hate God and His Anointed, and persecute unto death the saints of the Most High who confess and believe His truth. The last development of the so-called Christianised nations is the

manifestation of anti-Christ, the open and self-conscious rebellion against the Father and the Son. The end of this age is
judgment. The monarchies of the world are destroyed, and become like the chaff of the summer threshing-floors. Christ and
His saints appear in glory; the Son of man begins His reign;
and in His kingdom the nations of the earth honour and obey
God, and the Father's will is done here as it is in heaven.

The Church soon forgot the position which God has assigned
to her, and the object which she was continually to bear in view.
Instead of being a witness continuing the ministry of Christ,
endeavouring to save the lost sheep, and to gather those who were
of the truth into the fold; instead of relying on her spiritual
weapons, the influence of the Word, the converting and renewing
power of the Holy Ghost, the attraction of love and holiness, the
Church was dazzled by the outward Christianisation of kings and
princes; and, relying on the influence of worldly power, legislation, and fashion, rejoiced in the strong numerical accessions
which soon changed the Church from being a field of wheat in
which there were some tares, into a field of tares in which there
is some wheat. The papacy is, in its inmost essence, a false
anticipation of the kingdom, a confusion of the Church and the
Christocracy. As a German writer (Roos) says, "Rome usurped
as a harlot the position and rights which the Bride of the Lamb
shall possess in love and holiness." . . .

If we hold fast these truths, our position in the world is clear,
and our aim distinct. The object of the Church is not to Chris-
tianise the world. "Simeon hath declared how God at the first
did visit the Gentiles, *to take out of them a people for His name.*"
"This gospel of the kingdom shall be preached in all the world
for a witness unto all nations, and then shall the end come."
While the tabernacle of David is in ruins, while Jerusalem is
trodden down of the Gentiles, while instead of the theocracy there
is the witnessing and suffering Church, God is taking out from the
nations of the earth a people to know and serve Him. The
Church is an election; its character is elective, and not universal;
exceptional, and not general; we are the few, and not the major-

ity; strangers and pilgrims, and not established and dominant; waiting for the absent (yet spiritually present) Lord and Bridegroom, who will return and build again the tabernacle of David, and reign in peace and truth.

Our hope is Christ's return. We are not expecting days of peace and sunshine, but of storm and tempest; we are not looking forward to times of safety, of godliness and of truth, but to perilous times, in which worldliness and error shall become strong, attractive, and violent. We expect the days which preceded the Flood and the destruction of Sodom and Gomorrah. We believe God will gather many from among Jews and Gentiles into the Church, and bless His testimony to multitudes, ere the judgment comes. But our hope is nothing less and nothing else than the Lord Himself, who shall return to take to Himself the kingdom, according to the will of the Father. Our only anxiety, therefore, ought to be to remain faithful and loyal to Him; to maintain truth in its fulness and in the spirit of love, to seek not high or worldly things, but, like Jesus Himself, to rejoice and give thanks when the Father reveals His Son to "babes," and when sinners, however few and obscure, draw near to hear the beloved gospel of Divine grace.

How is the Church to fulfil her mission to the world, and to keep herself pure? The purity of the Church is not by isolation, but by aggressiveness; and the victory of the Church is not by world-conformity, but by purity. The more aggressive the Church is, the purer she will remain. The more courageously she attacks the world, the less injury she will receive from the poisonous atmosphere of unbelief and selfishness around her. If the Church wishes to keep herself unspotted from the world, and to grow in grace and heavenly-mindedness, she must enter into the mind of her Lord, who, sent by the Father, came to seek and to save that which is lost, who went about doing good, and declared to all, Pharisees and publicans, the evangel of divine love. The Church who feels no compassion for perishing souls, who is not constrained by the love of Him who died for the guilty, who does not walk in the footsteps of the great Deacon who came to minister unto others, has already become worldly; the spirit of selfishness and unbelief has already entered into her heart, and is endangering her very life.

The safety of the Church is in warfare. If she does not attack the world with the peaceful yet powerful weapons of the Spirit, she loses the faith which is the victory that overcometh, and the love which constrains the members of Christ to be ambassadors of the divine gospel. If the light does not shine before men, it will soon be extinguished; if the salt does not benefit the mass, the salt itself will soon be worthless and trodden under foot. The man who obeys not the command of his leader, and in cowardice and ignoble sloth stays away from the battle, does not merely deprive himself of a share in the joy and reward of victory, but is in danger of losing the approbation of him who has called him to be a soldier. . . .

The Church resists the world by conquering love. She keeps herself pure by going into the world, preaching glad tidings by word and work. And in this aggressiveness she is strongest when she is most pure. When loyal to her heavenly Bridegroom, she keeps herself unspotted from the world, she is most skilful and most blessed in gaining souls. She loves the world most, and is her true benefactor, when most obedient to the apostolic precept, "Love not the world." She cannot influence unless her standpoint is heavenly. As Archimedes said, "Give me where I can stand, and I will move the earth," the Church can attract and conquer only when she remembers her heavenly position and character. When we seek the praise, and yield to the spirit of the world, our light loses its light, our salt its savour. David cannot fight with Goliath in Saul's armour. Our sufficiency is of God; our weapons are spiritual.

Very comprehensive are the comparisons of Scripture to illustrate the wonderful position of the Church of Christ in the world. It is surely not accidental that these various comparisons comprise the *universe,* all the various spheres of the creation of God. Beginning with the inanimate, the Church is compared to the heavenly bodies, to the celestial luminaries — the Church is called the light of the world, and her ministers stars. She is compared unto precious stones, reflecting light in beauty; for by the electing love of God, the redemption of Christ, and the transforming power of the Holy Ghost, the saints, who were once children of wrath and disobedience, living in darkness, and without the hope of glory, are now filled with the Spirit, and beautified with the righteousness of Christ whose image they bear. The Church is compared to a building, believers being living stones, the Saviour Himself the foundation. For in the Church are strength and harmony; and while some are pillars able to sustain heavy weight, and chosen to be prominent and attractive, the exercise of love unites all, and renders the whole strong and fortified against the assaults of enemies, and the untoward and inclement influences of a hostile atmosphere. . . .

The primitive Church dwelt much on the Gospels and the Apocalypse. The Church of the Reformation gave prominence to the Epistles. *Let us return to the Gospels, and read them in the Pentecostal light of apostolic teaching.* He only who has died with Christ, and is risen with Him, can follow the Saviour in His life and walk. The natural, unrenewed man cannot follow Jesus; but when we know the grace of the Saviour, and the power of His resurrection, we understand the lessons of His life, and having received the Spirit of Christ, we can live and walk as the sons of God.

"From the life of Jesus," said the old Germans, "we can learn all things." We can learn Christ; and to know Him is to know all things that pertain unto life and godliness. Let us then continually study Him as the Model; we must represent Christ in our lives.

1. And first let us rememberr the object of Christ's life. He was sent. He never forgot that He came not to do His own will, but the will of the Father that sent Him. He teaches most emphatically and impressively that He had only one aim, one absorbing and dominant idea, one all-pervading law and rule. It was simply to do His Father's will. Motives which in themselves are pure and legitimate, and by which our minds may be naturally and

sinlessly actuated, such as benevolence and piety, and interest in the progress of God's kingdom, disappear before the all-important and central desire to honour the Father by obeying His command. Jesus spake the words which He heard of the Father; He did the works which the Father showed Him; He spake and acted whenever He knew that "the hour was come," the hour which the Father had appointed. Thus was He constantly the Servant of God, the Representative of the Father. Now *we* are sent by Jesus; and all that we are and have, all our words and works, are to be viewed in the light of mission and service.

In this unity and concentration of purpose was the strength of Jesus. His heart was *united,* as the Psalmist says, to praise God. "One thing I do," was in the fullest sense of the word true of the Saviour. And it was this exclusive reference to the Father, this living before Him and unto Him, which rendered the character and acts of Jesus enigmatic and obnoxious to the world, and sometimes unintelligible to His own disciples. How difficult is it for us to understand Him, who even in the good which He did sought not His own delight, and followed not His own thought, but simply the Father's glory and honour, the accomplishment of His will and purpose; who went into sufferings and death simply that the Scripture should be fulfilled, that the Father's commandment should be obeyed!

2. Jesus came in lowliness. His birth, infancy, childhood, and youth are characterized by the emblems of poverty and obscure humility. What a contrast between the power and splendour of Caesar Augustus and the glory of the Roman Empire, and Bethlehem, the small town of Judea, and the Infant who was born there of the poor and humble daughter of David. Jesus was called Nazarene, brought up in the despised Nazareth, that thus the whole tenor of prophecy might be fulfilled, which described Him as a root out of a dry ground, as coming in lowliness, without earthly pomp and power. Between the manger of Bethlehem and the humble home of Nazareth and His death on the cross, when He was numbered with the transgressors, we find nothing else but humility, poverty, and lowliness. "Foxes have holes, and

birds of the air have nests, but the Son of man hath not where to lay His head."

What are we to learn from this? Are we not to follow the Master? We may not be poor, but we are to love poverty. We ought not to trust in earthly riches and honour, in the things which the world esteems and pursues; we ought to remember that our influence and our power are spiritual, and that the garment of the true Church is that of a servant, of a stranger and pilgrim. When the Church becomes rich and strong, esteemed by the world, and dominant, the salt is in danger of losing its savour; spiritual objects are sought in a worldly spirit, and the mystery of the cross is obscured and forgotten.

For to the end of this dispensation the Church is as a widow, desolate and despised. She is hated of the world. But it is poor and persecuted Smyrna which, by her Christ-like poverty, maketh many rich. The glory of the Church is inward; the King's daughter, the bride of Christ, is all-glorious within.

3. Jesus was the Son of God. He came from above. He was poor, and yet all things were His; He was lowly, and yet all power was given to Him in heaven and earth, for He was the only-begotten of the Father. The Father was always with Him, and heard Him always. Thus the Church is born of God, of incorruptible seed. Her life is none other but the life of Christ, the risen Head, the life of the Spirit who dwelleth in us. We exert influence and power in the world simply by our being blameless and harmless, *the sons of God,* living Christ's life (which comes only out of the death and the crucifixion of the old man), manifesting the divine nature of which *we* are partakers who have escaped the corruption that is in the world through lust. The Church declares every Lord's day that the resurrection of Christ is her birthday, the source of her life and hope, and thus preaches to the world both the condemnation of the flesh, the utter helplessness of the first Adam and his seed, and the new and heavenly life, which in the Only-begotten of the Father, and the First-begotten of the dead, has come to all believers.

4. In this lowliness and in this power, the Church is able to

go to the whole world, with love and sympathy announcing substance in the midst of emptiness and vain shadows, eternal life and consolation in the midst of death and sorrow, peace to the heavy-laden conscience, love to the aching and thirsting heart, forgiveness and renewal, health and joy to the wounded and contrite. And while she loves all and intercedes for all, she is filled, like her Master, with a special love, intense and tender, for the brethren, towards His own who are in the world, and who are gathered to the Bishop and Shepherd of souls. Thanking God, as Jesus did, for the disciples whom the Father gives, she watches over the young and inexperienced, the weak and tempted, the lonely and afflicted. She seeks to build up, to cherish and to gladden the heritage of God, the fellow-heirs of life eternal.

The Church is Christ-like — sent from above, having one aim and motive, in lowliness, in divine power, in love and ministry. "He that hath seen Me hath seen the Father." Likewise ought we to be able to say, He that hath seen the Church hath seen Christ.

Christ is all in all, yet every member of the body, every Christian, has an individual life, work, calling, a name of his own, a position and a talent assigned to him, for which he is responsible to the Master. "Let *your* light so shine," saith He who is The Light. He means the light which God has given to each of us individually, according to our natural disposition and experience; the special *charisma* which we have received, be it knowledge or patience, or strength or skill, be it intellectual, or moral, or social. We possess each some features of His character, some gift of His Spirit, some power and influence out of His fulness. Each of us is placed in a position, surrounded by opportunities and endowed with gifts. Each one is individual, peculiar; no one else can do what the Master, the great Householder, has appointed and given him to be and to do. Let us remember that we are to let *our* light *shine*. Let us resemble the blessed Master in His loving wisdom, which directed men to what is easy and simple. Only the eye of faith can see that which is secret, spiritual, and rooted in the heart; but all can see the *manifestations* of

170

love. It is perfectly true that until the Spirit of God opens their
eyes men do not see Jesus; but in one sense they are able to see,
to judge, to appreciate; the world is able to see and to understand our good works; they can recognise the influence of God on
our lives and conduct; accordingly we find that the Lord Jesus
commands us so to let our light shine before men, that they may
behold our good works, and glorify our Father which is in heaven.

When meditating on the Church, we are always in danger of
forgetting our own duty, and of falling into feverish impatience
or indolent waiting for a sign from heaven. Let us rather believe
that the Lord is doing His work, and carrying out His purposes of
wisdom and love. Our own duty is clear before us. . . .

BIBLIOGRAPHY

William Beveridge: *Theological Works.* I. 1-25. 1842.
H. P. Liddon: *Easter in St. Paul's,* new ed., London, 1892, pp. 393-406
G. Campbell Morgan: *Westminster Pulpit.* IV. 33-40; VII. 217-224; IX. 209-
    216
William Rainy, in *Christian World Pulpit.* Vol. 43, pp. 300-303. May 10, 1893
Adolph Saphir: *Christ and the Church.* pp. 1 ff.; 37 ff.; 208 ff.
Charles H. Spurgeon: *Metropolitan Tabernacle Pulpit.* Vol. 7, 1861. No. 383.
    pp. 281-288

ADOLPH SAPHIR
(1831-1891)

Adolph Saphir is the only preacher whose sermons have been used in the first two volumes of this series who, if my memory does not fail me, was born in Europe, and even more, was of the Jewish race. His father was recognized as "perhaps the most learned Jew in Hungary and held in universal respect for probity and uprightness of character. He was in truth a sort of Gamaliel in the nation." The father's brother was Gottlieb Saphir, one of the great literary men of that period. There is no opportunity here to give the story with any detail, but the entire Saphir family, including Adolph, were brought to recognize Jesus Christ as their Saviour while they were living in Budapest, Hungary, by the visit of John Duncan, known as Rabbi Duncan, a Scotch Presbyterian Professor and master of Hebrew literature. He was returning from Palestine, a member of that famous Committee sent by the Scottish Church to look into the condition of the Jews in Palestine. Along with Adolph Saphir, Alfred Edersheim was also brought to Christ. Both of these young men moved to England, the latter ultimately writing the most important Life of Christ of the nineteenth century.

Saphir began to preach at the Laygate Presbyterian Church, South Shields, during which ministry he published his first book, *Conversion,* which immediately brought him to the attention of Evangelicals throughout England. He was asked to become Minister of St. Mark's Presbyterian Church, Greenwich, following the notable ministry of the Reverend George Duncan. Later on, many being convinced that he ought to be ministering to West London, he was invited to become the Minister at Kensington Park Road, an aristocratic area of that great city. It was here that he gave his famous Thursday morning lectures on the Epistle to the Hebrews, in the winters of 1873 to 1875, which, his biographer says, was "the greatest triumph of his career."

Book after book came from his pen, books that are still read with profit, especially *The Unity of the Scriptures,* and also *Christ in the Scriptures.* While his fame as a preacher and an expositor never waned, he became depressed in his latter days, while ministering at the Belgrave Presbyterian Church, and as his biographer admits, he was "often cast down and anxious."

It is very difficult to attempt to discover the secret of the ministry of a man like this, but one who heard him often in his Greenwich ministry, later wrote his own convictions as to the secret of Saphir's power, in words that I think should be quoted here for the encouragement and even rebuke of most of us. "What was the secret of it? a fine intellect? a splendid command of language? a wide and comprehensive knowledge of Scripture? All these he had, and they were blessed gifts of God; but the secret was, that Jesus was to him first and foremost. He saw Jesus from Genesis to Revelation, and this Jesus became transfigured (at least to one of the hearers), no longer the abstract mighty Being far away somewhere in heaven; but the living, loving, exalted, coming Son of man, yet to be glorified and owned in *this* world, where He is still despised, when all things, natural as well as spiritual, shall own His sway, and praise His Name. Ah! it was wonderful what a new light dawned through those burning words of his, and how God owned him to be His servant, by the way in which so frequently he answered the unspoken questions of the heart, clearly and concisely, as though they had been laid out in order before him, whereas he knew nothing, but his Master knew, and gave His servant the needed portion to distribute; or sometimes it was some trouble ahead, and even before it reached us, the needed words of comfort and strength had already been spoken, in readiness by God's faithful messenger.

"The short opening prayers, specially on Sunday mornings, have left a marked impression on my mind. They only lasted two or three minutes, and yet often I have felt, 'That is enough; I can go home now if need be' — it was so truly entering into the presence-chamber of the King. He loved to repeat that we had come to meet with Jesus, and claim the promise made to those gathered in His Name; we had come not because it was eleven o'clock on Sunday morning or because it was the Presbyterian Church, but *to see Jesus*."

LED OUT — LED IN

by

G. Campbell Morgan

"He led them out until they were over against Bethany: and He lifted up His hands, and blessed them." — Luke 24:50

After His Resurrection from among the dead, our Lord and Saviour, Jesus Christ, lingered on the earth for forty days, as though He were almost reluctant to leave it. He lingered, as we have no doubt, for very special purposes of revelation and manifestation; lingered in order to bridge over for His own first disciples the difficult period of the early days, when they would no longer have Him with them in bodily sight, and when it would be necessary, therefore, for the high faculty of the soul, faith, to be called into full play. He lingered for forty days, appearing occasionally, and disappearing. The second part of the statement seems as though it were unnecessary, but as a matter of fact, the disappearances were as important as the appearances, both in their manner and in their purpose. He appeared to them sometimes when together, gathered peculiarly as disciples; and sometimes to individuals. Coming suddenly and unexpectedly upon them, baffling them by the method of His coming, He yet always unveiled before their eyes some new wonder and glory of His own Personality and His own work. Then, with equal suddenness and strangeness of method, He vanished. This lasted, as I say, for forty days.

In the verse that I have taken as text, we have the account of the very last act of Jesus before His Ascension. This was His last appearance, as the last disappearance was the Ascension

173

itself. We are now to consider what these men saw in Him upon this occasion: "He led them out as far as Bethany: and He lifted up His hands, and blessed them."

This person, lifting His hands in blessing, is One who has been rejected in a three-fold rejection; rejected by the priesthood of the time; rejected by the earthly government which was in the ascendancy at the time; rejected by the people upon their own vote and claim. I am not now proposing to stay to discuss the reason of the priestly rejection, or the governmental rejection, or the democratic rejection. I simply face the fact as we look at this last appearing of Jesus. He was rejected.

Rejected, in the first place, by the priests of His time, and consequently, by priestcraft. Here, we pause for a moment, to consider this question of Priesthood in the light of Biblical revelation. In the divine economy as therein revealed, priesthood was really an accommodation to human weakness, and never a divine intention or provision. The history of the priesthood emerges in the most startling way. In the eighteenth chapter of Exodus, we discover that when God emancipated a people from slavery, and led them out with a high hand and outstretched arm into a large place, He brought them unto Himself; and the words that Moses was commissioned to speak to them were practically words of the New Testament, which came with greater meaning in the fulness of time: "I have chosen you to be unto Me, a kingdom of priests." In that declaration there is not the slightest suggestion of the creation of a caste of priests as within the divine economy and purpose; but rather the creation of a nation in which every individual was to be a priest. I will make you unto Me a kingdom of priests, was the divine original ideal for Israel. The people shrank from the high and awful function, were filled with fear in the presence of Jehovah, and naturally so; they were so filled with fear in the consciousness of their sinfulness and inability. Then the principle obtained that runs through all the Divine dealings with men, that of accommodation to human weakness. Because the people were not able to rise to the high level of realising their personal priesthood, a caste was created for awhile to fulfill the function of priesthood on behalf of the people.

Through the centuries, the story of priesthood runs on; and from beginning to end it is the story of failure, from beginning to end it is the story of corruption; of partial light eclipsed in darkness; of movement toward a higher for ever falling to a lower; until the last act of priesthood was the inspiration that resulted in the murder of the Son of God. As I look at Him standing on Olivet's slope I see One Whom priesthood had cast out.

I also see One here, Who had been cast out by government, by monarchy. Monarchy in Judaea at that time was a poor and insignificant thing, struggling to make its power great, when really it was entirely paralysed. Herod, and those associated with him in the governing authority of the Tetrarchies, were under the mastery of Rome; that brutal bully in human history that for once subdued the world by brute force, and initiated the Pax Romanum, which was but the pause of a palsied inertia resulting from war. When Jesus was born, He was born into that peace, a peace not worth the name, and which was happily disturbed by war, ere ever there had been long continuance of it.

But let me interpret this fact of government Biblically. What do we find concerning monarchy in the Bible? It was originally an accommodation to human weakness, just as priesthood was. I go back to this one nation that God chose, not in order that He might have a pet upon whom to lavish His love, but to be the illustration of His Kingdom in the world for the uplifting of the nations. He said to them: "I have called you unto Myself." In the first glimpse of the history of the people, who were in many senses rude, almost barbaric, there shines a glory such as the world had never elsewhere seen. It is the glory of a Theocracy, of a people governed by God, having no other king, and no other form of government. The history runs on for a little while, until there came a day in which this people said: "Give us a king like the nations." Then Samuel, broken-hearted by their failure, cried to God in complaint, and the answer of God, in the soul of Samuel, was this: "They have not rejected thee; they have rejected Me from being king. Therefore, go thou and anoint Saul, and give them what they ask." That was an accommodation to human weakness. Then followed the rapid exaltation and tragic fall of Saul, a king like the nations; the story of David, one gleam of light as to what kingship might be, ending in black failure; then that of Solomon, the most disastrous failure in the Old Testament. The kingdom was next disrupted, and entered upon a long period of conflict, until we see them once again, a remnant weak and small, and Zerubbabel, Ezra and Nehemiah setting them in order, after which they were locked up to law, until Christ. Government by monarchy in the Bible is thus marked as being a necessary accommodation to human weakness, a story of ghastly failure and loss, resulting in the crucifixion of the Lord of life and glory.

And what of the people? He was rejected by the people also. The people entirely failed; they submitted to the dominion of false rulership, so that they themselves caught up the cries of the false rulers, and hissed between closed teeth, "Crucify! Crucify!" The people! May God deliver us from a democracy which is not first a theocracy.

What is the history of the people according to the Bible? Their failure antedated that of priest or king. Babel is the first chapter of the federation of the people in order that they may manage themselves, and make themselves a great name in the world. From that first chapter, the movement runs on through all your Biblical literature until, thank God, the day is coming, which is not yet come, when the supreme anthem of earth's emancipation will take the form: "Babylon the great is fallen, is fallen!" "The kingdom of this world is become the kingdom of our Lord, and of His Christ."

I look then at this Man, with the little group gathered about Him on the slopes of Olivet. Priesthood has rejected Him, government has flung Him out, the people have given their vote, consenting to the self-same rejection.

Then I look at Him again, and what do I see? I see the one Priest of humanity, the great High Priest of the race, fulfilling the function of priesthood by the mystery of His Person, as it could not possibly be fulfilled in any human being. Jesus could never have been the High Priest of humanity merely within His human nature. By oneness with God, and identification with man, He can be that which Job in his agony sighed for — and in that cry the sigh for priesthood is found, perhaps, as nowhere else: Would that there were a daysman who might lay his hand upon God and upon me. That was the great cry of a soul for the meditation of one who is in himself in true fellowship with God; and in himself in perfect identification with humanity.

As I look I see that Jesus, as the One human Priest, the power of Whose Priesthood was created, as the Writer of the Letter to the Hebrews said, by the power of an endless life, which is more than a human life, but which is human in its qualification also. By His oneness with God, and identification with man, He is the One Priest of humanity.

I look again, and I see Him as the one and only Governor and King of humanity, the One upon Whose shoulder THE Government is to rest; the one King Whose kingship is based upon His eternal authority, and His temporal associations. — I did not say, temporary. I used my word with care. Associations that have to do with time. We have to do with time, and we shall always have to do with time. There is a sense in which we are not eternal nor can be. We have eternal life. We come into an atmosphere that keeps, and sustains, and enlarges; but we are not without beginning. To be eternal there must be no beginning. God is eternal. This King is One Whose authority is eternal, Who comes out of eternity, out of the necessity of things, out of the infinite wisdom that lies at the back of everything; the One Who initiates a law for a race, a nation, a man; which is not a law resulting from the manipulation of things as they seem, but which is a law resulting from the perfect knowledge of things as they are. His authority is based upon that. His authority is also based upon temporal association. He, Who is the Logos, the eternal, has been made flesh, has brought the eternal into the compass of the observation of the temporal. His Kingship is based now and for evermore, first, upon that eternal authority, and secondly, upon the fact that He tabernacled in the flesh, and walked the ways of men. God came into no closer sympathy with man by incarnation; but by incarnation God did reveal Himself in the exquisite tenderness and eternal strength of His sympathy. God, apart from incarnation, is an abstract idea, vast, terrific; but there is no warmth in it, there is no life in it, there is no inspiration in it. But, when I go to a King, and I know His word is the word of eternal authority, and yet hear it stated in the words that my mother taught me, and that I lisped when I was a baby, lo! I have found my King. I see Him, outside of the government of the world, but God's appointed Governor.

I see Him, again, as the ensign of the people, according to the prophetic word concerning Him: "Unto Him shall the gathering of the people be." It was but a little group about Him on Olivet; but think how many are gathered about Him today. Yes, let us think of that sometimes even today, when, it may be, we are almost tempted to imagine that the whole Christian ideal is being blotted out in blood. He is still the rejected One, but He is also the Crowned. He is even yet cast out of the councils of the nations. Ah! but He is considered and obeyed by a vast sacramental host, a sacramental host the extent of which we cannot measure by our Church statistics. His sacramental host includes the membership of churches, but runs far out beyond that membership, gathering into its ranks all souls pledged to name the Name and live according to His law. He gathers the people to Himself, for the realisation of a democracy under the reign of the one King; a democracy great, because a theocracy. So He stands on Olivet's slopes, rejected by the priests, the governors, the people. There He stands, the One Priest, the One King, the One to Whom the gathering of the peoples shall be.

Having thus looked at the principal matter, the Person, let us consider the statement, "He led them out." He took them towards Bethany. There were tender associations there. It was at Bethany that He found what was nearer to a home in His experience than any other place. There Lazarus lived, and Martha, and Mary, whom He loved. There He had often tarried; there He had spent those last tragic nights of the last terrific week.

He led them that way. There was no temple there, no kingly palace. It was not the place where crowds ordinarily assembled. He led them out to Olivet, to some slope from which Bethany could be seen. He led them out from the temple, and the priests' ministrations. He led them out from the government, and its protection. He led them out from the people, and their permissions. They would have to run counter to all these things in the coming days, as He Himself had done. The priests would seek to destroy them, and their testimony, as they had sought to destroy Him. The governors would be against them, and would even declare that they were seditious; and ere very long a corrupt emperor-master of the world would amuse himself and his licentious profligate friends by watching them burn. All these things He knew, and that leading out signified that He appealed to none of these things to protect His disciples when He was gone. By that leading out, He suggested to His own disciples that they were not to look for help in their propaganda from priests or governors or people. He led them out into association with Himself, in testimony to all that which He had set up, and which He came to make possible in human history.

He led them out from the temple and the priests; He led them into the true temple through a rent veil, where they might exercise their priesthood, as appearing in the presence of God, on behalf of humanity; and then passing out to appear in the presence of humanity on behalf of God.

He led them out from the protection of human governments; but He led them into the protection of His own Government, underneath His own sway and kingship and power.

He led them out from the promises and the voting of the populace; but He led them into association with the new democracy, consisting of all souls yielded to the Kingship of God, through Whom, at last, the Kingdom shall be established.

That leading out was thus, indeed, a leading in. As the writer of the Letter to the Hebrews says: He went outside the camp to suffer, to die; we must go after Him bearing His reproach. But the Writer of the Letter to the Hebrews also says: The veil was rent, and He opened the way into the holiest of all; we may go in with boldness. The people around Him are people led out to be led in; led out from the false into the true; led out from failure to the place of assured victory; led out from all the forces that disintegrate and break up humanity, and into association with all the forces that construct and build up humanity. So He led them out; and so He led them in.

From that day to this, He has been leading out and leading in. In proportion as we understand the occasion of that last appearing, we shall discover that the Church of God must never depend upon priesthood, or governments, or democracies, for her strength or protection. Every form and fashion of religion, every form and fashion of government, and all the hopes of the peoples, are centered in Him to Whom we have come; and in Whose Name we go with gladness, and singing, and hope, back to every form of religion, not to destroy it, but to fulfil the essential truth within it, and purge it of its dross; back to governments, not to proclaim anarchy, but to declare that every form of government must be finally related to the government through Whom it may realise its high ideals; back to the people, not to descend to the devilish barbarity of men who speak of them as *canaille,* but to love them, serve them, giving our own life-blood to lift them into the great Kingdom of our God. He led them out, not for their sakes alone, but in the infinite mystery of His marvellous work, for the sake of the very things from which He led them out.

His last act was the giving of blessing. He lifted up His hands and blessed them. In those Hands were arguments, scars of battle, stigmata of pain, the insignia of royalty. It was the High Priestly act. It declared that sin was atoned for, that death was vanquished; that sorrow was commandeered, captured, in order that finally it may do duty for the Kingdom of God. Henceforth sorrow is the most powerful agent in the sanctification of human life, in the deliverance of nations from their perils, and of individuals from their foolishness. That High Priestly act of blessing was the act of One Who had grappled with the darkness of sin, and mastered it, Who "Death by dying slew"; and He had apprehended sorrow, and taken it into His will in a gracious and infinite mystery. In the uplifting of those hands was no act of forgiveness; no act of intercession. Those acts also lie within the priestly function; but that was the uplifting of hands in blessing, and blessing means bestowment. He uplifted His hands upon men whom He led out from all the forces that seemed great in the world, denying to these men the protection of these forces; but He lifted up His hands, and blessed them; and as He did so, He gave them fulness of life; He gave them fellowship with God; He gave them perfect confidence for all the service that He was about to appoint to them.

Christ is thus seen to be the fulfillment, and, therefore, the centre of priesthood, of government, of humanity.

When He leads men out from things that seem so necessary; it is always to lead them into the possession of the real things. No man loses anything in his individual life; no society loses anything in the true passion that creates it a society; no nation loses anything of the underlying nobility of its national life, by being obedient to Christ. He fulfils. He is always leading out from things effete to Himself. Things effete are not necessarily things evil. They have become effete, but they were not in the first case things evil. Things effete are things that have done their work. He taketh away the first that He may establish the second. Yes; but He established the first. Yea! verily, but when it has done its work, He takes it away, that He might establish the second. Sacrifice and offerings Thou wouldst not! But He appointed sacrifices and He appointed offerings! Yea! verily; but when they had fulfilled their work, He destroyed them. That is the perpetual method of Christ. Things that were necessary, perchance for us in our individual lives as Christians at the beginning, when they have done their work, if we cling to them they will destroy the life they helped to make. Grave clothes are necessary for a dead man; but when he lives, loose him, and let him go! The law written upon tables of stone was necessary in the first period of religious revelation; but when the Spirit of God through the infinite mystery of the atoning work of Jesus comes into the life, and writes with the Finger of God upon the table of the heart, then I do not want tables of stone. When I put myself in bondage to a table of stone written with the finger of God two to four milleniums ago, then I am in bondage to a thing effete.

Christ ever leads men out. One of the greatest troubles of the Christian Church has been that she so clings to things that were necessary yesterday; forgetting that He ever leads forward, into something greater and grander. He led them out from things which in themselves had been necessary, and had their place: a place made necessary by the bitter necessity of accommodation; but when they had done their work He led them out. The mean- of what He did that day has been revealed in His teaching pre- viously. He said to a woman in Samaria: Believe Me, the hour cometh when neither in this mountain, Gerazim, nor yet in Jeru- salem shall men worship; the day is coming when you will not need a temple, but wherever the soul is in need it may find access to God.

Christ's last attitude, the last appearing, the last manifestation of Himself in these days of appearing and disappearing, was in the attitude of blessing, the attitude, not of the Aaronic priest- hood, but of that of Melchizedec. He is a Priest for ever, not after the order of Aaron, but after the order of Melchizedec. We find Melchizedec in the first book of the Bible. Melchizedec met Abram when Abram was weary from a warfare that he had con- ducted in answer to a demand for righteousness. Melchizedec brought forth bread and wine for him, and ministered to his need. Melchizedec blessed Abram, and then passed out of sight, and Abram confronted the king of Sodom. The king offered him part of the booty. In possession of that spiritual blessing which had come to new consciousness in his soul by the ministry of Melchizedec, Abram declined to take a hoof of anything that the king offered. Then God spoke to his soul: "I am thy shield, and thy exceeding great reward."

Jesus lifts up His hands in blessing upon the souls who dare to follow Him without the camp, bearing His reproach. He is the

High Priest Who brings bread and wine to refresh and renew us in our weariness. He is the High Priest that brings the consciousness, that steadies our faith in God, that enables us to say to every bribe that may be offered us: Not a hoof of anything. We have all we need in God.

BIBLIOGRAPHY

Isaac Barrow: *Theological Works.* Oxford. 1818. V. 39-63
George D. Boardman: *Our Risen King's Forty Days.* Philadelphia. 1902. pp. 162-186
W. M. Clow: *Idylls of Bethany.* London. 1919. pp. 178-190
H. P. Liddon, in *Christian World Pulpit.* 1884. Vol. 25, pp. 257-260
J. R. Macduff: *Memories of Bethany.* London, n.d. pp. 221-237; and *Memories of Olivet.* New York. 1868. pp. 341-354
Alexander Maclaren: *Expositions of Holy Scripture.* St. Luke XIII-XXIV. 388-399; and, *After the Resurrection,* 116-129; and, *The Secret of Power,* 174-186
Walter A. Maier: *Go Quickly and Tell.* St. Louis. 1950. pp. 272-292
G. Campbell Morgan: *Westminster Pulpit.* 1915. Vol. 10. pp. 265-272
Samuel M. Zwemer: *The Glory of the Empty Tomb.* New York. 1947. pp. 83-90.

THE ASCENSION OF JESUS
by
George G. Findlay

"Jesus saith to Mary Magdalene, Touch Me not; for I am not yet ascended unto the Father: but go unto My brethren, and say to them, I ascend unto My Father and your Father, and My God and your God." — John 20:17

Mary Magdalene had returned alone to the empty grave, after Peter and John paid their hasty visit. She stands there lost in grief: outrage is heaped on outrage; the body of Jesus has been removed, and there is denied to His friends even the poor consolation of paying the last rites of a hopeless love. The vision of the angels in the cave fails to rouse her from her stupor; only when Jesus speaks a second time, calling her by name, does she see through her tears who it is! Then with the cry, "My Master," she flings herself at His feet in a wild revulsion of feeling, reaching out her arms as if to grasp and hold Him fast. But He shrank from this too passionate embrace, as perhaps from some of our modern demonstrations sensuous and sentimental as they are, saying, "Touch Me not" — do not cling to Me thus! "For not yet am I ascended to My Father" — there will be other opportunities of meeting. "But go to My brethren and say to them, I ascend to My Father and your Father, and My God and your God!"

The Lord Jesus speaks as one upon a journey, with His face set toward another country. He has not returned to the mortal state, but looks in upon the way to reassure His friends and to tell them whither He is going. The old familiar relations of earthly companionship cannot be resumed; the deeper spiritual union with Him that awaits His disciples, is not yet established. Everything is in transition; and our Lord lingers by the way — certainly for our sakes, possibly also for His own — as He proceeds in two mighty strides from the Underworld to Earth, from Earth to Heaven, "travelling" on from world to world "in the greatness of His strength, mighty to save."

He travels alone, of the people none may be with Him; but He would have His brethren know of His movements, He directs their eyes to the goal of the journey. "Say to My brethren, I ascend!" Not downwards, but upwards in His march. Not defeat and death; but victory, eternal life, and power and glory, are the end of the ways of Jesus, for Him and for His.

This is the watchword of Ascension-tide, — the happiest, surely, of all the Christian festivals to a heart that shares the Saviour's joys and griefs: "If ye loved Me," He said, "ye would rejoice because I go to the Father!" While our hearts follow Him above the clouds, let us consider what His ascension means; let us ask ourselves in what character, and for what ends Jesus Christ has gone up to the heavenly places.

1. In the first place then, and as concerns Himself, *our Lord ascends as the Son of God returning to His proper place:* "Tell My brethren, I ascend unto My Father."

The ascent of Jesus is a final seal put upon His divinity; it consummates the resurrection, by which He was "declared to be the Son of God with power." It is the resurrection finished, as the incarnation of the eternal Son was, in a sense, His death begun. "What," He said once to His questioners. "if you should see the Son of man ascending up where He was before," would you still doubt His origin and challenge His authority? The mode of His exit certifies that He bore a supernatural life and was here upon a heavenly errand. He entered this world as never man did; He lived and spoke and wrought in it as never man did; He died, and rose again, as never man did; and He took His departure as no mere son of man ever did or could have done, — He who was "separated from sinners, and made higher than the heavens."

All is in keeping from first to last — pure, sublime, human at once and superhuman, full of Divine propriety and moral majesty. The history of Jesus, in conception and description, transcends human analogies and imaginings even as His departing feet rose above the earth and the clouds. "Touch Me not; I ascend!" it is the voice of the Son of God rising in His awful glory, before whose face the keepers of His grave fell like dead men, at whose feet His disciples joyously worship as He floats above them through the clouds.

How quiet and calm, in the deepest sense of the word how *natural*, the account of His departure which is given by another of the Evangelists. To the witnesses it must have seemed quite beautiful and in the fitting order of things that Jesus should thus part from them — as the ship casts off her cables and launches out to her own element. He breaks the chains of sense as naturally as He had burst the bands of death, for in neither case "was it possible that He should be holden of it" longer than He chose. "Earth to earth, ashes to ashes, dust to dust," is the sentence last pronounced upon our sinful bodies; but this doom cannot fall upon the Holy One of God, His flesh might not "see corruption." By the same law He gravitates upward — the heavenly heavenwards, the Divine to the Divine. The ascent of Jesus from the hill-top fronting Bethany is the manifest and due expression of this supreme affinity. As the bent bow returns to rest when its bolt is sped, as the son sets his face homewards when evening comes and the day's task is over, so Jesus goes back to His native sphere. "Now, Father," He cries, "I have finished the work which Thou gavest Me to do; and I come to Thee." The Son of God returns to the Father's house.

2. Jesus went up where He was before, but not as He was. He resumed the glory which He had with the Father before the world was; but He assumed a new glory hitherto unknown, that follows on His sufferings. We are to understand that *the Lord Jesus ascends as the glorified Son of man, as the acknowledged and exalted Christ.* He mounts upward as the Conqueror on our behalf of sin and death, the Head over all things to His Church.

In this sense the Church, by the mouth of St. Peter, at once interpreted the event: "Let all the house of Israel know assuredly that God hath made both Lord and Christ this Jesus whom ye crucified." So the apostle declared to the Jews on the day of Pentecost. For proof of this he pointed to the scene then enacted: "Being by the right hand of God exalted, and having received of the Father the promise of the Spirit, He hath shed forth this, which ye see and hear." The descent of the Spirit proved the ascent of the Lord Christ. The heir to some great property, who has been your friend in exile and obscurity, leaves you to take possession, promising to send you a splendid gift so soon as he has entered on his rights. In a short time that very gift arrives; and you know now that your friend's title is proved and that he is raised to the anticipated place of wealth and power. Thus the apostles reasoned; Pentecost verified to them the ascension of the Lord Jesus. By the coming of the Spirit of power on the disciples they knew, beyond a doubt, that their Master had reached His journey's end; that when He passed from their sight through the parting clouds above Olivet, He had not vanished into empty space, but had taken His seat on the Messiah's throne at God's right hand. His sacrifice for sinners is accepted; His promises to men are honoured by the Father; the crown is set upon His head, and henceforth "all authority" is His "in heaven and upon earth."

Now this is the issue of the ascension which supremely concerns ourselves, and the prospects of God's kingdom upon earth. For the Son of God did not come into this world on a visit of inspection, nor on a romantic adventure; He came to identify Himself with men, to redeem our race from iniquity, to proclaim and to found God's kingdom in this evil, rebellious world. What then does the departure of the Son of God mean, in view of this declared mission and enterprise of salvation? Is the attempt abandoned? has the task proved too great for our would-be Redeemer? Some such fear rose to the minds of His disciples, when Jesus first spoke of leaving them by death. It was not so much their personal loss, as the thought of His defeat and the failure of the

Messianic kingdom that distressed them. He has to show them that His going away is expedient, that He will be able to serve them better and to do more for the common cause when translated than if He had remained bodily present with His Church.

Instead of forsaking His work of redemption, He is now going to carry it on from heaven far more gloriously and effectively than hitherto. If He is, in appearance, quitting the field, He does so like some wise and confident military captain, who has struck for himself the decisive blow and then mounts the hill-top, from which, above the smoke and din of the conflict, he may survey the whole battle and in full command of his forces may direct the course of victory. Our Lord goes up with the government upon His shoulders, to wield on our behalf His new-won "authority in heaven," to direct and inspire from that lofty seat the work of His Church and the life of His people, to represent them evermore before the throne of God, while He draws forth from the depths of the Godhead new and infinite resources for the effecting of His purpose of salvation.

Jesus goes to His own place, the due place not only of the Son of God but of the representative and ruling Son of man, that He may "appear in the presence of God for us"; for He is the High Priest of mankind, now by His life and death identified with the race for ever and bearing the names of all the tribes upon His heart. The headquarters of the Church will henceforth be no longer at Jerusalem, nor certainly at Rome, but at the right hand of the Majesty in the heavens. There "He must reign, till He hath put all enemies under His feet."

Our Lord's departure therefore should afford us, instead of sorrow, the greatest comfort and satisfaction; as in fact it did afford to the apostles at the time, who, when they had witnessed it, "returned to Jerusalem with great joy." St. Paul in his wonderful outburst of praise in the first chapter of the Epistle to the Ephesians, grounds on Christ's ascension the entire hope of the Christian calling; he bids us measure God's "power to usward," the might of the forces at work for our salvation in Christ, by the sweep and lift of the Almighty Arm which raised Him from the dead and set Him on the topmost throne of heaven. Thus highly is the Captain of our salvation exalted and approved; such power and glory has God the Father given to Him as our Saviour, engaged in the very act of redeeming us from iniquity. It is the Son of man, in bodily human form, who has gone up on high; the Head of the Church, remaining incorporate with His earthly members, He has sat down by the Father's side. Our hopes and our rights are lifted as high as He has risen, for we are "joint-heirs with Christ Jesus." The ascension of the Lord Jesus means His earthly course not broken off but carried onwards and projected into the heavenly places, His plans and counsels of mercy not abandoned but endorsed as the policy of God, His incarnation and sacrificial death not rendered abortive but brought to their ripened and eternal fruitage in His heavenly rule by the mighty work of His Spirit throughout the earth and the ages. While thus translated He remains, on His own part, the same yesterday and today — the same Jesus teaching and healing amidst the multitude, sitting weary by the well-side, dying as the good Shepherd for His sheep, and seated now at the right hand of God in everlasting power and glory. When He says, "Tell My brethren, I ascend!" this is not to be defeated, exiled, forgotten, but to live for men and rule over men for ever.

Our lot and our work are cast in an age far removed from the time of these first events; and to many eyes the haze of distance obscures their glory and dims their certainty. Faith has its ebbs and flows; the heart of the Church is like the heart of a man, and has its hours of weariness, its moods of faintness and dejection. The Lord delays His coming; the battle is long, and the powers of evil make desperate and repeated rallies, beating back again and again the armies of the living God when victory appeared in sight. But we lift our eyes unto the hills. We "look away to Jesus, the Author and Perfecter of our faith," — from the Christ that was to the Christ that is, and again with restored assurance to the Christ that was and that is and that cometh. As we gaze upward to the Living One, where He sits at the right hand of the throne of God, the light of His glory returns to our eyes; the dimness passes from our vision, the despondency lifts from our hearts. There He sits, — His brow serene, His purpose sure, His power unbroken, His arm unwearied: "It is Christ Jesus that died, yea rather, that was raised from the dead, *who is at the right hand of God,* who also makest intercession for us."

The throne of God has not fallen; and while it stands, the dominion of Jesus is secure. His name is waxing and not waning through the earth. He is the King of the ages, and every prediction that set a limit to His ascendency has been falsified. He understands the twentieth century as perfectly as He did the first, and is master of the situation still. Our science and our art, our material progress and modern enlightenment, and the new powers and new forms of opposition that the advance of His kingdom has called into play, these are all within His grasp. The Church of God declares by the power of the Holy Ghost, standing in the midst of the proud and rebellious forces of the age, that "Jesus is the Lord," and that the day is coming fast when in every land of earth His crown shall flourish and to Him shall the gathering of the peoples be. It is the will of the Eternal "that in the name of Jesus every knee should bow, and that every tongue should confess that Jesus Christ is Lord."

3. Still another note sounds for us in this exultant word of Jesus. He ascends as *the Forerunner of His people, the Firstborn from the dead of many brethren.*

Had he coldly said, "I ascend to *My* Father and *My* God," and stopped there, it would have meant a severance, — His quitting the world that had disowned Him, shaking earth's dust from His feet and returning on His own account to His proper place. Had Jesus familiarly said, on the other hand, "I ascend to *our* Father and *our* God," He would have ranged Himself with men, claiming only such power and honour as might belong to the greatest of our race, ascending by Himself and leaving us to follow as we might by His example. But it is to be noted that, with all His humility and brotherhood towards men, the Lord never once uses this communicative expression, nor do the Evangelists by any chance put a word into His lips. It is always "My Father" or "your Father"; in the Lord's Prayer He bids us, "When *ye* pray say, Our Father which art in heaven"; but He never adopts the phrase in His own prayers. Always, even in His closest fellowship with men, there was at the back of the mind of Jesus Christ this distinction and reserve, the secret consciousness of a unique Sonship to God, which came out in His first recorded words spoken in boyhood.

But when He says, "My Father *and* your Father, My God *and* your God," there is the distinction in the union! We are redeemed, uplifted, dignified by Him just because He is so far above us. The eternal Son, the Heir of all things, returning to His throne and reassuming His Divine rank, is not ashamed to call us brothers — "Go, and tell My *brethren*, I ascend!" This is not the language of a child of earth, a human upstart, one of ourselves promoted, pushing his way (as one might speak) to the heavenly court; it is "the Son" who by this message "makes us free" of the Father's house where He is Lord, who assures us of a welcome and "prepares a place" for us, since He holds both with God and men, since He blends in Himself the two natures and links the two worlds. This brief conjunction comprises our Lord's whole work of reconciliation; the double "and" of the resurrection message — "My Father *and* your Father, My God *and* your God" — bridges the abyss which parted man from his Maker and earth from heaven.

Jesus Christ is our "way" to the Father, our Jacob's ladder with its foot set upon the grave-mounds and its top leaning against the stars. As He mounts upwards — the Son of God, the man Christ Jesus — every cloud parts, every door opens, every power yields homage; all the peers of the universe — thrones, lordships, principalities, dominions — bend before Him while He ascends from rank to rank, from realm to realm; and He virtually says, "Where I pass, My human brethren, My poor earthly friends, must pass too." The flaming sword that barred the path to Eden is put back into its sheath; the angel sentinels and heavenly warders are become "ministering spirits" the to the kindred of their Lord. None can hinder, nor would wish to hinder our admittance, since

He is not ashamed before His Father and the holy angels to call mankind His kinsmen.

The name of the ascended Jesus will be our password at the gates of Paradise and to the heaven of heavens. For the Son of God has said in our hearing, — has said it to the Most High God: "Father, I will that they whom Thou hast given Me, be with Me where I am."

G. G. FINDLAY
(1849-1919)

G. G. Findlay was born in 1849, the son of the Reverend James Findlay. From the time of his entering the Wesleyan ministry in 1870, his whole life was devoted to the teaching of the theological students of his church. For awhile he taught in Headingley and Richmond Colleges, and in 1881 he was made the Professor of Biblical Languages and Exegesis at the former of these two institutions located at Leeds. For almost all the years of his active life until near the very end, he carried for eight months, each year, a teaching schedule of eighteen hours a week. Out of this rich ministry came a number of invaluable works in the field of Biblical Exposition. This is the Dr. Findlay who wrote the commentary on Galatians in the *Expositor's Bible,* and the commentary on Colossians for the *Pulpit Commentary* Series, and then the famous commentary on First Corinthians in the *Expositor's Greek Testament.* To him was entrusted the writing of the Article on the Apostle Paul in *Hastings' Dictionary of the Bible.* My own opinion is that his commentary, or series of lectures, if you will, on First John entitled *Fellowship in Life Eternal* is one of the three greatest works on the Johannine Epistles in our language. Then one must mention a series of three volumes, which I am afraid are not too well known today, that would be a treasure for any library, entitled *Books of the Prophets.* A friend of his many years, the late Professor W. G. Moulton, said in an article on Professor Findlay at the time of his death, "For public life, Dr. Findlay had little inclination. He is probably the only Wesleyan minister who has ever declined the highest honor in the power of his brethren to give him, namely, the Presidency of the Wesleyan Conference." In reading again the other day the autobiography of Dr. Dinsdale T. Young, I came on this beautiful tribute to Professor Findlay, with which I would close this sketch.

"Dr. G. G. Findlay was the classical tutor during the major part of my College course. The learning, and humility, and sensitive kindliness of that great scholar and genius charmed me. And the charm multiplied with the years. His golden books are my constant companions. Dr. Findlay was always a sweetly gracious friend to me. I often consulted him on expository questions, and he always gave me sovereign help. All along my course he encouraged me. The last time I preached, in connection with a College Celebration, he said, 'You have inspired us all!' What a glorious man he was! In intellect and in heart he was magnificent. His power to sympathize with lines of life remote from his was positively wonderful. My great regret concerning this glorious man is that he was never the President of the Wesleyan Conference. We ought to have taken him by force and made him our king. I believe it would have done him good, both physically and in every way. But now he has outsoared earthly eminences. He lives and will live in the reverential and grateful love of a multitude of deeply indebted brethren."

THE GREAT COMMISSION
by
Brooke Foss Westcott

"That I may know him, and the power of his resurrection."
— Philippians 3:10

(actually on John 20:21-22)

We have seen that St. Luke and St. John have preserved for us the two complementary aspects of the first appearance of the Risen Lord to the representatives of His Church. St. Luke enables us to understand how He assured them of the reality of His Resurrection: how He offered His glorified humanity as the foundation of their abiding faith: how He gave them confidence in His unfailing sympathy, by showing that He bore even to the throne of heaven the marks of His dying love. St. John completes our view of this beginning of the Church. He sets before us clearly that the apprehension of the Gospel was at once followed by the charge to proclaim it: that the work of Christ finished in one sense was to be continued in another: that fresh powers were divinely provided for the fulfilment of fresh duties. St. John, so to speak, begins where St. Luke ends. In his narrative the joy of trembling expectation, which at first dared not believe, has passed into the joy of calm assurance, where there is no longer any question as to the Person of the Lord. The disciples were convinced as to the present: they were enlightened as to the past: the future still lay before them uncertain and unexplained. *Jesus therefore said to them again, Peace be unto you.* The Lord Himself used the salutation which He enjoined on His followers; and the greeting of Peace was repeated because it was now spoken

195

to new men under new circumstances. In the short time which had passed since the Lord stood among *the eleven and those that were with them,* they had been completely changed. The questionings, the doubts, the terrors by which they had been beset, were removed. They had tasted the powers of the spiritual world. They had gained peace for themselves, peace in the certainty that death had been overcome: peace in their restored fellowship with the Master whom they had lost: peace in the words of love which removed from them the burden of remorse and sin. But this was not all. There were fears and dangers without as well as within. The shut doors could not but remind them of a world hostile and powerful. And this world was to be met and conquered. Their communion with Christ was not yet made perfect. The message of Mary Magdalene forewarned them of a separation close at hand; yet they could not remain isolated or inactive. Therefore in the prospect of the vast work which they had not yet attempted: using the strength of the personal faith which they had gained: starting from the vantage-ground of quickened hope and reaching forth at once to the last issues of Christian effort, *Jesus said to them again, Peace be unto you. As the Father hath sent me, even so send I you. And when He had said this, He breathed on them, and saith unto them, Receive ye the Holy Ghost: whosesoever sins ye forgive, they are forgiven unto them; whosesoever sins ye retain, they are retained.*

The words thus uttered are the charter of the Christian Church. They define its mission: they confirm its authority: they reveal its life. They have indeed been so much obscured by glosses, and distorted by controversy, and misused by usurping powers, that it is very difficult for us now to rise to the perception of their original grandeur and breadth. But without entering upon any doubtful discussions, it will be enough for us to direct our attention to two or three facts in connexion with the passage, in order to place it in a truer light than that in which it is commonly regarded.

1. The words were not addressed to all the apostles nor to the apostles alone. Thomas was absent; and there were others assembled with the apostles, as we learn from St. Luke. The com-

mission and the promise were given therefore, like the Pentecostal blessing which they prefigured, to the Christian society and not to any special order in it.

2. The power which is described deals with sin and not with the punishment of sin. In essence it has nothing to do with discipline. It belongs to a spiritual world: and in regard to this it manifests the divine will and does not determine it.

3. The forgiveness and the retention of sins is represented as following from the impartment of a new being. The breathing upon the disciples recalls, even in the word used to express it, that act of creative energy whereby GOD breathed into the first man the breath of life.

4. The gift is conveyed once for all. No provision is laid down for its transmission. It is made part of the life of the whole society, flowing from the relation of the body to the Risen Christ. Thus the words are, I repeat, the charter of the Christian Church, and not simply the charter of the Christian ministry. They complete what Christ had begun, and could only begin, before His Passion. He had given to His disciples the power of the keys to open the treasury of the kingdom of heaven and dispense things new and old. He had given them power to bind and to loose, to fix and to unfix ordinances for the government of the new society. And now as Conqueror He added the authority to deal with sins. In saying this I do not touch upon the divine necessity by which the different persons and channels through which the manifold graces of the Christian life are administered were afterwards marked out. I wish only to insist upon the apostolic mission of all Christians, which no subsequent delegation of specific duties to others can annul. And it is surely most remarkable that St. John, by whom this commission is recorded, and St. Peter, to whom representative power was given, stand out among the writers of the New Testament as dwelling on the priestly office of all Christians. All Christians, as such, are indeed apostles, envoys of their Risen Lord. To ministers and to people alike, while they are as yet undistinguished, He directs the words of sovereign power in the announcement of His victory over death and sin, *Peace be unto*

you: as the Father hath sent me, even so send I you. Receive
ye the Holy Ghost: whosoever sins ye forgive, they are forgiven
unto them; whosoever sins ye retain, they are retained.

In this wider application of the words we can see a little more
of the meaning of the last most mysterious clause. The message
of the Gospel is the gladtidings of sin conquered. To apply this to
each man severally is the office of the Church, and so of each
member of the Church. To embrace it personally is to gain absolution. As we in our different places bring home to the consciences
of others the import of Christ's work, so far as we set them free
from the bondage in which they are held. There is therefore
nothing arbitrary in the fulfilment of the divine promise. He to
whom the word comes can appropriate or reject the message of
deliverance which we as Christians are authorised to bear. As
he does so, we, speaking in Christ's name, either remove the load
by which he is weighed down or make it more oppressive. For
the preaching of Christ cannot leave men as it finds them. If it
does not bring true peace, it disturbs the false peace into which
they have fallen. To this end all the sacraments and ordinances
of Christianity combine, to deepen the conviction of sin and to
announce the forgiveness of sin. In one way or other they bring
before the world the living lessons of the Passion and of the
Resurrection. And we all are charged to interpret them.

As the Father hath sent me, even so send I you. The exact
form of the language is most significant. Generally the words
express a resemblance of character between the mission of Christ
and the mission of His apostles, and not merely a resemblance of
form. At the same time there is a difference between the two
verbs equally translated 'send' which cannot be overlooked. The
first marks a definite work to be done; the second a personal relation of the sender and the sent. And in this connexion it is important to notice that Christ speaks of His mission as present and
not as past, as continuing and not as concluded. He says, *As the*
Father hath sent me, and not merely *as the Father sent me.* He
declares, that is, that His work is not over, though the manner in
which it is done is changed. Henceforth He is and He acts in

those whom He has chosen. They are in Him sharing in the fulness of His power: He is in them sharing in the burden of their labours. The promise of the Last Supper, the prayer on the way to Gethsemane, are accomplished. The disciples have entered on their inheritance of peace. They have beheld the glory of the Lord. And now it is their part to bear witness, that the world may believe.

We have only to realise the change which was wrought in the disciples within the short hours of the first Easter Day, in order that we may understand the substance and the authority of this witness which they had to give. They had known the defeat of death; they had received forgiveness; they had felt the breath of a divine life. Christ had inspired them with the power of His glorified manhood. He had given them the Holy Spirit through Himself. It was then their office to proclaim their experience, each according to the measure of his gift. And that office remains to be fulfilled as long as the Christian society exists. From the time of the apostles ever onwards the same blessings have been imparted to every generation of believers, and the blessings have brought and still bring with them the same obligations.

This fact lies at the foundation of our spiritual being. It is true that in the providential ordering of the Christian society various functions and graces have been variously concentrated; but all belong alike to the new life which the Risen Christ breathed into His Church. And whoever has consciously felt this life stirring within him, whoever has felt that it has brought rest in the midst of conflicts and light in the hour of gloom, whoever has felt that the faith in Christ's glorified humanity gives unity to the broken fragments of labour, and clothes our fleeting days with an eternal beauty, has heard, heard as truly as the disciples in the upper chamber, the words of the Lord: *As the Father hath sent me, even so send I you.*

As the Father hath sent me. Christ comes *not to destroy but to fulfil,* not to sweep away all the growths of the past, but to carry to its proper consummation every undeveloped germ of right. Even so He sends us to take our stand in the midst of things as they are: to guard with tender thoughtfulness all that has been consecrated to His service, and to open the way for the many powers which work together for His glory. Christ came in His Father's name, not of Himself, nor to do His own will. *Though He was Son, yet learned He obedience by the things which He suffered.* Waiting till the hour came, He bore all that the hour brought. Even so He sends us to crush down the promptings of our self-will, to discipline our impatience, to wait as well as to work, to listen for that divine voice which is articulate only to the still watchings of faith.

Christ came *not to be ministered unto but to minister, and to give His life a ransom for many;* not to win an easy battle, but to redeem through apparent defeat. Even so He sends us to reap what we have not sown, to sow what we shall not reap, to strive to learn and to work as believing that sacrifice alone is fruitful.

Christ came not to judge but to save, and still He came for a judgment; not *to send peace upon the earth, but fire and a sword.* His will was perfect love, but He did not veil the terrible law of His word, which kills if it does not quicken. Even so He sends us. The message which we have to bear will make the chains of evil more galling if it does not break them. The message of the Resurrection may be a message of peace: it may be a message of condemnation.

Christ came as *a light into the world,* bringing from another realm that which earth could not furnish, to illuminate, to vivify, to guide. Even so He sends us. We dare not dissemble that we are entrusted with a supernatural message. We have that to make known which is not of the world, but above it: that which cannot be measured or tested by limited standards: that which justifies itself simply by shining.

Christ came *to bear witness to the Truth:* to claim as His own everything that *is:* to claim the allegiance of every one that is of the Truth. Even so He sends us. In His name we take possession of every fact which is established by thought or inquiry. We fail in duty, we fail in faith, if we allow any human interest, or endowment, or acquisition to lie without the domain of the Cross.

Christ came *to seek and to save that which was lost, to call not righteous but sinners to repentance.* Even so He sends us to dare something for the Gospel, to believe that it has a power to arrest the careless, to raise the fallen, to find an answer in dull cold hearts, to move by a divine sympathy those whom the counsels of reason cannot reach.

As the Father hath sent me. Christ came to perfect, to serve, to enlighten. Such is the universal Christian mission. As we understand its character the knowledge becomes in us a spring of supplication; for the world around us shews that there is grievous need that we should all hear the divine call and answer it. The special duties, privileges, responsibilities of the Christian ministry remain undiminished and undisparaged when we recognise the common priesthood of all believers as sharers in the Life of the Risen Lord and charged to make known that which they have experienced. The greatest danger of the Church as present seems to be not lest we should forget the peculiar functions of ministerial office, but lest we should allow this to supersede the general power which it concentrates and represents in the economy of life. If only every Christian would have the courage to confess what he has found in his faith, simply and soberly, without affectation and without reserve; if, that is, our apostles were multiplied a thousandfold; we should not wait so sadly, so doubtingly, as we do, for the last triumph of Christ: we should rejoice to *hasten His Coming,* when He shall return in glory, the same Jesus who died and rose from the dead: we should, in a sense which we have not yet felt, *know Him and the power of His Resurrection.*

BROOKE FOSS WESTCOTT
(1825-1901)

The famous Greek scholar, exegete, and bishop, B. F. Westcott, was born in Birmingham, January 12, 1825, and was educated at Trinity College, Cambridge, where he had as colleagues, such young men as were destined to fame in Biblical studies, J. E. B. Mayor and J. S. Howson. Continuing there for a time as tutor, he had among his students, J. B. Lightfoot and F. J. H. Hort, the like of which cannot be found today in any one institution of England or our country. With a brilliant record, among other rewards, he won the Norrisian Prize in 1850, which he published the following year, with the title, *The Elements of the Gospel Harmony*. From 1852 to 1868, Westcott assisted the headmaster at the famous school at Harrow. There is a paragraph in the biographical sketch of Westcott by Professor V. H. Stanton, in the *Dictionary of National Biography*, which I cannot refrain from quoting here in its entirety. "By using every spare hour during the school terms and the greater part of the holidays for study and writing, Westcott succeeded in producing, while at Harrow, some of his best-known books and making a wide reputation as a biblical critic and theologian. In 1855 appeared his 'General Survey of the History of the Canon of the New Testament during the First Four Centuries'; in 1859 a course of four sermons preached before the University of Cambridge on 'Characteristics of the Gospel Miracles'; in 1860 his 'Introduction to the Study of the Gospels,' an enlargement of his early essay entitled 'The Elements of the Gospel Harmony'; in 1864 'The Bible in the Church,' a popular account of the reception of the Old Testament in the Jewish, and of both Old and New in the Christian, Church; in 1866 the 'Gospel of the Resurrection,' an essay in which he gave expression to some of his most characteristic thoughts on the Christian faith and its relation to reason and human life; in 1868, 'A General View of the History of the English Bible,' in which he threw light on many points which had commonly been misunderstood."

Westcott was made the Regius Professor of Divinity at Cambridge in 1870, having already been appointed Canon at Peterborough an office which he held until 1883. Westcott was a member of the Committee appointed for the revision of the New Testament in 1870 and in 1881 published, along with Professor Hort, the famous edition of the Greek New Testament, that was to be known thereafter as the Westcott and Hort Text, which exercised more influence over New Testament students in England for the next sixty years, than any other single volume. At the age of sixty-six, Westcott was appointed Bishop of Durham, following the great Lightfoot and succeeded by the saintly Bishop Moule.

Near the close of his life, on February 28, 1899, he addressed the Durham Junior Clergy Society on the subject of "The Study of the Bible." Inasmuch as we have in this address the ripe thought of one of the greatest Biblical scholars of his day, and inasmuch as the address itself is almost impossible to find, I am taking the liberty of quoting one of its most important paragraphs, from the biography of the Bishop by one of his sons. "I charge you, then, to prize and to use your peculiar spiritual heritage which was most solemnly committed to you at your ordination. Our English Church represents in its origin and in its growth the study of the Bible. In the study of the Bible lies the hope of its future. For the study of the Bible in the sense in which I have indicated is of momentous importance at the present time, and it is rare; there is much discussion about the Bible, but, as I fear, little knowledge of it. We are curious to inquire — and it is reasonable curiosity — when this book and that was written; but we are contented to be ignorant of what this book or that contains. We remain blind to the magnificent course of the Divine education of the world; and still less do we dwell upon the separate phrases of 'friends of God and prophets,' and question them and refuse to let them go till they have given us some message of warning or comfort or instruction. Such failures, such neglect seal the very springs of life. They deprive us of the remedies for our urgent distresses. Who does not know them? We are troubled on all sides by wars and rumours of wars, by the restlessness and anxiety of nations and classes; we ask impatiently if this wild confusion is the adequate result of eighteen centuries of the Gospel of Peace? We ask impatiently, and the Bible offers us an interpretation of a history and life not unlike our own, and helps us to see how the counsel of God goes forward through all the vicissitudes of human fortunes and human wilfulness. Our hearts again constantly fail us for fear *of the things which are coming on the world.* The Bible inspires us with an unfailing hope. We are yet further perplexed by conflicts of reasoning, by novelties of doctrines, by strange conclusions of bold controvertialists. The Bible provides us with a sure touchstone of truth, while

> The intellectual power, through words and things,
> Goes sounding on, a dim and perilous way,

and brings us back to a living fellowship with Him who is the Truth."

Of the Bishop's epochal writings, it is not necessary to speak in detail here. His commentaries on the Greek text of the Epistle to the Ephesians, Hebrews, and the Johannine Epistles, are still treasure houses for those who are fortunate to possess them. And, of course, his commentary on the Gospel of John probably had a greater circulation and influence than any work on the Fourth Gospel to be published in the last half of the nineteenth century, and is still worth studying and quoting.

No greater tribute could possibly be paid to the transparent character of the bishop and scholar than the fact that six of his sons were ordained into the ministry, four of whom went out as missionaries to India, and two of them becoming bishops themselves.

THE RESURRECTION INEVITABLE
by
H. P. Liddon

"Whom God hath raised up, having loosed the pains of death: because it was not possible that He should be holden of it."
— Acts 2:24

This is the language of the first Christian Apostle, in the first sermon that was ever preached in the Church of Christ. St. Peter is accounting for the miraculous gift of languages on the Day of Pentecost. After observing that it was, after all, only a fulfilment of the prophecy of Joel about the outpouring of the Spirit in the last days, he proceeds to trace it to its cause. It was the work, he says, of Jesus Christ, now ascended into heaven; — "He hath shed forth this which ye now see and hear." But Jesus Christ, he argues, had really ascended into heaven, because He had first really risen from the grave; and it is to St. Peter's way of accounting for Christ's Resurrection that I invite your attention today — as being the first Apostolic statement on the subject that was given to the world. And certainly, even if the point were only one of antiquarian interest, it would be full of attraction for every intelligent man to know how the first Christians thought about the chief truths of their Faith; considering the influence which that Faith has had and still has on the development of the human race. But for us, Christians, concern in this matter is more exacting and urgent. Our hopes and fears, our depressions and our enthusiasms, our improvement or our deterioration, are bound up with it. "If Christ be not risen, our preaching is vain, your faith is also vain." Let us then listen to what the Apostle

St. Peter says about a subject upon which his opportunities, to say nothing of higher credentials, qualified him to speak so authoritatively.

I.

First of all, then, St. Peter states the fact that Christ had risen from the dead. "Whom God hath raised up, having loosed the pains of death." Let us remember that he is preaching in Jerusalem, the scene of the Death and Resurrection of Christ, and, as his sermon shows, to some who had taken part in the scenes of the Crucifixion. Not more than seven weeks have passed since these events, — about the time that has passed since the Sunday before Ash Wednesday. And in Jerusalem, we may be sure, men did not live as fast as they do in an European capital, in this age of telegraphs and railroads. An event like the Crucifixion, in a town of that size, far removed from the greater centres of human life, would have occupied general attention for a considerable period. It would have been discussed and re-discussed in all its bearings. All that happened at the time, and immediately afterwards, the supposed disappointment of the disciples and ruin of the cause, as well as the agony and humiliation of the Master, would have been still ordinary topics of conversation in most circles of Jewish society. It was then to persons keenly interested in the subject, and who had opportunities of testing the truth of what he said, that St. Peter states so calmly and unhesitatingly the fact of the Resurrection. He states it as just as much a fact of history as the Crucifixion, in which his hearers had taken part. "Ye men of Israel, hear these words; Jesus of Nazareth, a Man approved of God among you by miracles and wonders and signs, which God did by Him in the midst of you, as ye yourselves also know: Him, being delivered by the determinate counsel and foreknowledge of God, ye have taken, and by wicked hands have crucified and slain:" and then he adds, "Whom God hath raised up, having loosed the pains of death." "This Jesus," he adds a little afterwards, "hath God raised up, whereof we all are witnesses." Not one or two favoured disciples; but all, even the doubter, all had seen their beloved Master. They had heard the tones of that familiar Voice; they had seen the wounds of the Passion; they had recognised in repeated conversations the continuity of heart, of thought, of purpose. It was the Jesus of old days, only invested with a new and awful glory. On the very day that He rose, He had been seen five times. And "He showed Himself alive after His Passion by many infallible proofs, being seen of His disciples forty days, and speaking of the things pertaining to the kingdom of God."

Some twenty-six years later, when St. Paul wrote his First Apostolical Letter to the Church of Corinth, there were, he says, more than two hundred and fifty persons still alive who had seen Jesus Christ after His Resurrection on a single occasion. The number of witnesses to the fact of the Resurrection, to whom St. Peter could appeal, and whom his hearers might cross-question if they liked, will account for the simplicity and confidence of his assertion.

In those days men had not learnt to think more of abstract theories than of well-attested facts. The world had not yet heard of that singular state of mind which holds that an *a priori* doctrine about the nature of things, or, stranger still, an existing temper or mood of human thought, is a sufficient reason for refusing to listen to the evidence which may be produced in favour of a fact. Nobody, it may be added, who professed to believe in an Almighty God, thought it reverent or reasonable to say that He could not for sufficient reasons modify His ordinary rules of working, if He chose to do so.

St. Peter then preached the Resurrection as a fact, and, as we know, with great and immediate results. But how did he account for the Resurrection? what was the reason which he gave for its having happened at all? This is the second point, to which I invite your attention; and it will detain us somewhat longer than the first

II.

St. Peter, then, says that Christ was raised from the dead, "because it was not possible that He should be holden of" death.

Thus St. Peter's first thought about this matter is the very opposite to that of many persons in our day. They say that no evidence will convince them that Christ has risen, because they hold it to be antecedently impossible that He should rise. St. Peter, on the other hand, almost speaks as if he could dispense with any evidence, so certain is he that Jesus Christ must rise. In point of fact, as we know, St. Peter had his own experience to fall back upon; he had seen his Risen Master on the day of His Resurrection, and often since. But so far was this evidence of his senses from causing him any perplexity, that it only fell in with the anticipations which he had now formed on other and independent grounds. "It was not possible," he says, "that Christ should be holden, or imprisoned, by death." It will do us good, my brethren, as fellow-believers with St. Peter, to spend some little time upon his grounds for saying this; to consider, so far as we may, the reasons of this Divine impossibility.

And here, first of all, we find the reason which lay, so to speak, closest to the conclusion, and which was intended to convince the Apostle's hearers, in the sermon itself. "It was not possible that Christ should be holden of death; *for* David speaketh concerning Him." It was then Jewish prophecy which forbade Christ to remain in His grave, and made His Resurrection nothing less than a necessity. As to the principle of this argument there would have been no controversy between St. Peter and the Jews. The Jews believed in the reality and force of prophecy — of that variety of prophecy which foretells strictly future events — just as distinctly as did Christians. The prophets, in the belief of the Jews, were the confidants of God. He whispered into their souls, by His Spirit, His secret resolutions for the coming time. "Surely," exclaims the prophet Amos, "surely the Lord will do nothing, but He revealeth His secret unto His servants the prophets." And when once God had thus spoken, His word, it was felt by Jews and Christians, stood sure. His gifts and calling were without repentance. The prophetic word became, in virtue of God's Moral Attributes, a restraint upon that liberty of which it was the product, until it was fulfilled. It constituted within the limits of its application a law of necessity, to which men and events, and, if need were, nature had to bend. And for all who believed in its Author the supposition that it would come to nothing after all, was, to use St. Peter's phrase, "not possible." It could not return empty; it must accomplish the work for which God had sent it forth; since it bound Him to an engagement with those who uttered and with those who heard His message.

Obviously enough, the true drift of a prophecy may easily be mistaken. God is not responsible for the eccentric guesses as to His meaning in which well-meaning men of vagrant imaginations may possibly indulge. We have lived in this generation to hear some very confident guesses, based on the supposed meaning of prophecy, respecting the end of the world, or some impending general catastrophe. But the dates assigned for such occurrences have passed. And religion would be seriously discredited, if the Sacred Word itself were at fault, instead of the fervid imagination of some incautious expositor. But where a prediction is clear, it does bind Him Who is its real Author to some fulfilment, which, in the event, will be recognised as such. And such a prediction of the Resurrection of the Messiah St. Peter finds in Psalm XVI., where David, — as more completely in Psalm XXII., — loses the sense of his own personal circumstances in the impetus and ecstasy of the prophetic spirit, and describes a Personality of Which indeed he was a type, but Which altogether transcends him.

"Therefore My heart is glad,

And My glory rejoiceth:

My flesh also shall rest in hope.

For Thou wilt not leave My Soul in hell;

Neither wilt Thou suffer Thine Holy One to see corruption.

Thou wilt show Me the path of life:

In Thy Presence is fulness of joy;

At Thy Right Hand there are pleasures for evermore."

David, so argues St. Peter, utters these words; but they are not strictly true of David. "David," he says, "is both dead and buried, and his sepulchre is among us unto this day." Or, as St. Paul states, when appealing to this very Psalm in his sermon at

Antioch in Pisidia, "David, after he had served his own generation by the will of God, fell on sleep, and was laid unto his fathers,
and saw corruption. But He, Whom God raised up, saw no
corruption." The meaning of the Psalm was so clear to some
Jewish doctors, that, unable as they were to reconcile it with
David's history, they invented the fable, that his body was
miraculously preserved from corruption. David, however, was
really speaking in the Person of Messiah. And his language
created the necessity that Messiah should rise from the dead; or,
as St. Peter puts it, his language made it impossible that Messiah
should be holden by death. God had spoken, in other passages,
no doubt. But He spoke with great clearness in this. And His
Word could not return unto Him empty.

Observe, here, that St. Peter had not always felt and thought
thus. He had known this Psalm all his life. But long after he had
followed Jesus Christ about Galilee and Judaea he had been
ignorant of its true meaning. Only little by little do any of us
learn God's truth and will. And so lately as the morning of the
Resurrection, St. John says of both St. Peter and himself that
"as yet they know not the scripture, that He must rise again from
the dead." Since then the Holy Spirit had come down, and had
poured a flood of light into the minds of the Apostles and over
the sacred pages of the Old Testament. And thus a necessity for
the Resurrection, which even Jews ought to recognise, was not
abundantly plain to them. May that same Eternal Spirit teach
us, as then He taught our spiritual forefathers, the full meaning
of His Word!

A second reason which would have shaped St. Peter's language
lay in the character of his Master Jesus Christ. It was our Lord's
character not less assuredly than His miracles which drew human
hearts to Him, and led or forced them to give up all that this
world could offer for the happiness of following and serving Him.
Now, of our Lord's character a leading feature was its simple
truthfulness. It was morally impossible for Him to hold out
prospects which would never be realised or to use words which
He did not mean. Nay, He insisted upon simple sincerity of

language in those who came into His company. He would not allow the young man to call Him "Good Master," when the expression was a mere phrase in His Mouth. He would not accept professions to follow Him whithersoever He went, or aspirations to sit on His Right Hand and on His Left in His kingdom till men had weighed their words, and were sure that they meant all that such words involved. Unless then He was like those Pharisees whom He censured for laying burdens upon others which they would not touch themselves, it might be taken for granted that if He promised He would perform; that His promise made performance morally necessary, and non-performance morally impossible. This was the feeling of His disciples about Him. He was too wise to predict the impossible. He was too sincere to promise what He did not mean.

Now Jesus Christ had again and again said that He would be put to a violent death, and that after dying He would rise again. Sometimes, as to the Jews in the Temple, when He cleansed it in in the early days of His ministry, He expressed His meaning in the language of metaphor. "Destroy," He said to them, "this Temple, and in three days I will raise it up." The Jews rallied Him on the absurdity of undertaking to reconstruct in three days an edifice which it had taken forty-six years to build. The drift of the words may have been made plain to the disciples by a gesture which accompanied them; and in later years they understood the sense in which He termed His Body a Temple, namely, because in Him dwelt all the fulness of the Godhead bodily. Sometimes He fell back upon ancient Hebrew history, and compared that which would befall Himself to the miraculous adventure of the prophet who shrank from the mission assigned to him by God. When the Pharisees, irritated at His stern rebuke of their blasphemous levity in ascribing His miracle on the blind and dumb man to the activity of Beelzebub, asked Him for a "sign," that is, for some credential of His mission, He contented Himself with saying that as Jonah had been three days and three nights in the whale's belly, so would the Son of Man be in the heart of the earth. In other words, His right to speak and act as

He did would be proved by His rising from the dead. With His disciples He used neither metaphor nor historic parallel. He said simply, on three occasions at the least, as the hour of His sufferings approached, that He should be crucified, and should rise again from death. Peter himself had, on the first of these occasions, rebuked Him, as we know, and had been rebuked in turn. Thus He was pledged, if we may reverently say so, to this particular act. He was pledged to the Jewish people, pledged to its ruling classes, pledged especially to His Own chosen band of faithful followers. He could not have remained in His grave — I will not say without dishonour, but — without causing in others a revulsion of feeling such as is provoked by the exposure of baseless pretensions.

It may indeed be urged that the Resurrection foretold by Christ was not a literal resurrection of His dead Body, but only a recovery of His ascendency, His credit, His authority; obscured as these had been for a while in the apprehension of His disciples and of the world, by the tragedy of the Crucifixion. The word Resurrection, according to this supposition, is in His Mouth a purely metaphorical expression. It is used to describe not anything that affected Jesus Christ Himself, but only a revolution of opinion and feeling about Him in the minds of others. Socrates had had to drink the fatal hemlock; and the body of Socrates had long since mingled with the dust. But Socrates, it might be said, had risen, in the intellectual triumphs of his pupils, and in the enthusiastic admiration of succeeding ages; the method and words of Socrates had been preserved for all time in a literature that will never die. If Christ was to be put to death by crucifixion, He would triumph, even after a death so shameful and degrading, as Socrates and others had triumphed before Him. To imagine for Him an actual exit from His tomb, is said to be a crude literalism, natural to uncultivated ages, but impossible, when the finer suggestiveness of human language has been felt to transcend the letter.

An obvious reply to this explanation is, that it arbitrarily makes our Lord use literal and metaphorical language in two successive clauses of a single sentence. He is literal, it seems, when He predicts His Crucifixion; there is no doubt about that. The world has always agreed with the Church as to the fact of His being crucified. Tacitus mentions His death as well as the Evangelists. But if our Lord is to be understood literally, when He foretells His Cross, why is He to be thought metaphorical when He foretells His Resurrection? Why should not His Resurrection, if it be only Metaphorical, be preceded by a metaphorical crucifixion; a crucifixion of thought, or will, or reputation, — not the literal nailing of a human body to a wooden cross? Why does this fastidious temper, which shrinks from the idea of a literal rising from a literal grave, not shrink equally from a literal nailing to a literal cross? It is impossible seriously to maintain on any grounds consistent with an honest interpretation of His Words, that our Lord Himself could have meant that He would be literally crucified, but would only rise in a metaphorical sense. Surely He meant that the one event would be just as much or just as little a matter of fact as the other. And any other construction of His Words would never have originated except with those who wish to combine a lingering respect for His language, with a total disbelief in the supreme miracle which has made Him what He is to Christendom. No; it is clear that, if Jesus Christ had not risen from the grave He would not have kept His engagement with His disciples or with the world. This was the feeling of those who knew and loved Him best. This was the feeling of St. Peter, ripened no doubt but lately into a sharply-defined conviction, but based on years of intimate companionship; — when Christ, so scrupulously truthful and so invariably wise, had once said that He would rise from death, any other event was simply impossible. All was really staked on His rising again. And when He did rise, "He was declared to be the Son of God with power, in respect of His Holy and Higher Nature, by the Resurrection from the dead." Those who cling to His human character, yet deny His Resurrection, would do well to consider, that they must choose between their moral enthusiasm and their unbelief; since it is the character of Christ, even more than the language of prophecy, which made the idea that He would rise after death impossible for His first disciples.

Not that we have yet exhausted St. Peter's reasons for this remarkable expression. You will remember, my friends, that in the sermon which St. Peter preached to a crowd, after the healing of the lame man at the Beautiful gate of the Temple, he went over much of the ground which is traversed in this first sermon on the Day of Pentecost. He told his hearers among other things that they had "killed the Prince of Life, Whom God raised from the dead." Remark that striking title, "The Prince of Life." Not merely does it show how high above all earthly royalties was the Crucified Saviour in the heart and faith of His Apostle. It connects the thought of St. Peter in this early stage of his ministry with the language of his Divine Master on the one side, and that of His Apostles St. Paul and St. John upon the other. Our Lord had said, "I am the Way, the Truth, and the Life;" He had explained the sense of this last word "Life" by saying that "as the Father hath Life in Himself, so hath He given to the Son to have Life in Himself." He had complained to the men of His time, "Ye will not come unto Me that ye might have life." And St. John said of Him that "in Him was Life:" and St. Paul, in today's Epistle, calls Him "Christ, Who is our Life." When, then, St. Peter names Him the "Prince of Life," he is referring to this same truth about his Master. And it is in fact the keynote of the Gospel.

What is life? That is a question which no man even now can answer. We do not know what life is in itself. We only register its symptoms. We see growth; we see movement; and we say, Here is life. It exists in one degree in the tree; in a higher in the animal; in a higher still in man. In beings above man, we cannot doubt, it is to be found in some yet grander form. But in all these cases it is a gift from another: and having been given, it might be modified or withdrawn. Who is He in Whom life resides originally; He Who owes it to no other; He from Whom no other can withdraw it? Only the Self-Existent lives of right. He lives because He cannot but live; He lives an original as distinct from a derived life. This is true of the Eternal Three, Who yet are One. But Revelation assures us that it is only true of the Son and the Holy Spirit, because by an unbegun, unending communication of Deity, They receive such Life from the Eternal Father. Hence our Lord says, "As the Father hath Life in Himself, so hath He given to the Son to have Life in Himself." Not merely Life, but "Life in Himself." Thus, with the Eternal Giver, the Eternal Receiver is Fountain and Source of Life. With reference to all created beings, He is the Life, — their Creator, their Upholder, their End. "For," says St. Paul, "by Him were all things created, that are in heaven, and that are in earth, visible and invisible; whether they be thrones, or dominions, or principalities, or powers: all things were created by Him, and for Him: and He is before all things, and by Him all things consist."

This then is the full sense of St. Peter's expression, "The Prince of Life." And in the truth which it teaches as to our Lord's jurisdiction over life, based on the truth of His Eternal Nature, we may trace a third reason for St. Peter's expression in the text. How could the very Lord and Source of Life be subdued by death? If, for reasons of wisdom and mercy, He subjected the Nature which He had made His Own to the king of terrors, this was surely not in the course of nature; it was a violence to nature that this should be. And therefore when the object had been achieved, He would rise, St. Peter implies, by an inevitable rebound, by the force of things, by the inherent energy of His irrepressible Life. From St. Peter's point of view, the real wonder would be if such a Being were not to rise. The pains of death were loosed, — not by an extraordinary effort, as in your case or mine — but because it was impossible that He, the Prince of Life, should be holden of it.

Observe, then, my friends, how St. Peter deals with this great subject. He now looks at it from above, so to say, rather than from below. He here asks himself what his faith about the Son of God points to, rather than what history proves to have taken place. He is for the moment more concerned for his Master's honour than with the significance and value of His acts for us.

To St. Peter it is less strange that there should be an innovation upon nature such as the resurrection of a dead body than it would be if such a Being as Jesus Christ, having been put to death, did not rise. St. Peter is very far from being indifferent to the proof that Christ did rise; indeed he often and earnestly insists on it. But just as St. John always calls Christ's miracles His "works," meaning that they were only what such an One as He might be expected to do; so St. Peter treats His Resurrection from the dead as perfectly natural to Him; nay, as an event which any man or angel with sufficient knowledge might have calculated beforehand, just as astronomers predict unerringly the movements of the heavenly bodies. God hath raised Jesus from the dead, he says, because it was impossible that death should continue to hold Him.

III.

Yes. The Buried Christ could not really remain in His grave. He was raised from it in virtue of a Divine necessity; and this necessity, while in its original form strictly proper to His case, points to kindred necessities which affect His servants and His Church. Let us in conclusion briefly consider them.

Note, first, the impossibility, for us Christians too, of being buried for ever in the tomb in which we shall each be laid at death. We too, after the death and burial which awaits each one of us, shall rise; nay, we must rise. In this, as in other matters, "as He," our Lord, "is, so are we in this world." To us as to Him, although in a different way, God has pledged Himself. There is a difference indeed, such as might be expected between our case and His. In Him an internal vital force made Resurrection from death necessary; in us there is no such intrinsic force, only a power guaranteed to us from without. He could say of the Temple of His Body, "I will raise it up in three days:" we can only say that God will raise us up, we know not when. But this we do know, that "if the Spirit of Him that raised up Jesus from the dead dwell in you, He that raised up Christ from the dead shall also quicken your mortal bodies by His Spirit that dwelleth in you." This we do know, that "we must all be made manifest before the judgment-seat of Christ, that every one may receive the things done in the body, according to that which he hath done, whether it be good or bad." The law of justice and the law of love combine to create a necessity which requires "a resurrection of the dead, both of the just and of the unjust."

It is not always easy even for believing Christians to do justice to this solemn and certain truth. The gradual decay of vital force during illness, the dissolution and corruption of the body after death, the chemistry not less than the pathos of the grave, combine to make us forget Whose word it is that warrants for each one of us a Resurrection. And yet He "will change our vile body, that it may be fashioned like unto His glorious Body, according to the mighty working whereby He is able even to subdue all things unto Himself." Death is not an eternal sleep; the tomb is not the final resting-place of the bodies of those whom we have loved. The empty sepulchre at Jerusalem on Easter morning is the warrant of a new life, strictly continuous with this, and, if we are faithful, much more glorious.

See here, also, the principle of moral resurrections in the Church of Christ. As with the bodies of the faithful so it is with the Church of Christ. The Church of Christ is, according to St. Paul's teaching, Christ Himself in history. St. Paul says as much when he tells us that "as the body is one, and has many members, and all the members of that body, being many, are one body, so also is Christ." The Church is Christ's Body, the fulness of Him That filleth all in all. But the force of this language is limited by the fact, equally warranted by Scripture — that the Church has in it a human element, which, unlike the Humanity of Christ, is weak and sinful. The Church of Corinth itself, to which St. Paul wrote the sentence which I just now quoted, was filled with strife, irreverence, even worse sins than these. Again and again in the course of her history large portions of the Christian Church have seemed to be dead and buried, — away in some one of the lumber-rooms of the past. And the world has gone its way, rejoicing as if all was over; as if henceforth unbelief and ungodliness would never be disturbed in their reign on earth by any protest from heaven. But suddenly the tomb has opened; there has been a moral movement, a profound agitation in men's consciences, a feeling that all is far from right. And then has arisen a new spirit of devotion, social stir, literary activity, conspicuous self-sacrifice; and, lo! the world awakes to an uneasy suspicion that "John the Baptist has risen from the dead, and that mighty works do show forth themselves in him." The truth is that Christ has again burst His tomb and is abroad among men. So it was after the moral degradation of the Papacy in the tenth century; so it was after the recrudescence of paganism by the Renaissance in the fifteenth; so it was in this country after the great triumph of Puritan misbelief and profanity in the seventeenth century, and of indifference to vital religion in the eighteenth. The oppression, the degradation, the enfeeblement, of the Church of Christ is possible enough; too generally, the world only binds and makes sport of Samson, because Samson has yielded to the blandishments of Delilah. But there is a latent force in the Church of Christ, which asserts and must assert itself, from generation to generation. If the Crucifixion is re-enacted, in the Holy Body; if, as St. Paul puts it, we fill up, from century to century, that which is behind of the afflictions of Christ; the Resurrection is re-enacted too. It is not possible that the Body of Christ, instinct with His force and vital Spirit, should be holden of death; each apparent collapse and failure is followed by an outburst of energy and moral glory, which reveals the Presence of the Living Christ; His Presence Who, if crucified through weakness, yet liveth by the Power of God.

Thirdly, note here what is or ought to be the governing principle of our own personal life. If we have been laid in the tomb of sin, it ought to be impossible that we should be holden of sin. I say "ought to be;" because, as a matter of fact, it is not impossible. God only is responsible for the resurrection of the Christian's body, and for the perpetuity, through its successive resurrections, of the Christian Church; and therefore it is impossible that either the Church or our bodies should permanently succumb to the empire of death. But God, Who raises our bodies whether we will or not, does not raise our souls from sin, unless we correspond with His grace; and it is quite in our power to refuse this correspondence. That we should rise then from sin is a moral, not a physical necessity; but surely we ought to make it as real a necessity as if it were physical. For any who feels in his soul the greatness and love of Jesus Christ it ought to be morally impossible to remain in the tomb: "Like as Christ was raised from the dead by the glory of the Father, even so we also should walk in newness of life." If Lent is the season for mourning the past, Easter is the season for those bracing definite resolutions and vigorous efforts which control the future. If we were unaided and alone, such efforts and resolutions would be failures indeed; like the vain flutterings of a bird against the wires of the cage which imprisons it. But He Who has "broken the gates of brass, and smitten the bars of iron in sunder," will not fail us, if we ask and seek His strength; and the permanence and splendour of His Life in glory may, and should be, the warrant of our own.

One word more. A real Resurrection with Christ will make and leave some definite traces upon life. Let us resolve this day to do or leave undone some one thing which will mark a new beginning: conscience will instruct us, if we allow it to do so. If any of you are looking out for a way of showing gratitude to our Risen Saviour, let me suggest that you should send the best contribution you can afford to the Mission at Zanzibar on the east coast of Africa. There a small band of noble men, under the leadership of a bishop of Apostolical character, is making efforts worthy of the best days of the Church to propagate the Faith among races, to whom no depths of degradation and misery that are possible for human beings are unknown, but who are as capable as ourselves of rising with Christ to a new life of moral and mental glory. According to accounts which have just reached this country, at the very moment when new and unanticipated opportunities are presenting themselves, and such an inroad upon heathendom, and the slavery and vices which mark its empire, is possible, as has never been possible before, their scanty means altogether fail these noble missionaries. They literally have not enough to eat; much less can they attempt the new enterprises of Christian charity which their circumstances imperatively demand. Shall we leave them to despondency, to retreat, to failure; with the heathen before them stretching out their hands unto God, and with the impure imposture of the false prophet hard by, ready to take a cruel advantage of our supineness? Surely it cannot but be that some who hear me will make an effort worthy of our Easter gratitude in behalf of an object, than which none can well be imagined more truly Christian and philanthropic, more worthy of men who humbly hope that they have part in the First Resurrection, and in all that it implies.

BIBLIOGRAPHY

S. H. Kellogg: *The Past a Prophecy of the Future*. London. 1904. pp. 249-261
H. P. Liddon: *Easter in St. Paul's*. pp. 62-76 and 407-421
G. Campbell Morgan: *Westminster Pulpit*. Vol. 9. pp. 145-152.
Robert South: *Sermons Preached Upon Several Occasions*. Philadelphia. 1844. II. 18-30
Charles H. Spurgeon: *Metropolitan Tabernacle Pulpit*. Vol. 47 (1901), No. 2707. pp. 13-24

THE UNDYING ONE
by
H. P. Liddon

"Christ being raised from the dead dieth no more."
— Romans 6:9

Easter Day is a day on which the best Christians are hardly in a mood for sermons. Their hearts are full of joy, and they come to church, as they would go to a wedding; to make their congratulations; to utter their hymns of joy and praise to the King of kings on the anniversary of His great victory. Their hearts say more to them than any fellow-man can possibly say; and much of what their hearts tell them cannot well be rendered into human language. They wish to be left alone with their joy: sermons, they say, are very well in seasons and on days of penitence: but when the heart is bursting with triumphant emotion, sermons either lag behind our feelings or are out of harmony with them. And for this kind of reason, I suppose, it has been said that a sermon on Easter Day requires an apology.

It is not my business to dispute the existence of a state of mind such as this. There are Christians, no doubt, who in some sort, in varying degrees, even while here on earth, anticipate heaven. They know what may be known about invisible things; about God, about conscience, about the future. They enjoy not merely light, but love. They feel as angels feel rather than as men; and human voices or human experiences can do, for such as they are, little or nothing. We need not doubt that such Christians exist; but the immense majority of us, you and I, are on a very different level. We are the children of time all over; at least as yet. We are entangled in difficulties, greater or less; we have to battle with weakness in our wills and with darkness in our understandings. For us, too, in our measure, Easter is a day of joy: we catch the inspiration which moves higher and brighter souls around us; we keep pace, as we can, with the loftier feeling of the time. But, at least for us, it is a great help to have definite points to fall back upon as the reasons for our joy: and, with a view to this, we cannot do better than place ourselves under St. Paul's guidance this afternoon, in those words which are so familiar to us from childhood, as forming part of the Easter anthem, "Christ being raised from the dead dieth no more."

In these words are two assertions which lie at the bottom of all Easter satisfaction. First, The reality of the Resurrection; "Christ being raised from the dead." Secondly, The perpetuity of Christ's Risen Life: "Christ being raised from the dead dieth no more."

I.

The Resurrection then asserts a truth which is by no means always written legibly for all men on the face of nature. It tells us that the spiritual is higher than the material; that in this universe spirit counts for more than matter. There are no doubt abstract arguments which go to show that this is the case. But the Resurrection is a palpable fact, which assures us that the ordinary laws of animal existence may be altogether set aside in obedience to a higher spiritual interest. It was, we all know, no natural force like that of growth which raised our Lord Jesus Christ from His grave. And such a fact as this is worth much more than abstract arguments. It can always be fallen back upon, when we are in no mood for speculative thought; and it leaves less room for mistake or self-deception.

"Christ being raised from the dead." The Resurrection is not merely an article of the Creed: it is a fact in human history. That our Lord Jesus Christ was begotten of the Father before all worlds is also an article of the Christian faith. But it has nothing to do with human history, and it cannot be shown to have taken place, like any event, say in the life of Julius Caesar, by the reputed testimony of eye-witnesses. It belongs to another sphere; it is believed on account of the proved trustworthiness of Him Who has taught us this truth about His Own Eternal Person. But that Christ rose from the dead is a fact which depends on the same sort of testimony as any event in the life of Caesar; with this difference, that no one ever thought it worth while to risk his life in order to maintain that Caesar defeated Vercingetorix or Pompey. Our Lord, as you know, was seen five times on the day that He rose from the dead. Mary Magdalene saw Him in the garden. She saw Him again, with the other Mary and Salome, when He allowed them to hold Him by the Feet, and to worship Him. At a later hour in the day He appeared to Peter. In the afternoon He discovered Himself to Cleopas and another disciple who were walking on the Emmaus road. In the evening He was with the Apostles, excepting Thomas. He showed them His Hands and His Feet, as those of the Crucified; He ate before them; He gave them the power of remitting and retaining sins. And after this first day, six separate appearances are recorded; while it is implied that they were only a few of those which actually occurred. After the interval of a week, He appeared again to the Eleven. Thomas then was with them; and He convinced Thomas that He was really risen. On another occasion they saw Him on a mountain in Galilee. On another He was seen by five hundred persons, more than one half of whom were still living when St. Paul described the fact to the Corinthians. On another He appeared to St. Peter, St. Thomas, St. Bartholomew, St. James the Great, and St. John, with two others, on the shore of the lake of Tiberias. On another He had a private interview with St. James the Less. Once more, He was with all the Apostles at Jerusalem, before He led them out to Bethany, gave them His last promises and benediction, and went up to heaven before their eyes.

And when He was gone, His Apostles went forth to do and teach, no doubt, a great deal else, but especially, they went forth as "witnesses of His Resurrection." That was a fact of which they were certain; they were prepared to attest its truth, if need were, with their blood. We learn from the Acts of the Apostles that the earliest Christian preaching was a constant assertion that Christ had really risen. The reality of His Resurrection was so certain that it emboldened and indeed forced His followers to address themselves to the conversion of the world. "We cannot but speak the things," they said, "which we have seen and heard."

If the testimony which can be produced in proof of the Resurrection concerned only a political occurrence, or a fact of natural history witnessed eighteen centuries ago, nobody would think of denying its cogency. Those who do reject the truth of the Resurrection quarrel, for the most part, not with the proof that the Resurrection occurred, but with the supposition that such a thing could happen under any circumstances. No proof would satisfy them; because they have made up their minds that the thing cannot be. Certainly, on the face of it, the Resurrection is a miracle; nay, we may well say, it is the greatest of Christian miracles. As such it is unwelcome to those who make their limited personal experience of the physical world the measure of all spiritual as well as physical truth. Look, they say, at the fixed order of nature: day after day, year after year, it is what, within our memories, it always has been. The day waxes and wanes; the seasons follow each other; the apparent caprices of nature are, upon closer observation, more and more easily referred to the empire of law; the life of every animal obeys a fixed order from birth to death; and man, he too,however he may flatter himself, is no exception to the general rule; he too obeys this universal order; whether he will or no, he obeys, alike in life and in death, those physical laws which govern the course of animal existence. So that, when man dies, he lies down to mingle his body with the dust for good and all; he does not, so far as we see, break the bonds of death. It is the fixed order of nature.

The fixed order of nature! Surely, brethren, we in this age are, at least as much as our less scientific forefathers, the slaves of phrases! The fixed order of nature, you say. Fixed, I ask, by whom or by what? By some fated necessity, do you say? But you yourselves, out of the experience of that existence which minute by minute you enjoy, can dispose of this phrase about a fixed order. You know that you can speak, move, act, or refrain from acting, moving, speaking, as, minute by minute, you will, and without any allegiance whatever to a supposed necessity. This is a fact within your experience: and what you know about yourselves to be experimentally true, you reasonably think may well be true, on a much greater scale, of beings higher than yourselves, of the highest Being of all. For that such a Being exists, as the Cause of all else, nature itself assures you by its existence; and that He is not a mindless cause, but an ordering and disposing Intelligence — I do not forget recent attempts to set aside the argument from design — the order and symmetry of nature assure you too. If then you believe in God, you confess that the order of nature is fixed not by necessity or a fate, but by a Will which can at pleasure innovate upon or reverse it. He Who made life and nature what they are, could have made, and can make them otherwise. The power to work miracles is implied in the Power Which created nature. Miracles, to say the least, are not antecedently incredible for any rational believer in God.

'God can work them,' you say; 'but will He? Are not miracles a libel upon the wisdom and far-sightedness of God? How should the All-providing Mind have to supply deficiencies? How should the Perfect Wisdom consent to break in upon the settled order of His work? God in creation is the Supreme Engineer: it is only the unskilful workman who, having set his machine in motion, has to thrust in his hand in order to correct some defect, or to communicate some new impulse for which no provision was made originally.'

Here you run a risk of manufacturing argument out of mere metaphor. To say that God, in creation, is an Engineer or an Artist, is a very pardonable phrase. Within certain narrow limits it expresses a truth about His relation to the universe. It reminds us that all the resources and provisions of nature are due to His contriving Mind. But such an expression must not be pressed so as to obscure or deny other, and higher, truths about God, and about His work. The universe is something more than a machine: since it contains not merely matter but minds; not merely inanimate masses, governed by rules which they unconsciously obey, but free spirits, able consciously to yield or to refuse obedience to the true law of their being. And God is much greater than a Supreme Engineer. He is, before all things, a Moral Governor; He is a Father. His first care is for His intelligent offspring: and the universe of matter was framed not for its own sake, but for the rational beings who were to tenant it. If no such being as man had been created, miracle might have been superflous. The universe might then well have been nothing more than a perfect machine, admitting of no interference, for any cause whatever, with its ordinary working. But if the education, the improvement, the rescuing from darkness and from evil, of a created rational mind or soul be God's noblest purpose in creation, then, if we believe Him to be Wise and Good, as well as Almighty, we shall expect Him to make the world of matter instruct and improve us, by deviating, if need be, from its accustomed order, as well as by observing it. No one who considers carefully what a mind endowed with freedom of choice is, and how various is the discipline and teaching which it needs, will say lightly that it needs no lights or aids to its true perfection and development, but such as an unvarying order of nature can supply.

We may indeed go further than this. The order which is observable in the natural world teaches no doubt a great and precious lesson to the man who already has a firm faith in the Living God; it teaches him that order is a law of the Divine Mind. But for thousands upon thousands of human beings, who have indistinct and fluctuating ideas of God, in all countries and in all generations, and not by any means least in our own, the order of nature paralyses the spiritual sense. Perhaps, if it were possible to watch a fellow-creature continuing undeviatingly a single movement during a period of twenty years, we should come to look at him also as a machine which worked unconsciously, instead of as a free agent who might at any moment hold his hand. And undoubtedly men whose minds, or rather whose imaginations, are controlled mainly by impressions derived from sense; who mark how regular God's work is, how undeviating; and who instinctively presume that it must always be what it has hitherto been; — such men gradually come to think of this visible scene of things as the whole universe of being. They drop out of mind that more wonderful world beyond it; they forget Him Who is the King of this world as well as of that. Nay; let us own that there are times in the lives of many of us when the physical world lies like a weight, or like a nightmare, heavy upon our thoughts; when we long for some higher promise of blessedness and perfection than any which a fixed order of nature can give; when we would fain rise in spirit beyond this material sphere, —

> "But still the wall impassable
> Bars us around with senual bond;
> In vain we dive for that beyond;
> Yet traverse o'er and o'er the bound
> Walking on the unseen profound.
> Like flies, which on my window pane
> Pace up and down, again, again,
> And though they fain would break away
> Into th' expanse of open day,
> They know not why, are travelling still
> On the glass fence invisible:
> So dwell our thoughts with the unseen
> Yet cannot pass the bourne between."

This, then, is the happiness, which is bestowed on many a human mind by the fact of Christ's Resurrection. It breaks down the iron wall of uniformity which goes so far to shut out God. It tells us that matter, and the orderly arrangement of matter, is not the governing principle of the universe. It assures us that matter is controlled by Mind; that there is a Being, a Will, to Which matter can offer no effective resistance; that He is not bound by the laws of the universe; that He is their master. God had said this before to men who had ears to hear and eyes to see. But

He never said it so clearly as in the Resurrection of our Lord. If ever there was a case which might be expected to warrant summary interference with the common order of the world on the part of a moral God, here was one. When Jesus died on Calvary, the purest of lives seemed to the eye of sense to have ceased to be. The holiest of doctrines appeared to have died away upon the air, amid the blasphemies which raged at the foot of the Cross. Apart from the question who the Sufferer was, there was the question whether a righteous God did really reign on earth and in heaven. And the Resurrection was an answer to that question. It was the finger of God visibly thrust down amid the things of sense; disturbing their usual order; bidding matter bend itself to proclaim the supremacy of spirit; bidding brute human force, as well as physical order, own the superiority of goodness; bidding us men know and feel that the truths which Christ has taught us about God and about the soul are higher and deeper than any which are written on the face of nature. Christ has risen. "This is the day which the Lord hath made: let us rejoice and be glad in it."

II.

But today's festival is also significant as commemorating the beginning of an Undying Life. The Resurrection was not an isolated miracle, done and over, leaving things as they had been before. The Risen Christ is not like Lazarus; marked off from others by having visited the realms of death, but knowing that he must again ere long be a tenant of the grave. Christ rises for eternity: "Christ being raised from the dead dieth no more." His Risen Body is made up of flesh, bones, and all things appertaining to the perfection of man's nature. But It has superadded qualities. It is so spiritual that It can pass through closed doors without collision or disturbance. It is beyond the reach of those causes which slowly or swiftly bring down our bodies to the dust. Throned in the heavens now, as during the forty days on earth, It is endowed with the beauty and glory of an eternal youth; — "Christ being raised from the dead dieth no more."

Nor is this, in itself, a new miracle. The real miracle, perhaps, was that the sinless Christ should have died at all. Death was an innovation upon the true conditions of His existence; and the Resurrection was but a return to His rightful and normal immortality. Let us recall the truth which, within our limited range of experience, we may verify for ourselves, namely, that bodily pain, disease, death, came at first, as they often come now, to man in the train of the disease and death of man's spiritual nature. Adam died, because he sinned. If Adam had not sinned, he would not have died. Men point, I know, to the presence of disease and death among the lower creatures. But, not to enter upon the difficult question of their relation to the Fall, who shall say that these creatures too may not be under the same law of pain following upon such a measure of wrong-doing as their natures are capable of? And if we are told of fossil human remains, of a much higher antiquity than that of the Adam of Genesis, it may be observed that, supposing the fact to be certain, it is consistent with the Revealed Account to hold that, between the original act of creation, and the present outfit of this our planet, ages upon ages may have elapsed during which the earth may have been peopled by races like our own, who had their period of probation, and finally passed away in some great geological catastrophe. In any case, what we say is that "by one man," of our present race, "sin entered into the world, and death by sin, and so death passed upon all men, for that all have sinned." But when the Second Head of our race appeared, cut off from the entail of corruption by His supernatural birth of a Virgin Mother, and exhibiting in His Life absolute conformity to eternal Moral Law, He was, by the terms of His Nature, exempt from the law of death. Therefore He died, not as a matter of course, but by violence. He consented, for the sake of others, to undergo the violence which was to kill Him. In His case, death was a momentary innovation upon the true law of being. "I am," He says, "the Living One, and I became dead, and behold, I am alive, for evermore." God loosed the pains of death because it was impossible that He should be holden of it. And therefore when He had paid the mighty debt which the human family, represented by because impersonated in Him, owed to the deeply-wronged Righteousness of God, Life resumed its suspended sway in Him as in its Prince and Fountain. "Christ being raised from the dead dieth no more."

Now observe how the perpetuity of the Life of the Risen Jesus is the guarantee of the perpetuity of the Christian Church. Alone among all forms of society which bind men together, the Church of Christ is insured against utter dissolution. When our Lord was born, the civilised world was almost entirely comprised within the Roman Empire. That vast social power might well have appeared, as it did appear to the men of our Lord's day, destined to last for ever. Since then the Roman Empire has as completely vanished from the earth as if it never had been. Other kingdoms and dynasties have risen up and have in turn gone their way. Nor is there any warrant or probability that any one of the states or forms of civil government which exist at present will always last. And there are men who tell us that the Kingdom of Christ is no exception to the rule; that it too has seen its best days and is passing. We Christians know that they are wrong; that whatever else may happen, one thing is impossible; the complete effacement of the Church of Jesus Christ. And what is our reason for this confidence? It is because we Christians know that Christ's Church, although having likeness to civil societies of men in her outward form and mien, is unlike them inwardly and really. She strikes her roots far and deep into the World Invisible. She draws strength from sources which cannot be tested by our political or social experience. Like her Lord, she has meat to eat that men know not of. For indeed she is endowed with the Presence of Christ's Own Undying Life. "Lo, I am with you alway, even unto the end of the world." Christ's superiority to the assaults of death is the secret of His Church's immortality: our confidence in the perpetuity of the Church is only one form of our faith in the unfailing Life of the Risen Jesus.

Certainly, although the Church of Christ is insured against dissolution, she is not insured against vicissitudes, not even against corruption, more or less extensive. Her Lord is Divine: but the beings who compose her are human. She has not always tri-

umphed: she has through weakness fallen back before an impure
fanaticism like Mohammedanism, as in North Africa and Western Asia. She has been corrupted, as we know too well, sometimes by large and unwarranted additions to the original Creed
of Christendom; sometimes by forgetfulness of truths which were
constantly on the lips of Apostles and Martyrs. And upon corruption, division has followed, so that she no longer presents a
united front to the powers of evil. And there have been times
when it has seemed as if the world was right, and the Church
was on the point of disappearance from among men; so great has
been the weakness or the corruption of her representatives. To say
that she would perish would have been reasonable if she had
been only a human society, founded by some human genius, who
had passed away. That which is so striking in her history, making
it unlike that of any other society whatever, is the power of self-
restoration — so men term it — which she has again and again
developed, partially or as a whole. The tendency to dissolution
has clearly been arrested by an inward Influence against which
ordinary circumstances and causes could not prevail. What is this
but the presence of Him Who, being raised from the dead, dieth
no more? And who shall forecast the future? She may or may
not, here or elsewhere, enjoy the friendship of civil governments;
she may be welcomed in high places or persecuted in catacombs.
This only is certain: — she will exist while the world shall last.
"God is in the midst of her, therefore shall she not be removed:
God shall help her, and that right early. The heathen make much
ado, and the kingdoms are moved: but God hath showed His
voice, and the earth shall melt away."

It may indeed be said, 'Why should I rejoice on Easter Day in
the perpetuity of the Church? Why should I grieve at her failure,
if my personal Christian life remained? To me Christianity is
not a political or ecclesiastical, but a personal matter; and I cannot affect such enthusiasm for the institution which only embodies
and transmits it.' My brethren, if you hold this language, you
do not yet know what it is, in the fulness and reality of the term,
to be a Christian. Your isolated, or as you call it, your "personal"

Christianity, is not the Christianity of the New Testament. If one thing is clear in that blessed Book, it is that Christ came to found a Divine Society, and that the life of Christians comprises duties to, and privileges intimately bound up with that Society. What! is it nothing to be welcomed into a vast association of souls, extending through so many centuries, so many countries, reaching up into the world invisible, reaching from our homes and hearths to the very throne of Christ? Is it nothing to have a home and refuge for the solitary spirit, where we again find father and mother, and brother and child, who in the order of nature may have passed away? Is the endurance of this Church of God a matter of indifference to any who have felt its place in the Divine counsels; to any who have known what it is to have come unto Mount Sion, and to the city of the Living God, and to an innumerable company of angels, and to the general assembly and Church of the firstborn, and to Jesus? I trow not. Glorious things are spoken of thee, thou city of God; because thou art the home of saints, the home of angels, the home — so an Apostle teaches — of the Living Christ; because, as in thy chequered story of shame and honour, of failure and victory, thou traversest the centuries, thou dost always bear with thee, in thy assured and indestructible vitality, the certificate of thy Lord's deathless Life.

III.

Lastly, the great event of this day reveals the secret, as it displays the model, of perseverance in the life of godliness. Christ risen from death, Who dieth no more, is the model of our new life in grace. I do not mean that absolute sinlessness is attainable by any Christian. "If we say that we have no sin, we deceive ourselves, and the truth is not in us." But at least faithfulness in our intentions; avoidance of known sources of danger; escape from presumptuous sins; innocence, as the Psalmist has it, of the great offence: these things are possible. And they are necessary. Lives which are made up of alternate recovery and relapse: recovery perhaps during Lent, and swift relapse after Easter; or even lives lived, as it were, with one foot in the grave, without any strong vitality, with feeble prayers, with half-indulged inclinations, with weaknesses which may be physical, but which a regenerate will should away with; lives risen from the dead, yet without any seeming promise of endurance, what would St. Paul say of them? "Christ being raised from the dead dieth no more." Just as He left His tomb on Easter morning, once for all, so should the soul, once risen, be dead indeed unto sin. There must be no hovering about the sepulchre, no treasuring the grave-clothes, no secret hankering after the scent and atmosphere of the guilty past. If any of you who hear me humbly hope that you have by God's grace during this Lent attained to a spiritual resurrection; if in your case the words have been fulfilled, "The hour is coming, and now is, when the dead shall hear the voice of the Son of Man, and they that hear shall live;" then, be well assured that you have great need to see that you persistently set your affections on things above; that you desire passionately to live as those who are alive from the dead, "yielding your members as instruments of right-eousness unto God."

Depend on it, Christians, the Risen Life of Jesus tells us what our own new life should be. Not that God, having by His grace raised us from death, forces us whether we will or no to live on continuously. That great company of associated souls, which we call the Church, has indeed received from the King of kings a charter of perpetuity. But to no mere section of the Universal Body, and much more to no single soul on this side the grave, is it said that "the gates of hell shall not prevail against" it. Judas, after sharing that Divine companionship, may sell his Master if he wills to do so. Demas, after his friendship with St. Paul, may forsake him at pleasure, through love of this present world. The Galatians, among whom Christ has been evidently set forth crucified, may yet be bewitched by the fascinations of a plausible falsehood. Paul himself may for a moment tremble, lest having preached to others, he himself should be a castaway.

No force is put upon us; no man is carried up to heaven mechanically if he prefers to go downwards, or even does not sincerely desire to ascend. God allows us to employ that freedom of choice, in which our peril and our dignity as men consists, against ourselves, against Himself, if we choose to do so.

234

But how, you ask, can we rejoice in our Risen Lord, if we are so capable, in our weakness, of being untrue to His example? I answer, because that Life is the strength as well as the model of our own. "If the Spirit of Him that raised up Jesus from the dead dwell in you, He that raised up Christ from the dead shall likewise quicken your mortal bodies, by His Spirit that dwelleth in you." The Risen Christ in us is "the hope of glory." And God gives us His grace, not to withdraw it, but to continue it to us, if we will not resist Him and sin it away. "If any man love Me, My Father will love him, and We will come unto him, and make Our abode with him." "He that eateth My Flesh, and drinketh My Blood, dwelleth in Me, and I in him." "No man," says our Lord of the elect, "is able to pluck them out of My Father's hand." "Who," asks St. Paul, "shall separate us from the love of Christ?" Plainly God desires our salvation; He gives us, in and for the sake of His Blessed Son, all necessary grace; but it is for us to say whether we will respond to His bounty.

Pray today, brethren, then, in the spirit of this text, that at least you may persevere, in anything you have learnt of the life of God. Perseverance is a grace, just as much as faith, or hope, or charity. The secret strength of perseverance is a share in the Glorified Life of Jesus. Perseverance may be, it will be, won by prayer for union with our Risen Saviour. Say to yourselves with the Psalmist, "It is good for me to hold me fast by God." Cling to the Risen Lord, by entreaties which twine themselves round His Person; by Sacraments, the revealed points of vital contact with His Human Nature; by obedience and works of mercy, through which, as He says Himself, you abide in His love. Invigorate your feeble life, again and again, by that Divine Manhood which, reigning on the throne of heaven, can never more sink into the grave; and then, not in your own strength, but in His, "likewise reckon ye also yourselves to be dead indeed unto sin, but alive unto God through Jesus Christ our Lord."

The above sermon is from Canon Liddon's *Easter in St. Paul's,* pp. 156-168. No research I have been able to undertake has revealed any other sermon on this text worth inserting in a bibliography.

THE PIOUS DEAD ARE LOST —
LIVING BELIEVERS ARE MISERABLE
by
Robert S. Candlish

"Then they also which are fallen asleep in Christ are perished. If in this life only we have hope in Christ, we are of all men most miserable." — I Corinthians 15:18, 19

This is the climax and close of the apostle's argument concerning the resurrection, in its negative form. He reasons with the deniers of the possibility of a resurrection, after the manner of what is technically called in logic *reductio ad absurdum;* pointing out the conclusion in which their doctrine must, by a few short and necessary steps, inevitably land them.

This is a perfectly legitimate and warrantable mode of reasoning, if, in using it, I avoid the too common unfairness of imputing to my adversary the actual holding of dogmas, or principles, which may seem to me to follow from the proposition he is maintaining, but which he himself does not see or admit to be implied in it. To candid minds, it is a mode of reasoning fitted to be very convincing. Show me that my views, if reasoned out, or acted out, lead to consequences from which I recoil as much as you do; and I cannot but be moved to reconsider the grounds on which I have adopted them.

In the present instance, it is a most fair, and what is more, a most affectionate, appeal.

Have you thought seriously of the bearing of your new belief on your Saviour's work, and on your own faith and hope? Study it, and look at it, in that light. Surely you must perceive, that at all events, and in the first place, it involves a denial of the resurrection of Christ. However you may try to explain the fact of the Lord's empty sepulchre, and these strange words, reported to have been uttered by him, "Handle me, and see, for a spirit hath not flesh and bones, as ye see me have," it must have been a spirit after all that spoke. It might be Christ as he disappeared, when having cried with a loud voice, "Father, into thy hands I commend my spirit," he gave up the ghost. It could not be Christ with anything about him of that material frame which thereafter hung for a little longer, empty, on the cross, and was then hastily buried in Joseph's tomb. Your doctrine, that there is no resurrection of the dead, with the ground on which you defend it, — the essential vileness of matter, and its incompatibility with a perfect state of being, — makes that impossible. Plainly, if there be no resurrection of the dead, Christ is not risen. Are you prepared to face such a result of your philosophy?

Then you must be prepared to face also what immediately follows from it. I do not speak of your virtually giving the lie to our testimony as apostles; a testimony which can be corroborated, if need be, by five hundred other witnesses. That might be comparatively a small matter. But you cut up by the roots the gospel which we preach, and your own faith founded upon it. For of what use is your faith, uniting you to Christ, and giving you an interest in Christ, as dying for your sins, if the death which they entailed on him has not been wholly reversed, undone, destroyed? If in any respect, and to any effect, with reference to any part of his person, these sins of yours, for which, and in which, he died, have proved permanently fatal to him, how can he redeem you from them? "If Christ be not raised, your faith is vain; ye are yet in your sins."

And if it be so with you, what of those who are dead and gone? You still live, and may try some other way of getting quit of your sins, if that which has hitherto satisfied you now fails. You may try some new doctrine or discipline of perfection, based on that very spiritualizing of the resurrection which upsets your old faith in the atonement. But alas! for your brethren and friends, who have perilled their all on what now, it seems, turns out to be an error; — "Then they also which are fallen asleep in Christ are perished." Our case, in fact — the case of all of us, living and dead — is sufficiently deplorable; — "If in this life only we have hope in Christ, we are of all men most miserable."

I. "Then they also which are fallen asleep in Christ are perished." This does not mean that upon the supposition made, they have ceased to exist. The question of the continued existence of men after death is not raised in the argument. It is a mistake to say that in reasoning on the subject of the resurrection of the body, the apostle loses sight of the distinction between that particular doctrine and the general doctrine of man's immortality. It is a mistake also to think that in this verse he is teaching the dependence of either doctrine on the admission of the fact of Christ's resurrection. His statement is not put thus: Then they also which are fallen asleep in Christ shall never rise again; their bodies shall never be raised. That would be a true statement. It is an inference or deduction of which Paul may afterwards make use. But it is not his point here. Neither is his statement put thus: Then they also which are fallen alseep in Christ, have undergone total and final annihilation. That idea is not once suggested in the whole of this chapter. The glorious resurrection of the bodies of his believing people may be connected with the resurrection of Christ; so that if his resurrection, as a matter of fact, is denied, their resurrection, as a matter of doctrine, must be denied also. But it does not follow that their spiritual immortality or continued existence out of the body, is on that account denied. It does not follow that they must have perished, in the sense of ceasing to exist.

The fact is, what the apostle has in his view as to those who are fallen asleep in Christ, is not their perishing, in the sense of ceasing to exist, either in the body or out of the body; but their perishing in the sense of not being saved, but being lost. It is a far more solemn and awful conclusion that he asks you to face concerning the pious dead than either of these two: — either first, that they are not to live again in the body, or secondly, that they are not to survive and live after death at all.

The first of these conclusions, as flowing from the denial of the fact of Christ's resurrection, a spiritualist, jealous of physical impurity, and enamoured of an ideal immaterial perfection, might rather hail and welcome, than repudiate. Such a consequence deduced from his belief would not alarm or shock him. The second of these conclusions, again, he would deny to be logical or legitimate. I do not see, he might urge, how the fact, if it be a fact — and you say it must be a fact, upon my view of the resurrection being present and spiritual, not future and corporeal; — I do not see how the fact of there having been no corporeal resurrection in the case of Christ, any more than I expect that there will be a corporeal resurrection in the case of his followers, implies that they cease to exist after death, any more than that he ceased to exist after death. He would have had an immortal life, even if his body had not been raised. So they may have an immortal life also in him, even although you shut me up into the admission that his body has not been raised.

Such might have been a fair rejoinder or reply, if the apostle's argument in this eighteenth verse were to be understood as having reference to the mere continuance of life, embodied or disembodied, in the other world. Do you mean to argue thus: If Christ be not raised, then they also who have fallen asleep in Christ have perished — in this sense, that nothing of those corporeal frames of theirs which we bury is afterwards to reappear, and be revived? I accept that result. Or do you mean to argue thus: That upon that supposition they perish, in the sense of not surviving at all, but being altogether annihilated? I do not see how that follows. The spiritual part of me may live on for ever, though all that is material about my person perish, — and perish irrecoverably.

What the apostle really reasons about is not immortality, whether spiritual or corporeal, but salvation. The conclusion to which he shuts up those with whom he is arguing, is not that they who have fallen asleep in Christ have perished, in the sense of not living again in the body; nor that they have perished, in the sense of not continuing to live at all; but that they have perished in the sense of their being lost as guilty and unsaved sinners; irremediably lost; hopelessly consigned to everlasting perdition.

The statement or argument, in short, concerning believers who have died, is immediately connected with the statement or argument concerning believers who are living. "If Christ be not risen," ye who still live, although you believe in Christ, "are yet in your sins." "If Christ be not raised," your departed brethren, although they fell asleep in Christ, must have died in their sins, and must even now be reaping the fruit of their sins, in condemnation and utter ruin — and that for ever. If Christ be not raised, you now believe in vain; you believe in one who cannot save you from your sins, seeing that he is not himself saved from them. And your friends who have fallen asleep in Christ have believed in vain. They fell asleep believing in one who could not save them. They are lost, therefore, finally; they have perished.

Are you prepared for that consequence, inevitably flowing from this speculation of yours about the resurrection? Are you prepared, not only to make void your own faith, which hitherto has sustained you in the hope of your salvation from your sins, but to make void also the faith of venerated fathers, beloved brothers and sisters, whose peace, as they fell asleep in Jesus, depended altogether on the assurance of justification through his resurrection from the dead? Was it a lie that these holy men and women grasped in their right hand, when they walked so fearlessly through the valley of the shadow of death? And are their eyes now opened in that other world to the sad and awful truth, that for all their faith in Christ, they are yet in their sins; that they have believed in one who died, indeed, for their sins, but is not, to this hour, himself extricated from them? Is theirs, as well as yours, the melancholy complaint of disappointment and despair — "We trusted that it had been he who should have redeemed us?"

Surely this is a startling appeal, well fitted to make the boldest innovator pause.

II. For in truth the innovation involves us all, the dead and the living, who have believed in Christ, in one common ruin; — "If in this life only we have hope in Christ, we are of all men most miserable."

Is there exaggeration in this utterance? — the exaggeration of rhetoric or of feeling? Is it an overstrained emotion, partly of enthusiasm — partly, also, of vexation and annoyance — that here breaks out?

So it might seem, if the point at issue were either the resurrection of the body, or the immortality of the soul; if the question were merely, Are we to live again in the body? or even, Are we to continue to live after death at all?

Thus, as to the first of these questions, why should believers in Christ be of all men most miserable, even though it should turn out that they are not to live again in the body? There is enough, surely, in that immortal blessedness into which they enter when they depart and are with Christ, "absent from the body and present with the Lord," to be a compensation, and far more than a compensation, for all the toil, hardship, self-denial, and persecution which, for a few short years, their faith in Christ may entail upon them here. They may be more in trouble than other men; they may be more plagued than other men; there may be "bands in their death" from which other men are exempt. But if, when all on earth is over, the Lord Jesus receives their spirits, even though their bodies are to be wholly left behind for ever, — if that is their hope, — they cannot well be said to be "of all men most miserable."

Nay, take even the other supposition. Let the case put be that of their not continuing to live at all. Let that be the conclusion to which the denial of Christ's resurrection shuts us up; namely, that we have no evidence or assurance of even the spiritual part of us surviving our bodily dissolution. Still, believers in Christ need not be condoled with; — they are scarcely entitled to condole with one another; — as being "of all men most miserable." They have, at least, as good prospects and presumptions with reference to the life to come, as that great Roman orator and philosopher had, who, in the evening of life, amid the wreck and ruin of earth's holiest ties, would not let go his grasp of immortality. "If it prove to be a dream, I can be none the worse for it; meanwhile, by means of it, I have fellowship with the excellent who are gone." And — which is more than the wisest and best heathen ever had — they enjoy, in their experience, or imagination, of peace with God and reconciliation to him, what may well make their present life not wretched, but most enviable, even though it should be a life of incessant trial, and a life that is to terminate conclusively at death.

What, then, is the precise ground of the apostle's earnest ejaculation, "If in this life only we have hope in Christ, we are of all men most miserable?"

It is in entire accordance with his previous argument. It proceeds upon the inference or deduction, that if Christ be not raised, the very peace and reconciliation, which make this life at its worst not only tolerable, but even desirable to believers in Jesus, are themselves a delusion. In this life we have hope in Christ. And there may be pleasure in such hope in Christ while it lasts. But it is a hope which, if there be, as there assuredly is, a hereafter, will be found to be utterly hollow and untrue. For it is the hope, it is the faith, of our being saved from our sins. But we are not saved from our sins "if Christ be not raised." On the contrary, we "are yet in our sins." Whatever hope we have in Christ, as regards our being saved from our sins, rests on what, it seems, is an error and a fable. It cannot last beyond this present life. At death, if we survive death, even although we fall asleep in Christ, we shall too surely discover — as "they which have fallen asleep in Christ" before us have already discovered — that our faith is vain, and our hope delusive; that since Christ is not raised, we are yet in our sins; and alas! must continue in our sins for ever.

Is not this truly a miserable case? If it is really ours, are we not deeply to be pitied? Are we not "of all men most miserable?"

The "hope in Christ," then, of which Paul speaks, is not the hope of the resurrection; — nor even the hope of immortality; — but the hope which has for its object the pardon, the favour, the approbation, the love of the Most High. It is the hope which cheers the broken heart of the man whose sin has found him out, when first, amid the anguish of his godly shame and sorrow, his eye fixes itself on Jesus lifted up on the cross, a sacrifice for sin. It is a hope which, if it be well founded, it is rapture to him to cherish, for present peace and pure joy in God, apart from all thought of what is to befall him in the future.

Yes! If it be well founded. But if you fling a cold doubt across that great fact on which it is built; if he to whom the Holy Ghost has been moving me to look as dying for my sins, may, after all, not have risen again; if my sins are still upon him, keeping his body in the tomb; if, through his bearing my guilt, the precious dust of that holy human frame, which the Holy Ghost prepared for him in the Virgin's womb, is lost inextricably and irrecoverably in the common dust of this doomed earth, the ground cursed for man's sin: — if thus the great Redeemer himself has failed to procure, even in his own case, a reversal of the sentence, dust to dust; — if the very "ransom God has found to deliver from going down to the pit" is itself marred, and the person of Emmanuel is no more complete, as it was when it was formed within the womb of his mother Mary; — if the grave has triumphed, and the expiation has broken down; in a word, if Christ is not raised, and they who have believed on him for the remission of their sins, are in their sins still, and die in their sins, and perish in their sins; — Oh! what better is my hope to me than the hope of the hypocrite, whose "soul, whatever he has gained, God taketh away!"

"If in this life only we have hope in Christ!" Any hope we can have in Christ respecting the forgiveness of our sins, must, on the supposition now made, be a hope which we can have only in this life. We may cling to it, and lean on it, for a little longer, while we live. We may desperately grasp it as the only solace of our anxious souls. We may try earnestly to persuade ourselves that there is for us an atonement — that there is for us a pardon in Christ. But the atonement; what is it? — the pardon; where is it? — if our sins, for which Christ died, are upon him still, subjecting him still to the power of death?

The bubble must one day burst. The fond persuasion, the flattering hope, must be cut off. At death, if not before, we must be awakened to the discovery that, believing in Christ for the saving of our souls from sin, we have believed in vain. We are yet in our sins after all. We perish, as they who have fallen asleep in Jesus have perished, hopelessly and for ever. If this be so, "Are we not indeed of all men most miserable?"

The Apostle is not here formally comparing himself and his fellow-believers with the rest of mankind. When he calls himself elsewhere the "chief of sinners," he is not measuring himself by others. It is of himself alone, and of his own aggravated guilt, that he is there thinking. So it is here. It is himself and his fellow-believers alone, and not any others, that he has in his mind, when, using the strong language of seeming comparison, he cries — "If in this life only we have hope in Christ, we are of all men most miserable!"

Yes. We are so! We who have had our eyes opened to see the exceeding sinfulness of sin, and the infinite preciousness of salvation from sin! If our hope is dashed; if it is found to be a hope which, however we may cling to it for a while, must fail us at the last; we cannot fall back again upon the fat, contented slumber of easy unconcern and worldly security. Our natural peace has been broken. Our consciences have been pricked. Our hearts have been stirred. We have been made to know ourselves, and to know God. We have been forced to feel what every sin of ours deserves, and how terrible a thing it is to "fall into the hands of the living God."

We had got a hope, a trembling hope, of the forgiveness of sin, and the favour of God, being ours. It was a hope based and built on a satisfying atonement having been offered on our behalf by the Eternal Son, through the Eternal Spirit, to the Eternal Father; — offered on our behalf, and accepted too. Our conviction of its having been accepted — rested on this belief, that whatever our sins, when he died for them, brought on Christ, had been undone.

But you tell us, no. The ruin of his body was irreparable. Our sins slew his body, and it lies slain to this hour.

Then where is our hope? Where is the hope we so fondly cherished, that our sins were fully atoned for; their guilt expiated, their condemnation thoroughly taken away? They still keep Christ under the power of death, the death he died for us. They must keep us in the doom which we, wicked as we are, brought on him, the Righteous One. It is, on that supposition, a doom from which he is not himself completely delivered. How than can he deliver us? They must keep us, these sins of ours — they must keep us as well as him, in that doom of guilt and ruin evermore.

Is not that enough to make us miserable, "most miserable?" What matters this present life, with its gleam, its spark of hope, kindled by the death of Christ, if that is to be the end of it? Touch our hope, as you do touch our hope, of the full, free, everlasting forgiveness of our sins, through Christ dying for our sins and rising again, and what refuge have we? We cannot in any other way find rest or peace. We cannot lay any flattering unction to our souls, as if we might, somehow, otherwise be saved. We cannot do without the atonement.

And must it not be misery unspeakable to conclude that, after all, he whom we have admired, believed, trusted, loved, cannot save us? — that in spite of his dying for our sins, we are yet in our sins? — that, like others who have gone before us, when we fall asleep in him, we perish?

But it is not so. Christ is risen from the dead. He who was dead is alive for evermore. Therefore, we live now; — we who believe in him. And they live too; — they who have fallen asleep in him. Death could not hold him: no; not any part of him. Sin could not destroy him: no; not any part of him. He goes down to the pit. But see! He comes forth, leaving no part of him behind. Therefore, guilt is expiated. Therefore, the ransom is sufficient. Therefore, the redemption is complete. Therefore we, as well as our predecessors in the life of faith, have a hope which neither death nor sin can touch.

They have not perished. Though absent from the body, they live now. In the body they are to live hereafter. No part of them has fallen, or is to fall, a victim, either to death or to sin.

We, also, believing, are not in our sins. No wrath for sin is upon us now. No death for sin awaits us at last. Our now is a life in Christ, free from the doom of guilt. When we fall asleep in Christ, we do not perish.

In the risen Saviour, then, let us rejoice to hope. In the risen Saviour let us rejoice to have fellowship, in our hope, with all them that have already fallen asleep in Christ. They have fallen asleep, as we hope to fall asleep, not to perish, but to have everlasting life.

BIBLIOGRAPHY

David J. Burrell: *Christ and Progress*, New York, 1903, pp. 175-185

Robert S. Candlish: *Life in a Risen Saviour*, 2nd ed., Edinburgh, 1859, pp. 54-68

R. E. Golladay: *Life Forever*, Grand Rapids, 1940, pp. 41-53

Martin J. Heinecker, in Alton M. Motter: *Preaching the Resurrection*, Philadelphia, 1959, pp. 42-56

H. S. Holland: *On Behalf of Belief*, London, 1889, pp. 1-24, 25-49

Hugh Price Hughes: *The Philanthropy of God*, London, 1890, pp. 175-184

H. P. Liddon: *Easter in St. Paul's*, new ed., London, 1892, pp. 1-11

G. Campbell Morgan: *Westminster Pulpit*, Vol. I (1906), No. 23; Vol. III (1908), pp. 137-144

Lewis A. Muirhead, in *Christian World Pulpit*, 1891, Vol. 40, pp. 102-104

Joseph Parker: *City Temple Pulpit*, Vol. IV, pp. 261-268

James S. Stewart: *The Gates of the New Life*, London, 1940, pp. 160-169

ROBERT S. CANDLISH
(1806-1873)

Like Dinsdale T. Young, Robert S. Candlish, born at Edinburgh, in 1806, was the son of a physician. He was adequately educated at home in his earlier years so that when he went up to the University of Glasgow, he at once stood out as a student of unusual brilliance. His preaching gifts were soon discovered, and in 1833, when he was only twenty-seven years of age, he was appointed Minister of St. George's, Edinburgh, the most influential congregation in that city. Little did he know then of the great part he would play in the mighty struggle that was soon to develop over the matter of an established church, which led to the formation of the Free Church of Scotland, an event which was marked by 470 ministers leaving the State Church of Scotland, and forming themselves into the Free Church. One of his biographers says that "from this time, or at least, from the death of Chalmers (1847), till close on his own death, in 1873, Candlish may be said to have been the ruling spirit in the Free Church." He continued as the Minister of St. George's Free Church to the end of his life, and, in addition, was made the Principal of New College. In 1861, he was the Moderator of the General Assembly.

Candlish's writings are still worth reading, even those two volumes now seldon seen, *Contributions Toward the Exposition of Genesis,* (1842). Probably the greatest expository series he ever delivered was published in his large volume, *Expository Discourses on I John,* which gives some idea of his great theological ability and his brilliant style. Some of these chapters are simply unequaled in the depth of meaning which he discovers in this Johannine writing.

DEATH A PARENTHESIS IN LIFE
by
F. B. Meyer

"And when I saw him, I fell at his feet as one dead. And he laid his right hand upon me, saying, Fear not; I am the first and the last, and the Living one; and I was dead, and behold, I am alive for evermore, and I have the keys of death and of Hades."
— Revelation 1:17, 18

Death was a very familiar thought to the little church at Ephesus, from which the holy apostle had been torn. It was no uncommon experience for young maiden or aged men to be suddenly transferred from the ranks of the militant to those of the triumphant church. There was therefore a special aptitude in this vision of One who had Himself become dead, but was living on the other side of death, in all the radiant glory of an assured victory. It showed that the enforced plunge into the sullen waters of the dark cave of death would conduct the diver under the teeth of the black portcullis into a summer sea.

The Christian doctrine of resurrection differs altogether from Plato's reasonings about the immortality of the soul. Deep in the heart of man there rises the spring of an immortal hope. As corn is indigenous to every soil, so belief in the immortality of the soul is part of the constitution of every child of Adam. It is instinctive, necessary, universal. It may be tampered with, and almost crushed out of existence, but it will at any moment arise and assert itself. It played a very distinct and important part in the reasonings of the old Greek philosophers.

But immortality is not the same thing as resurrection. *Plato* was wont to say that at death the soul would leave the body like

247

248

an emancipated eagle, to soar into the empyrean; but he had no conception of a future state which included the upraising of the body from the dust of death. *Christ* taught that in the resurrection the body was immortal as well as the soul; that there was a germ of life hidden somewhere in this body of humiliation, as there is a life-germ in each corn of wheat cast into the ground, and that at His summons it would yield a body like unto His glorious body. In other words, Christ taught that not a part of man, but the whole, was destined to pass through death unto the life eternal; and it was for this reason that He appeared to John, in this significant vision, with head as white as snow, and feet that glowed like fire, and hands holding the stars — the attributes of the human form. Man was created with spirit, soul, and body. As such he has been redeemed, as such he will be restored. The Creator and the Redeemer is one; and there is naught that death shall hold as its prey, saving what is temporary and earthly. This mortal shall put on immortality, this corruptible incorruption; "then shall be brought to pass the saying that is written, Death is swallowed up in victory."

The Scripture doctrine of resurrection is attested by one-well-ascertained fact.

In Plato's charming dialogue of the *Phaedo,* the reader will find an account of the last conversation which Socrates had with his friends. On the day of his execution his disciples went to see him early in the morning. Among other things, Socrates gave this commission to Cebes (one of the party present) :

"Tell Evenus to follow me as quickly as he can, if he is wise. I, it seems, shall depart today; for that is the will of the Athenians."

Then he considered the question, "Why, in a case where death is better than life, a man should not hasten his own end." He finds the answer to be, "Because man is a prisoner, and has no right to release himself, being in fact a sort of possession of the gods, who will summon him at their pleasure."

"Then," says Cebes, "the wise man will sorrow and the fool rejoice at leaving his masters the gods, and passing out of life."

"Not so," is the reply, "for I am persuaded that I am going to other gods, who are wise and good, and also (I trust) to men departed, who are better than those I leave behind; therefore I do not grieve, as otherwise I might, for I have good hope that there is yet something awaiting the dead, and, as has been said of old, some far better lot for the good than for the wicked."

This is very beautiful, especially when we consider the poor flickering torch by the light of which the speaker groped to such a conclusion; but we cannot fail to notice the uncertainty which lies upon his words, as morning haze over the landscape. *I trust, I have good hope, I am persuaded* — these are his strongest words. Whereas the Christian is able to say, "I *know* in whom I have believed," annd anticipates resurrection and eternal life with the assurance with which a man refers to facts that have happened within his certain knowledge.

We do not need to argue from nature, or the inequality of reward and punishment in the present life, or the intuitions of the soul, when we attempt to establish the resurrection. It is enough to point to the empty but well-ordered grave in Joseph's garden. On the night of the day of crucifixion they brought a lifeless body there, and wrapped it in the swathing-bands of death, as Mary had wrapped it in the swaddling-clothes of babyhood. All the next day it lay there; when the next morning broke it was gone, the stone rolled from the mouth of the grave, the linen clothes lying well wrapped together, the keepers trembling with fear. And those who knew Him best had been compelled to recognize that He was with them again, in a body that differed indeed from the one with which they had been so familiar, though it was clearly identical with it; just as the perfect flower differs from the bulb you sow in the wintry soil, and yet is unmistakably the same.

Our religion rests on this fact of Christ's resurrection. Therein He was declared to be the Son of God with power; therein all His own statements were verified; therein the Scriptures were fulfilled; therein the sufficiency of His sacrificial work was substantiated and approved; therein resurrection took its place among the facts and phenomena of the world, the law of which might not be understood, but its certainty was beyond question.

But perhaps He had not really died! John, what do you say to this? "I witnessed His last moments; standing beneath His cross, I heard His last deep sigh as He bowed His head on His breast and gave up the ghost; shortly afterward a soldier pierced His side, and as he withdrew his spear-head, blood and water gushed out, and attested His death as being already accomplished. This, indeed, was so evident that the Roman soldiers did not think it worth their while to break one of His bones; and the Roman centurion had no hesitation in certifying Pilate that His body might be handed over to His friends."

Perhaps His body was stolen! John, what do you say to this? "When the thief rifles the house of the living, or the last home of the dead, he leaves everything in disarray — the drapery of the room disheveled, the casket of the jewels broken, all that is loose and light tossed in confusion or borne away. But when we entered into the deserted tomb we found all so orderly and neat that we were convinced that the foot of violence or haste had not entered there; surely our Master with His own hand had wrapped together the cerements of death, which loving hands had wrapped about His body."

Notice the remarkable manner in which death is here referred to by the Master of life. "I am He that liveth," or, as the Revised Version puts it, "the Living One." These words tell the mystery of His eternal being. This is the life which was with the Father, and was manifested unto us, which had neither past nor future, neither beginning nor end, and is separated by an impassable gulf from the highest life of the creature. This life, emerging from reaches of being which have no limit or shore, came down from the far eternities to the cross, reared on the place of a skull. All the life of the Son of God, which He had shared with the Father from eternity, is comprehended in this expression.

"Behold, I am alive forevermore." This life is slightly different from the former; it is not so much the essential life of the Godhead as the life of the God-man, who has taken into Himself our nature, weaving it into His own in an indissoluble union, and wearing it forever. "Thou art a priest forever." "He ever liveth to make intercession." "Not after the law of a carnal commandment, but after the power of an endless life." The divine and eternal are both present, but they have taken on them a flavor and tone borrowed of the earthly life of the Lord, just as the waters of a mighty river will be affected by the soil over which they flow.

Between these two great words, indicating the life of the eternal God and that of the Mediator, who is God with man, there is inserted the one mysterious phrase, "I became dead." We need say nothing of the idea of voluntariness which these words convey, and which leads us to compare them with the Master's own assertion that He laid down His life of Himself. It is rather our purpose to emphasize their suggestion that death is not a condition but a doorway, not a state but a transition, not a long home but an experience, a birth, a stepping across the frontier, the traversing of a bridge which it takes but an instant to cross, and conducts, not, as in Venice, from a palace to a prison, but the reverse. The traveler who pierces the Alps leaves behind the precipices, dashing streams, and wild grandeur of Switzerland, to emerge, after a brief period of darkness, in the radiant sunshine of Italy. Death is just that — the passing through a shadow from the light of life which comes to its edge on the one side, into the light of life which comes to its edge on the other. The expression used by the Lord clearly indicates that, in His case, death was the slightest possible parenthesis between two realms of life.

We speak of the dead; but, in point of fact, there are no dead except such as are dead in trespasses and sins. Those whom we call dead are such as have died. They have passed through death, bowing their meek heads beneath its frowning portal, and passing out into a broader, freer, gladder life. So with ourselves. We are living now in the enjoyment of light and air, and the energy of life. If the Lord do not first come, we shall pass through the physical phenomenon that closes this mortal life, as we passed through that which commenced it, and probably shall be as unconscious of the one as we were of the other. After the briefest possible interval, such as the Bible calls "the twinkling of an eye," we shall wake up to find ourselves amid the sights and sounds of eternity.

Beyond the article of death, our Savior lives forever. Lives to make intercession for the weakest and feeblest for those that are ignorant and out of the way. Lives as our representative and priest, bearing our names before God. Lives to welcome each wayworn pilgrim as he passes through the gateway and lifts a wan, tear-worn face to be kissed by those gentle human lips. Lives to be the fountain of life, of which we may drink more abundantly forevermore. Lives to lead us, as a shepherd his flock, ever farther into the heart of the country where the sun never sets, because the Lord has become an everlasting light.

There is life beyond death for all His saints. In the circle of His life they live. In the presence of His glory they are enlightened. The little child, taken from its fond mother; the aged Simeons and Hannahs, strong soldier-spirits and weak, tender ones; such as were saved through a storm of trouble, and those who came into harbor with every sail spread — they are all there, and await our coming. All live unto Him. We go not to death, but to life. The sun dips for a moment under the rim of the horizon, and then springs up as a bridegroom emerges from his chamber, to traverse the boundless circles of immortal and infinite existence.

The living Christ holds the keys of death and Hades. In death He destroyed the devil and abolished death. There was a transference of power from the prince of darkness to the Lord of life; from those strong hands which had grasped the keys with such indomitable energy since the time of Adam's fall until they were wrenched from them by a stronger than he. Smiting him to the ground, the Saviour cried, "I will be thy plague, O death; thy destruction, O grave!" And from that moment the supreme control of death and the grave and the resurrection has been vested in the Son of man, who holds it as the arbiter of our destinies and the representative of our highest interests.

The keys of death! Then not one of us can pass the portal till He unlock the door. The malice of our foes may force us toward that small slit in the long dark wall that shuts out the unseen, but they cannot force us through until Jesus turns the key; and He will not turn it until the predestined moment has struck.

The keys of death! Then not one of our dear ones passes from us apart from His will and choice. Did the door open the other day, and let your beloved pass through, while a momentary flood of light lit up the chamber of his departure? Jesus was there. You might have detected Him had not your eyes been holden. Do not repine too bitterly, lest you sin against His perfect wisdom and hurt His tender heart.

The keys of death! Then He has the key of every grave in the quiet country parish or the crowded city cemetery. Precious in His eyes are those mounds of earth which hold the bodies He redeemed. Not one key shall be mislaid or lost. You may keep a grave decked with sweet flowers, but He is the custodian of its treasure. At the moment of resurrection He will unlock the door, and bid the imprisoned body arise in the likeness of His own.

The keys of Hades! He went there when He died, and passed through the dim world, announcing His victory, asserting His supremacy. With Him dwell the spirits of the departed. Each is intrusted to His custodianship. Where they are, what they are doing, their spheres of bliss, *all* lie under His appointment. In a sublime sense we may apply to Him some olden words that acquire a new meaning in this application, remembering only that Hades is palace rather than prison: "The keeper of the prison committed to Joseph's hand all the prisoners that were in the prison; and whatsoever they did there, He was the doer of it."

The keys of Hades! Our beloved are with Him. They sleep in Jesus. We shall be with Him also, if that is His will, rather than to abide till His coming again. He will keep His hand on the door until the time appointed for its opening, that through it myriads of redeemed spirits may issue forth to accompany Him to the closing scenes of human history. Then He will open it.

254

When the full procession is prepared upon the other side, and
the destined hour has struck, the wards of the lock will yield before the pressure of His key, and the Lord shall come with ten
thousand of His saints, descending into the air, coming to take to
Himself His great power and reign.

The keys of death and Hades! Then it must be within His
power to deal finally with each. At His word death and Hades
shall give up the dead which are in them, before they are themselves cast into the lake of fire. This is the second death, to
escape which we must be identified with the eternal life. On
all such death hath no power, Hades no permanent hold, but
they shall live and reign with God and the Lamb forever. Because He lives they shall live also!

BIBLIOGRAPHY

W. Hay M. H. Aitken: *Eastertide*. London, n.d. pp. 225-240
T. H. Darlow, in *Great Texts of the New Testament*. pp. 142-152
Thomas A. Gurney: *Alive for Evermore*. London, n.d. pp. 233-250; and, *The
 Living Lord and the Opened Grave*. London. 1901. pp. 112-132
F. B. Meyer: *Through Fire and Flood*. New York. 1896. pp. 146-162
Charles H. Spurgeon: *Metropolitan Tabernacle Pulpit*. Vol. 46 (1881), No.
 2689. pp. 397-406
James Stalker, in *Christian World Pulpit*. Vol. 47 (1895). pp. 280-282
Samuel M. Zwemer: *The Glory of the Empty Tomb*. New York. 1947. pp.
 73-82

F. B. MEYER
(1847-1929)

This saint, preacher, writer, and, preëminently, man of God, was born in London, April 8, 1847. Unlike such men as G. Campbell Morgan, Joseph Parker, Charles H. Spurgeon, and others, he had the privilege of attending college, graduating from Regents Park College. Like many others, his great gifts were recognized when he was still young, and he was called to be the Assistant of the Reverend C. M. Birrell at Pembroke Chapel, Liverpool, in 1870, when only twenty-two years of age. His various pastorates do not need to be detailed here. Strange to say, four of his pastorates were confined to two churches. After a four year's ministry at Regents Park Church, 1888-1892, he followed Dr. Newman Hall as minister of Christ Church, Westminster Bridge Road, London, 1892-1907, and then crossed the Thames River again to serve at Regents Park from 1909 to 1915, when once more he ministered at Christ Church, until 1921, when he was appointed Pastor Emeritus. It was while Dr. Meyer was in Liverpool that D. L. Moody received his first official welcome to Britain, and a rich friendship was established that remained until the death of the great evangelist.

I think rather than attempting a summary of Mr. Meyer's ministry myself, it would be far better to quote from a contempory of his, also a distinguished preacher of that day, Dr. Shakespeare. "There are half a dozen men in our generation who amaze their contemporaries by the persistency of their toil, and the enormous amount of work they are able to do. To very many F. B. Meyer has become a synonym for tireless industry. The most casual observer is able to discover that he plays many parts, each of which would be enough to tax the energy of an ordinary man. He is the Pastor of a large church with great traditions; he is the centre and inspiration of a vast Church organisation; an author whose books are read and prized throughout the world; a member of many very important committees, in which his presence is always a directing and controlling force;

he has been President successively of our greatest religious and interdenominational organisations — and for him to be President is no sinecure, as he at once devotes an astonishing amount of energy to the position; he is well known at Keswick and at Northfield; he is a leader in national movements, of which just now the chief is education; one of the three Free Church ministers asked for at every big demonstration; a Councillor of the Borough of Lambeth; a friend and helper to whom countless perplexed and distressed souls repair for guidance and help; a punctilious correspondent; last, but not least, the President of the Baptist Union, devoting every possible day to its work and interests. We may well rub our eyes in amazement at such a programme, and ask, How is all this done?

"I understand the secret of it better than I did. I have known Mr. Meyer for thirty years, but during the last few months I have learnt a great deal about him which I did not properly understand. Without any hesitation I should place first that he carries out the injunction to pray without ceasing, in the sense of prayer as dependence upon God. He is never in a hurry; he always seems to have time for some fresh task. He does one thing at once, and it has for the moment all his mind, for it is the thing which the Father has given him to do."

Dr. Meyer was probably the most influential devotional writer during his lifetime. His biographical works on Old and New Testament characters, such as Abraham, Joseph, Elijah, the Apostles Peter and John, etc., somehow remarkably met the need of great multitudes of Christians in that day, as well as his expositions, such as that of Exodus in the *Devotional Commentary Series*. It is said that up to the time of his death not less than five million copies of his writings had been published.

RESURRECTION OF THE BODY
by
John R. Broadus

Will you examine with me the 15th chapter of the first
Epistle of Paul to the Corinthians? The subject of this grand
chapter is the resurrection of the body. There were some of the
professed Christians in Corinth who denied that there is any such
thing as a resurrection of dead men. They might naturally do
so for the obvious reasons which occur to many people now. But
besides, it is probable that some of them were influenced by a
curious speculative theory which in the next century is called
Gnosticism. We see that theory appearing in the errors condemned by Paul in writing to the Colossians, and by John in his
Epistles. It seems far away from us, but it was a very proud
philosophy in its day, boasting of itself as science. The fundamental position of the Gnostics was that matter is necessarily
the seat of evil: all evil resides in matter, and no matter is free
from evil. We can at once see how they would deny the possibility
of a resurrection of the body, because that would involve the
perpetuating of evil. However this may be as to the Corinthians,
there were some of them who not merely questioned the doctrine of a general resurrection, but positively denied that there
is any such thing as a resurrection of dead men. The Greek has
no article. It is not strictly "resurrection of the dead"; but they
said, "there is no resurrection of dead men" — as Eschylus long
before had declared: "When a man has once died there is no
resurrection to him."

Now, in the first section of the chapter — verses 1-19 — the
Apostle says: To affirm that there is no resurrection of dead men

is to deny the resurrection of Christ, and thus to destroy Christianity. He begins by reminding them that the Gospel which he originally preached to them — from which they derived all their knowledge of Christianity — involved and rested upon the fact that Christ had been raised from the dead. "For I delivered unto you first of all . . . that Christ died for our sins according to the Scriptures; and that He was buried; and that He hath been raised on the third day according to the Scriptures." Both His death and His resurrection were in accordance with the predictions of the Old Testament. Then the Apostle proceeds to speak of witnesses to the risen Christ: First, Cephas, whom we call Peter. Second, the twelve. Third, above five hundred brethren at once, "of whom," he says, "the greater part are still living." It had been no great interval of time. We know most exactly that this Epistle was written in A. D. 57 — it cannot have been more than a year earlier or later. Most probably our Lord's resurrection was in A. D. 30, with a possible variation of one or two years. So it had been about twenty-seven years since His resurrection. Consider a moment. It is twenty-eight years since our great civil war began, and twenty-three years since it ended. The older persons present remember with perfect familiarity all its events from beginning to end. And there had been only the same lapse of time in the case of these witnesses whom Paul mentions. No class of skeptics at the present day will think of denying that Paul wrote this Epistle: and he declares that more than half of those five hundred witnesses were still living. Afterwards he adds that Christ appeared to James, and then again to all the Apostles, and finally to Paul himself. This statement of the testimony of our Lord's resurrection is surely remarkable, and is to be added to the evidence furnished in the four Gospels, in the Acts, and in the other Epistles. Allow me to say as a student of history desiring to speak calmly: If I don't know that Jesus of Nazareth rose from the dead, then I know nothing in the history of mankind. It is a great assured fact; and rightly considered it carries with it the truth of Christianity in general. And not merely is our Lord's resurrection a pillar of Christian evidence, but it is a part of His work of salvation. In 2 Corinthians 5:15 we read: "He died for all, that they which live should no longer live unto themselves, but unto Him who for their sakes died and rose again." He did not merely die for them; but for them He both died and rose again. And in Romans 4:25: "Who believe in Him that raised Jesus our Lord from the dead, who was delivered up for our trespasses, and was raised up for our justification." I cannnot now elaborate this thought; but these passages plainly teach that our Lord's resurrection is a part of His saving work. He died and rose again for our salvation. Now, let us see the Apostle's argument: "If the resurrection of Christ is a cardinal part of Christianity, how say some among you that there is no resurrection of dead men?" Observe: this was not the general belief of the Corinthian Christians, but only of some, who are carefully distinguished elsewhere in the chapter also, from the general body of the brotherhood. The Apostle declares that to deny a resurrection of dead men will necessarily exclude the resurrection of Christ. Notice the argument in verse 13. He doesn't say: "Unless it is true that there is a resurrection of the dead in general, then Christ is not risen." That wouldn't be sound logic — for Christ might have risen as an isolated fact. But he says — and the Greek shows the difference plainly: "If it be true, as some among you maintain, that there is no resurrection of dead men, then Christ is not risen."

Again and again he repeats this — verses 14-17 — showing that to deny a resurrection of dead men is to deny Christ's resurrection, which overthrows Christianity and destroys all the hopes founded on it. And that not only as to the living, but — in verse 18 — as to those who are fallen asleep in Christ. Their existence has ceased — they are perished if what these men say be true. As to ourselves also (verse 19): "If in this life only we have hoped in Christ, we are of all men most miserable." The word "miserable" used to signify, not as now "wretched," but "pitiable"; and the Revised Version here says: "We are of all men most pitiable." If we have simply hoped in Christ in this life, and it will turn out to be all a delusion — there being no future life — then we are of all men most to be pitied, because we have cherished such a delusion. I have heard good men sometimes say: "If Christianity be a delusion, I should wish to cherish it still, because it makes me happy." But I say: "No! I want no delusions — no happiness coming from delusions. I want truth — reality. My soul was born to know truth, and to love truth. And, blessed be God! He has given me the means of learning truth through His Spirit; and I don't wish to be cheated with delusive hopes." It is to that feeling the Apostle here appeals. To deny the Christian's hope of a future existence is to make his a pitiable lot.

Now comes the second section of the chapter — verses 20 to 28. Before completing his argument the Apostle turns to the other side in a manner quite characteristic of him. He says: "But now Christ *is* risen from the dead, and this secures the resurrection of His people." He proceeds to speak only of the resurrection of Christ's people. We know full well that he believed in a general resurrection of all mankind. A little more than a year later — in Acts 24:15 — we find him saying before Felix that he expects a resurrection of the dead, both of the just and unjust. But in our passage he confines his view to the resurrection of the just, and declares that of this Christ's resurrection is the pledge and assurance. Christ was the first-fruits, and the first-fruits of the harvest gave promise of all that should follow. So he proceeds to remind us that death came through Adam, and in like manner the resurrection comes in Christ. It is wholly beside the mark to quote as teaching universal salvation the statement in verse 22: "As in Adam all die, even so in Christ shall all be made alive"; for the whole connection shows plainly that he speaks of bodily death and bodily resurrection. And so he declares that Christ's people will all rise at His coming. Having mentioned the coming of the Lord, he declares that then Christ will deliver up the kingdom to God, and will Himself also be subject to God, "that God may be all in all." This does not conflict with the plain teaching elsewhere that Christ is Himself Divine. The reference is to the authority delegated to Him as the God-man — the Mediator. As He told the disciples just before His ascension: "All authority in Heaven and in earth was given to Me"; so here we are told that this delegated Mediatorial authority will at last be turned back again to God who gave it, and Messianic dominion will be merged in the general dominion of God.

In the third section of the chapter — verses 29 to 34 — the Apostle gives further arguments against these persons at Corinth who denied the resurrection. This section needs to be closely connected with the end of our first section at verse 19. The Apostle here practically identifies the question of a resurrection with that of a future existence. We know that he believed in and taught a conscious existence of the spirit between death and the resurrection of the body. In 2 Cor. 5:6-8 he declares: "We are always confident, knowing that whilst we are at home in the body we are absent from the Lord. We are confident, and willing rather to be absent from the body and to be present with the Lord." Here he distinctly asserts a conscious existence in the presence of Christ while absent from the body; but in the passage with which we are dealing he speaks only of the re-embodied existence, and points out that for them to deny a resurrection is to deny a future existence. The Corinthians would make no distinction. The first argument he here presents has awakened much disputation, and I have thought all the trouble arises from the unwillingness of many readers to take the passage in its plain and obvious sense. I don't know how you have found it, but I think one of the commonest sources of difficulty in understanding the Bible is a certain unwillingness to let the Bible mean what it wants to mean. We don't fancy the obvious meaning of some passage, and we say, "Oh, it cannot mean that," and proceed to look for another meaning. Then the plainer the language is, the more difficulty we find in drawing from it any other meaning; and so we call the passage extremely difficult. I do not say that you have ever done this, but certainly I have, and have become conscious of it again and again. Now, the obvious meaning of this passage — verse 29 — is that some persons among this party at Corinth had been baptizing living persons instead of those who had died without baptism. There is a great disposition in human nature to magnify the externals of Christianity. This would easily arise among Jews and among Greeks. We know that a disposition to exaggerate the importance of Christian ceremony existed not many generations after this, and it might easily have existed at the beginning among some persons. And as to this particular matter, we know from several Fathers that there were in the second century certain professed Christians who did actually practise the baptism of a living person for the benefit of one who had died without baptism. Of course, that is all nonsense from the Christian's point of view; but I pray you to observe that the Apostle doesn't present this as his own argument in favor of his own teaching — he presents it as what the logicians call an argument *ad hominem:* an argument specially applying to the persons addressed. He wishes to show them how inconsistent it is for some of them to be practising this baptism for the dead when they say that men will never live again. He carefully distinguishes the persons who do this from himself and from the Church in general. It is not, "What shall we do who are baptized for the dead?" but, "What shall *they* do?" Before and after he speaks of the Christians in general as *"we."* All the difficulty about this passage appears to have arisen from a failure to observe that the Apostle introduces it only as an *ad hominem* argument, to silence captious objectors; even as he tells Titus concerning certain unruly persons, that their mouths must be stopped. Our Lord used a similar argument when they charged Him with casting out demons by a league with Beelzebub, and He said: "Well, then; by whom do your sons cast them out?" It was a mere argument *ad hominem* to silence unreasonable controversialists. The Apostle then proceeds to further considerations addressing themselves to all Christians. "Why do we also stand in jeopardy every hour — constantly exposed to peril, to death, in the service of Christ — if there be no future life?" For his part he declares that his sufferings amount to daily death. And why should he have fought with beasts at Ephesus if there be no resurrection? We don't know whether he means that he has literally fought with beasts, or means it figuratively; and it doesn't at all matter for the understanding of his argument. He had encountered great perils and sufferings in the service of Christ; and what was the use of bearing all this if there be no future? Naturally enough might one then say, as the wicked Jews had said long before — Isaiah 22:13: "Let us eat and drink, for tomorrow we die." People would very generally say this if they abandoned all belief in a future existence. But the Apostle checks them: "Be not deceived. Don't adopt any such ruinous notion. Don't allow the people who assert that there is no resurrection to communicate their ideas to you." And then he quotes a line of a Greek poet. We don't know whether he was quoting directly from the poet, or the saying had become proverbial. It is a little difficult to translate. "Communications" is not indeed the word. The revisers say "evil company." It means evil intercourse or conversations. And the word rendered "manners" signifies both morals and manners. We have no term that denotes both at once, as they have in German — "Sitten." The thought is surely one of great importance — perhaps especially to the young: "Evil conversations and intercourse corrupt good morals and manners." The Apostle has repeatedly quoted Greek poets, as a missionary in China now likes to quote some saying of Confucius, because that will take hold upon his hearers.

The remainder of the chapter presents a reply to objectors. The first objection, which is answered in verse 35-49, turns upon the inquiry: "How can the same body be raised?" The Apostle introduces it in a manner characteristic of his writings, by representing some individual objector as speaking. "But some one will say, How are the dead raised? and with what kind of body do they come?" Now, this is not the question of a sincere and anxious inquirer wishing to have difficulties removed out of the way of his faith. It is the question of a curious and hostile objector. We see that from the harsh term with which the Apostle introduces his reply. He says: "Thou fool!" — a strong expression, which an inspired teacher might employ because he would know that it was deserved, and could use it without improper feeling on his own part. There are occasions on which for us also this would be the most appropriate answer to use; but we feel a difficulty in making it. Apart from the matter of civility, there is danger of wrong judgment or wrong feeling on our part; so we sometimes have to shrink from saying: "You are a fool, and you know you are," — or: "You are a fool, and have not sense enough to know it" — although at times that would be the only logical reply. To this silly objector the Apostle now answers that there are many different kinds of bodies in the world; and so the risen body may be very different from the present body, and yet be in some just sense the same. He illustrates this, first, from sowing wheat. The grain of wheat that we sow must die in order to be made alive. The body that grows out of it: the stalk, the leaves, the head, the blossoms, and many grains — are in one sense the same as the single seed we planted, though in another sense they are very different. Again, there are many kinds of flesh, he declares: flesh of men, flesh of beasts, flesh of fishes, flesh of birds. There are also many bodies: bodies celestial and terrestrial; and the celestial bodies widely differ in glory. You see the point of all these illustrations. The risen body may be in a true sense the same, while yet in the conditions of its existence exceedingly different. It will be incorruptible, glorious, powerful — a spiritual body. You ask just what the spiritual body is; and I answer: We don't know — we are at the end of our information on the subject. But you see at once that there is no propriety in questioning or denying the resurrection on the ground that the matter composing the body becomes widely scattered — even enters into new bodies, and that the same body contains entirely different matter at different periods of its existence, and all that. The risen body will not be in the strict sense a flesh and blood body: it will be incorruptible and spiritual; so the objection is cut off, and that is what the Apostle undertook to do. He is not attempting to define for us the nature of the risen body, but only to meet the objector by showing that it will be exceedingly different from the present one.

The second objection — in verses 50-57 — asks how it will be with those living when Christ shall appear. That difficulty might well present itself at the beginning. People would say: "Grant that the dead will rise again. How about those whom Christ finds alive?" The Apostle declares that they will immediately be changed without passing through the experience of death. They must be changed, because flesh and blood unchanged cannot inherit the kingdom of God, and the corruptible must become incorruptible. So, when the dead shall have been raised, and the living at that moment shall have been changed, then all the consequences of death will have been destroyed. Then — as written in Isaiah 25:8 — death will be swallowed up in victory. And, borrowing from the prophet Hosea, the Apostle breaks into an outburst of rejoicing: "O death, where is thy sting? — O grave, where is thy victory?" It is a triumph which Christianity warrants — a victory which Christianity promises. He adds: "The sting of death is sin; and sin cannot be overcome by the law: nay, the law gives strength to sin" — a thought here mentioned in passing, and to be developed a few months later in the 7th chapter of the Epistle to the Romans. The law has no power to take away the sting of death by conquering sin; but the Gospel has this power. And so he adds: "But thanks be to God, who giveth us the victory through our Lord Jesus Christ."

The conclusion of this great chapter — in verse 58 — contains a twofold exhortation, and a great encouragement. He exhorts, first, to be fixed in Christian convictions. "Be ye steadfast, unmovable." Second: To be active in Christian work — "always abounding in the work of the Lord." Only fixed convictions will produce permanent Christian activity; and only those who are actively at work will maintain fixed convictions. The two may stand together: either attempted alone will fail. Observe how strong is the expression here: not merely "engaged" in the work of the Lord; but *"abounding* in the work of the Lord," and *"always* abounding." Then he adds the encouragement to steadfastness and activity: "Forasmuch as ye know that your labor is not in vain in the Lord." It is not in vain, because it shall not fail of good results. Labor in the Lord is never in vain. Speak any word for Christ in public or in private, that is in accordance

266

with the Bible, and pray God's blessing upon it, and it will, and must, and does do good. You are engaged in a cause which cannot fail — which is destined to success. Your King must reign till He hath put all enemies under His feet. And it is not in vain, because you shall not fail of eternal reward. There is a resurrection — a future life — and in that future life will God recompense for all sacrifices and all toil in the Saviour's service. Brother, don't talk about the sacrifices you have made for Christ; but think only of what you may do in the future. Ah, if there be sorrow in the home of the glorified, methinks the keenest sorrow with which we shall look back upon our earthly life will spring from remembering that we did not make more sacrifices and engage in greater toils for the good of men and for the glory of Christ.

The above address is to be found in a work of scarcity, *College Students at Northfield*. New York. 1888. pp. 150-161.

JOHN R. BROADUS
(1827-1895)

This distinguished American Baptist clergyman, professor, preacher, and writer was born in Culpeper, Virginia, January 1, 1827. After some experiences of teaching, he entered the University of Virginia at Charlottesville, of which it was said that at that time "it offered the most thorough education to be had in this country in the 40's." He became minister of the Baptist Church at Charlottesville, Virginia, in 1850, and at the same time served as an assistant instructor, teaching Ancient Languages in the University of Virginia. In 1858, he went to Greenville, North Carolina, as Professor of New Testament and Homiletics, in the new Baptist seminary there, a ministry that was interrupted by the Civil War. In 1870, the school was removed to Louisville, Kentucky, and there Broadus began his work of teaching and writing, which made him one of the outstanding homiletical professors in America, as well as a preacher of unusual gifts. No less a person than the famous New Testament Greek scholar, Dr. A. T. Robertson, has said of Broadus that he was "the greatest teacher of his time. No one in this country could equal him in the marvelous projectile force and in the inspiring momentum which he gave to his pupils. His old pupils sought in vain among the teachers of Germany for his equal. With one accord they all pronounce him the greatest of teachers. . . . Doctor Broadus could not brook slipshod work either in the classroom exercises or examinations. He held himself to the most severe ideals of exact scholarship even in the most minute matters. The high standard of scholarship through the years at the Seminary is due to his ambition in this direction. But he was no Doctor Dry-as-Dust. He showed that learning need not be dry. He was popular in the true sense."

In 1870 he published his well-known volume, *The Preparation and Delivery of Sermons,* which went through innumerable editions, year after year, and I think is recognized on every hand as being the greatest single volume on this important subject that has ever appeared in the English language. (Strange to say, this title of his most important book is not in the biographical sketch in the *Dictionary of American Biography*). The most important commentary on the Gospel of Matthew written by an American scholar was the one that Broadus wrote for the American Commentary Series in 1886. In 1889 he delivered the Lyman Beecher Lectures at Yale on Preaching, and the verdict of one who heard him, also a well-known scholar, Dr. H. C. Vedder, might here well be quoted. "Men of considerable reputation have come and gone without their presence being known to any but the few immediately concerned. Such has not been the case with the visit of Doctor Broadus and the delivery of his lectures. He has made marked impression on the life and thought of the University, outside of the Divinity School, to which he has been especially lecturing. Every available seat in Marquand chapel not reserved for students, has been occupied each day, considerably before the hour for the lecture, and after all available spaces have been filled by chairs many have crowded into the corners left and listened standing. To judge from appearances, the audience might have been doubled or quadrupled if there had been room for those who would have gladly come."

The material I have here used of Dr. Broadus does not show him at his best as a preacher, but I have chosen it because, better than any other one sermon I know of, it gives a comprehensive view of the basic teaching of the 15th chapter of First Corinthians.

I. A CLASSIFICATION OF PASSAGES IN THE NEW TESTAMENT RELATING TO THE RESURRECTION OF CHRIST and the DOCTRINE OF THE RESURRECTION

A. CHRIST'S PREDICTIONS OF HIS RESURRECTION
I. IN THE EARLY JUDEAN MINISTRY

1. "Destroy this temple and in three days I will raise it up," John 2:19-22. This bold statement, misunderstood, formed one of the charges against Jesus, nearly three years later — Matthew 27:40, 63, 64; Mark 15:29.

II. IN HIS GALILEAN MINISTRY

2. "As Jonah — so shall the Son of Man be three days and three nights in the heart of the earth," Matthew 12:40. Though this verse does not actually contain words indicating resurrection, all agree that it is of such that Jesus is speaking.
3. "The third day be raised up," Matthew 16:21; Luke 9:22. "After three days rise again," Mark 8:31.
4. After the Transfiguration. "Tell . . . no man, until the Son of Man be risen from the dead," Matthew 17:9; Mark 9:9.
5. Shortly thereafter, Matthew 17:23; Mark 9:31.

III. DURING THE PEREAN MINISTRY

6. "After three days He shall rise again," Matthew 20:19; Mark 10:34; Luke 18:33.

IV. ON THURSDAY OF PASSION WEEK

7. "After I am raised up, I will go before you into Galilee," Matthew 26:32; Mark 14:28. They would see Him again, John 16:16, 17, 19, 22.

    It is in regard to such statements as these that the angel said to the women at the tomb — "He is not here, but is risen: remember how He spake unto you when He was yet in Galilee, saying," etc. Luke 24:6, 7; Matthew 28:6.

B. THE TEN POST-RESURRECTION APPEARANCES OF CHRIST

I. ON EASTER SUNDAY
  1. To Mary Magdalene, John 20:11-18; Mark 16:9-11.
  2. To a group of women at the tomb, Matthew 28:9, 10.
  3. To Simon Peter, Luke 24:34; I Corinthians 15:5, 7.
  4. To two disciples on the road to Emmaus, Mark 16:12, 13; Luke 24:13-35.
  5. To the Ten in an upper room, Mark 16:14; Luke 24: 36-43; John 20:19-25; I Corinthians 15:5.

II. ONE WEEK LATER
  6. To the Eleven, John 20:26-29.

III. THREE SUBSEQUENT APPEARANCES
  7. To James, I Corinthians 15:7.
  8. To seven disciples at the Sea of Galilee, John 21:1-24.
  9. To eleven disciples on a mountain in Galilee, Matthew 28:16-20; Mark 16:15-18.

IV. AT THE TIME OF HIS ASCENSION
  10. Mark 10:19, 20; Luke 24:44-53; Acts 1:1-9; I Corinthians 15:6.

C. CHRIST'S TEACHINGS ABOUT RESURRECTION

I. DURING THE GALILEAN MINISTRY
  1. In the astonishing statement recorded in John 5:25-29, Christ speaks of the time when
    a. "the dead shall hear the voice of the Son of God";
    b. "all that are in the tombs shall hear His voice and come forth";
    c. there will be "the resurrection of life," and, "the resurrection of judgment." With this compare the resurrection "of the just and the unjust" in Acts 24:15.

  Note: — Many interpret this passage as referring to a spiritual resurrection, i.e., to new birth.

2. That Christ would raise up all whom the Father had given Him, "at the last day," John 6:39, 40, 44.

II. DURING THE PEREAN MINISTRY
3. Of Lazarus — "thy brother shall rise again," John 11: 23.

III. ON TUESDAY OF PASSION WEEK
4. In replying to the insincere question of the Sadducees, Matthew 22:23-33; Mark 12:18-27; Luke 20:27-38, our Lord affirms that
   a. in the life to come there will be no marriage relationship;
   b. they will then be "sons of the resurrection," Luke 20: 37.

D. TITLES OF CHRIST IN RELATION TO RESURRECTION

I. GIVEN BY CHRIST
1. "I am the Resurrection and the Life," John 11:25.

II. GIVEN BY THE APOSTLES
2. "Firstborn from the dead," Colossians 1:18.
3. "The First Begotten of the dead," Revelation 1:5.

E. SUBSEQUENT TESTIMONY TO THE GREAT FACT OF CHRIST'S RESURRECTION

I. THE TESTIMONY OF THE ANGELS ON EASTER MORNING
Matthew 28:6, 7; Mark 16:6; Luke 24:6, 7.

II. THE TESTIMONY OF JOHN THE APOSTLE
"after He was risen from the dead," John 21:14.

III. THE TESTIMONY OF THE APOSTLE PETER
1. In discussing the choice of a successor to Judas, Acts 1:22.

    2. In his preaching, Acts 2:24, 31, 32; 3:15; 4:10; 5:30; 10:40; regarding which the priests and Sadducees were "grieved," 4:2.

    3. In his First Epistle
       a. by His Resurrection we are begotten again unto a living hope, 1:3, 21;
       b. concerning which baptism is a type, 3:21.

IV. ALL THE TWELVE WERE TO BE WITNESSES TO THE FACT OF CHRIST'S RESURRECTION
Acts 1:22; 2:32; 3:15; 10:41.

V. THE TESTIMONY OF THE APOSTLE PAUL

    1. In his preaching
       a. at Antioch in Pisidia, Acts 13:29-34. Note that while Paul does not specifically state that the tomb in which the body of Jesus was placed was empty on Easter morning, v. 29 certainly implies such;
       b. in Thessalonica, Acts 17:3;
       c. in Athens, Acts 17:18, 31.

    2. In his various defences
    It is significant that in the numerous references to this truth, the text states Paul's assertions concerned the doctrine of resurrection, rather than the Resurrection of Christ, 23:6; 24:15, 21; 26:6-8; but that actually he did also refer to Christ's Resurrection is clearly implied in the words of Festus to Agrippa in 25:19.

    3. In his Epistles
    Here I would list only those passages in which simply the fact of Christ's Resurrection is stated. I have thought Paul's doctrine of Resurrection warranted a separate division in this outline study.

VI. THE TESTIMONY OF THE WRITER OF THE EPISTLE TO THE HEBREWS
Hebrews 13:20.

VII. THE TESTIMONY OF THE RISEN LORD
Revelation 1:18. While the actual nomenclature of resurrection is not here, the fact is clearly implied. I believe this is the only reference to the Resurrection of Christ in the Apocalypse.

F. THE TEACHING OF ST. PAUL REGARDING THE RESURRECTION

I. IT IS GOD WHO RAISETH THE DEAD
II Corinthians 1:9.

II. THE FACT OF CHRIST'S RESURRECTION
Romans 4:24; 6:4, 9; 7:4; 8:34; 10:9; I Corinthians 6:14; 15:12, 20; II Corinthians 4:14; 5:15; Galatians 1:1; Ephesians 1:20; Colossians 2:12; I Thessalonians 1:10; II Timothy 2:8.

III. SOME CONSEQUENCES OF CHRIST'S RESURRECTION
1. He was thus declared to be the Son of God, Romans 1:4.
2. He is thus Lord both of the dead and of the living, Romans 14:9. In this passage only do we have a verb (anazaoo) meaning to *revive,* used in reference to Christ's resurrection. It is the verb used in Revelation 20:5.
3. He makes our justification possible, Romans 4:25.
4. Because He was raised from the dead we will be also, Romans 6:5; I Corinthians 6:14; 15:21; II Corinthians 4:14.

IV. THE APPALLING CONSEQUENCES IF CHRIST HAS NOT RISEN FROM THE DEAD
I Corinthians 15:14-19.

V. THE RESURRECTION OF BELIEVERS
1. Time — at the coming of Christ, I Thessalonians 4:16.

    2. The nature of the resurrection body, I Corinthians 15: 42-48, 52; II Corinthians 5:1-5 (in this passage the actual term for resurrection is not used); Philippians 3:21.

    3. In the factors that urged Paul on in his service for God, Philippians 3:11.

VI. THERE WILL BE A RESURRECTION "BOTH OF THE JUST AND THE UNJUST"
Acts 24:15.

VII. THE *PRESENT* EXPERIENCE OF "RESURRECTION" AS NEWNESS OF LIFE
Romans 6:13; Ephesians 2:6; Philippians 3:10; Colossians 2:12. It is generally held that Romans 8:11 is to be so interpreted, but some affirm this refers to actual bodily resurrection. (See also Ephesians 5:14).

G. *THE TESTIMONY OF THE NEW TESTAMENT TO THE FACT THAT RESURRECTION WAS TAUGHT IN THE OLD TESTAMENT*

I. IN GENERAL

1. "That the dead are raised up even Moses showed," Luke 20:37.

2. Abraham believed God would, if Isaac were sacrificed, raise up Isaac from the dead, Hebrews 11:19.

3. Paul frequently refers to the belief of Israel that God would raise the dead, Acts 23:6; 24:15, 21; 26:8, 23.

4. "Women received their dead raised to life again," Hebrews 11:35.

5. Our Lord drew from the revelation that God is not the God of the dead but of the living the truth that there *must* therefore be a resurrection, Matthew 22:31, 32; Mark 12:26, 27; Luke 20:37, 38. See Exodus 3:6, 15, 16; etc.

II. SPECIFICALLY — IN RELATION TO THE
RESURRECTION OF CHRIST
   6. His Resurrection was "according to the Scriptures,"
   Luke 24:46; I Corinthians 15:4; Acts 17:3.
   7. The Psalms are declared to contain prophecies of Christ's
   Resurrection
      a. Psalm 2:7 — Acts 13:33.
      b. Psalm 16:8-11 — Acts 2:25-31; 13:34-37.

H. *PASSAGES IMPLYING RESURRECTION BUT NOT
USING SUCH WORDS*

   I. OF JESUS, WHEN STATING HE WOULD LAY
   DOWN HIS LIFE, ADDED "I take it again," John
   10:17, 18.

   II. "HE SHEWED HIMSELF ALIVE," Acts 1:3
   With which compare the assertion that Paul "affirmed
   (Jesus) to be alive," Acts 25:19.

   III. TWO PASSAGES IN THE EPISTLE TO THE
   ROMANS
      1. That God will "quicken our mortal bodies," 8:11.
      2. All Christians are waiting for "the redemption of the
      body," 8:23.

   IV. THREE ADDITIONAL PASSAGES
      1. The intricate declaration regarding our having "a build-
      ing of God," II Corinthians 5:1.
      2. "Who shall change our bodies of corruption," etc.,
      Philippians 3:21
      3. Christ was "put to death in the flesh, but quickened by
      the Spirit," I Peter 3:18.

   V. WORDS OF THE RISEN LORD
   "I was dead . . . I am alive," Revelation 1:18; 2:8.

I. RESURRECTION IN THE NEW TESTAMENT APART FROM THAT OF CHRIST

   I. IN GENERAL
"The dead are raised up," Matthew 11:5; Luke 7:22; compare the commission of Jesus to the Twelve, Matthew 10:8.

   II. CERTAIN INDIVIDUALS DURING THE MINISTRY OF JESUS
1. The son of the widow of Nain, Luke 7:11-17.
2. The daughter of Jairus, Matthew 9:18, 19, 23-26; Mark 5:22-24, 35-43; Luke 8:41, 42, 49-56.
3. Lazarus, John 11; 12:1, 9, 17.

   III. AN UNIDENTIFIED GROUP, AFTER CHRIST'S RESURRECTION
Matthew 27:52, 53.

   IV. DORCAS
Acts 9:36-42.

   V. A *FUTURE* INDIVIDUAL RESURRECTION WILL BE THAT OF THE TWO WITNESSES
of Revelation 11:11.

J. SOME MISCELLANEOUS STATEMENTS

   I. THE SAMARITANS BELIEVED IN A RESURRECTION John 11:24.

   II. THE DOCTRINE OF THE RESURRECTION SHOULD BE A FOUNDATION TRUTH FOR BELIEVERS
Hebrews 6:2.

   III. ONCE IN THE NEW TESTAMENT WE HAVE THE PHRASE "THE FIRST RESURRECTION"
Revelation 20:5, 6.

K. ERRONEOUS OPINIONS CONCERNING RESURRECTION

I. THE SADDUCEES — "WHO SAY THAT THERE IS NO RESURRECTION,"
Matthew 22:23; Mark 12:18; Luke 20:27; Acts 23:8; I Corinthians 15:12.

II. THAT JOHN THE BAPTIST WAS RISEN FROM THE DEAD
Mark 6:14, 16; Luke 9:7.

III. THAT THE RESURRECTION IS PASSED,
II Timothy 2:18.

IV. IN ATHENS, WHEN THEY HEARD PAUL PREACHING THE RESURRECTION "SOME MOCKED,"
Acts 17:32.

In the above classification, I have sometimes used a passage in relation to two different aspects of this subject, and in four cases, I have used a passage three times — Acts 24:15; I Corinthians 3:21; and Colossians 2:12. In estimating the totals which I am about to give, I have reckoned, for example, the three Gospel accounts of the raising of the daughter of Jairus as three different passages. I feel one is justified in speaking of separate passages on the Resurrection in identifying six of them in the 15th chapter of I Corinthians. In the enumeration that follows, it will be discovered that in the Four Gospels, there are fifty-seven different references to the Resurrection and the Resurrection of Christ, embracing 172 verses. In Acts, there are 21 separate passages, totaling 43 verses. In the Epistles of St. Paul, there are 36 references, totaling 54 verses, and in the remaining books of the New Testament, there are 12 passages, totaling 13 verses. Thus, we find there are 126 different passages in the New Testament referring to the subject of the Resurrection and the Resurrection of Christ, totaling 282 verses.

LIST OF PASSAGES REFERRED TO IN THE ABOVE OUTLINE

Matthew	9:18, 19, 23-26; 10:8; 11:5; 12:40; 16:21; 17:9, 23; 22:23-33; 26:32; 27:40, 52, 53, 63, 64; 28:6, 7, 1-8, 9, 10, 16-20
Mark	5:22-24, 35-43; 6:14, 16; 8:31; 9:9, 31; 10:19, 20; 12:18-27; 14:28; 15:29; 16:1-8, 6, 9-11, 12, 13, 14,15-18
Luke	7:11-18, 22; 8:41, 42, 49-56; 9:7, 21; 18:33; 20:27-38, 37; 24:1-12, 6, 7, 13-35, 34, 36-43, 44-53, 46
John	2:19-22; 5:26-29; 6:39, 40, 44; 10:17, 18; 11:1-57, 23, 24, 25; 20:1-10, 11-18, 19-25, 26-29; 21:1-24, 14
Acts	1:1-9, 3, 22; 2:24-31, 31, 32; 3:15; 4:10; 5:30; 9:36-42; 10:40, 41; 13:29-34, 33, 35-37; 17:3, 18, 31, 32; 23:6, 8; 24:15, 21; 25:19; 26:6-8, 23
Romans	1:4; 4:24, 25; 6:4, 5, 9, 13; 7:4; 8:11, 23, 34; 10:9; 14:9
I Corinthians	6:14; 15:4, 6, 7, 12, 14-19, 20, 21, 42-48, 52
II Corinthians	1:9; 4:14; 5:1-5, 1, 15
Galatians	1:1
Ephesians	1:20; 2:6
Philippians	3:10, 11, 21
Colossians	1:18; 2:12
I Thessalonians	1:10; 4:16
II Timothy	2:8, 18
Hebrews	6:2; 11:19, 35; 13:20
I Peter	1:3, 21; 3:18
Revelation	1:15, 18; 2:8; 11:11; 20:5, 6

AN ALPHABETICAL LIST OF SUBJECTS RELATED TO THE RESURRECTION NARRATIVES

Angel
Appearances
Ascension
Bethany
Body
Burial
Cleopas
Commission, the Great
Emmaus
First Day of the Week
Joanna
Joseph of Arimathaea
Mary Magdalene
Mary the Mother of James
Napkin
Predictions of Christ Relative to the Resurrection
Prophecies of Christ's Resurrection in the Old Testament
Resurrection
Salome
Seal
Sepulchre
Simon Peter
Stone
Third Day
Thomas
Tomb
Twelve, the
Watch, the
Witnesses

BISHOP GOULBURN ON THE MEANING OF THE GREEK WORD ANASTASIS

There are, no doubt, more extensive examinations of the Greek word translated *resurrection* than the following by Dr. Goulburn, but they are not known to me, and I thought many would profit by this careful study.

"The word *anastasis* gives simply (if its etymology be consulted) the notion of rising up, after a previous period of recumbency — it expresses the change of posture from lying or sitting to standing. Thus its cognate verb is applied to Levi's rising up from the receipt of custom at which he was sitting when Christ called him; to our Lord's rising up a great while before day for the purpose of solitary prayer; and to the rising of blind Bartimeus, who had been previously sitting by the highway side, a petitioner for the alms of passengers. It is, however, worthy of notice that notwithstanding the frequent usage of the cognate verb to express an ordinary change of posture incidental to the course of every day life, the derivative noun *anastasis* seems set apart and consecrated to express the high Verity of the Resurrection. This noun is never applied to the rising up out of a recumbent position — nay, it is never even used to denote the miraculous reanimation of the old natural body, except in one solitary instance, where the distinction between this mere reanimation and resurrection is carefully pointed out — 'Women received their dead raised to life again' and 'others were tortured not accepting deliverance that they might obtain a *better* resurrection' (Heb. 11:35). And another remark may be made confirmatory of the observation that this word *anastasis* is appropriated to the expression of that Verity which is the theme of our present discussion. Often as the moral nature of man is spoken of as the subject of quickening spiritual influences — obvious as is the transition of thought from the awakening of the naturally dead to that of those who are dead in trespasses and sins — and much therefore as we might expect to find the same word interchangeably used of either process, the word *anastasis* is never applied to the Spiritual Resurrection. The single exception (if exception it be) to this remark, is of such a nature as rather to confirm the rule. It is to be found in that celebrated chapter of the Book of Revelations where mention is made of the first (which according to the Augustinian interpretation is the Spiritual) Resurrection. The other and more literal interpretation of that passage being adopted, we have not a single instance in the whole compass of the New Testament in which the word *anastasis* denotes the quickening of man's moral nature. May we conjecture that the vivid bodily reference inherent in the etymology of the term precluded a spiritual application of it?" — Edward Meyrick Goulburn: *The Doctrine of the Resurrection of the Body as Taught in Holy Scripture*, Bampton Lectures, 1850, Oxford, 1850, pp. 6-8.

A NOTE CONCERNING TOYNBEE'S "CHRISTUS PATIENS."

In regard to the resurrection, there is a very remarkable fact revealed concerning its uniqueness in no less a work than Toynbee's *Studies of History*. In Volume VII is a famous section of some 160 pages, entitled "Christus Patiens," which has a sub-heading "Correspondences between the Story of Jesus and Stories of Certain Hellenic Saviours." Toynbee here attempts to find eighty-seven incidents in the life of Christ which are parallel in various myths and stories in Greek mythology. There are 87 of them. Indeed the last 38 all have reference to the incidents of our Lord's trial, condemnation, suffering, and death. As an illustration, the last, the 87th so-called parallel, reads as follows: "The executor's conversion is partly due to the two-fold influence of a martyr who is devoted to the dead hero's person and of a sage who is sympathetic to the dead hero's ideas." (p. 405). Now the interesting thing about all this is that Toynbee ends his parallels with the death of Christ. He does not even hint that there is anything in Greek mythology, not to mention Greek history, or the biography of any great Greek hero, paralleling the resurrection of our Lord. Probably Toynbee does not believe in the resurrection of Christ, but that is neither here nor there. His historical acumen prevents him from attempting even to indicate any such a parallel. In other words, the resurrection of Christ is an absolutely unique event, without parallels anywhere, in spite of what some of the German rationalists of the nineteenth century were accustomed to insist upon. Mohammed is dead. The Greek gods, of course, have all vanished. The Greek heroes, the Roman heroes, the emperors, the great scientists, the states-men, the philosophers — all are in their tombs today, their bodies moldering in the dust. So also with the founders of re-ligious cults in our own country, but the body of Jesus is not disintegrating in the tomb of Joseph of Arimathaea. He came forth in His own body from that tomb on Easter morning and He dieth no more.

A BIBLIOGRAPHY OF WORKS RELATING TO THE
RESURRECTION OF CHRIST

A full bibliography of relevant data bearing upon the inexhaustible subject of our Lord's resurrection, even were it confined to material in the English language, could easily fill a volume of four hundred pages, because of the many ramifications of the subject, and because of the various theological disciplines in which the subject of the resurrection of Christ must be considered. Of course, all of the standard biographies of Christ will have chapters on Christ's Resurrection, some quite important. So likewise volumes treating such subjects as New Testament Theology, the Teaching of Christ, the Speeches of the Apostles, Pauline Theology, Eschatology, the Apostles' Creed (as well as other creeds), Biographies of New Testament Characters, and, especially, all the more important biographies of the Apostles Peter, James, John, and Thomas. In addition, there are those numerous volumes devoted to the exposition of certain passages in which the resurrection is the major theme, as for example, the exquisite work by H. C. G. Moule, *Jesus and the Resurrection,* which carries the interpreting sub-title, *Expository Studies of St. John XX, XXI,* (4th ed., London, 1905). At the conclusion of this bibliography, will be found a brief list of books which are devoted to an interpretation of the 15th chapter of First Corinthians.

I have purposely omitted rationalistic works, because the volume for which I have constructed this bibliography is not as such a study of the historicity of Christ's resurrection, the nature of the resurrection body, etc., but a collection of great sermons on the Resurrection of Christ, and rationalistic works which deny the Resurrection will not be of any value to one wishing to preach with conviction the great truths related to this glorious theme.

The two most important volumes on the Resurrection of Christ to be published down to the middle of the nineteenth century appeared within a period of less than twenty years, one by an Anglican Bishop, and the other by an English layman of literary gifts. In 1729, in answer to the attacks upon the Resurrection of Christ by the Deists of his day, Bishop Thomas Sherlock (1678-1761), published his famous work, *The Tryal of the Witnesses of the Resurrection of Jesus Christ*. The Bishop published the work anonymously and followed it with a *Sequel* in 1749. It was immediately received with enthusiastic acclaim so that within forty years, fourteen editions appeared and an uncounted number of later reprints even down into the twentieth century. The attack of the Deists was dealt a mortal blow by this volume, so that in subsequent years, the Deistic literature faded away while the work by Sherlock was issued by the thousands.

Gilbert West (1703-1756), identified with various positions in the government of his day and a friend of Lord Lyttleton, of the great statesman Pitt, etc., issued in 1747 his volume, *Observations on the History and Events of the Resurrection* of Jesus Christ. This also went through a number of editions and found a place in the fifth volume of Bishop Watson's famous *Collection of Theological Tracts*. The work won for Mr. West the honorary degree of D.C.L. from Oxford in 1748. Both of these works on the Resurrection, together with memoirs of these and other writers may be found in an invaluable work published in London in 1849, *Christian Literature: Evidences,* A Collection of Famous apologetic works edited by J. S. Memes.

The following titles are arranged in (approximately) chronological order:

Bishop Samuel Horsley: *Nine Sermons on the Nature of the Evidence of the Resurrection,* 1815, pp. 250
George Moberly: *The Sayings of the Great Forty Days,* 2nd ed., London, 1846, pp. lxvi, 312
Bishop Edward M. Goulburn: *The Doctrine of the Resurrection of the Body as Taught in Holy Scripture,* Bampton Lectures, Oxford, 1850, pp. xv, 377. A profound work.
William Landels: *The Sepulchre in the Garden,* London, 1866, pp. 355
Robert Macpherson: *The Resurrection of Jesus Christ,* Edinburgh, 1867, pp. 515
Brooke Foss Westcott: *The Gospel of the Resurrection.* London, 1st ed., 1867, pp. xxxiii, 261
Revelation of the Risen Lord, 1st ed., 1881, pp. xxxvi, 199. These

two volumes, by the great scholar, bishop and commentator, probably exercised more influence over British thought concerning the resurrection than any other volumes written during the century.

Eliphalet Nott: *The Resurrection of Christ: A Series of Discourses*, New York 1872, pp. xi, 157

R. J. Cooke: *Outlines of the Doctrine of the Resurrection — Biblical, Historical, and Scientific*, N. Y., 1884, pp. 407

Edgar R. M'Cheyne: *The Gospel of a Risen Saviour*, Edinburgh, T. & T. Clark, 1892 pp. xv, 376, with an exhaustive index. This remarkable volume is today hardly known in this country. In many ways, it is unique. For every chapter there is an extensive bibliography of English, French and German titles. The subjects dealt with are generally of a more profound nature than in most such books. The concluding nine chapters have the following suggestive titles: "The Demonstration of the Spirit — Christ Risen in the History of the Church," "The Demonstration of the Critics — the Risen Saviour Among the Doctors," "The Risen Saviour — the Gospel Regarding God," "The Risen Saviour — the Gospel Regarding Man," "The Risen Saviour as the Reconciler," "The Risen Saviour as Master-Moralist," "The Risen Saviour and His Gospel Regarding the Body," "The Risen Saviour as a Quickening Spirit." "The Risen Saviour Shedding Light on the Last Things."

Henry Latham: *The Risen Master*. Cambridge, England, 1901, pp. xvi, 488, with an exhaustive index of texts. For the most part, this work is taken up with a detailed scholarly consideration of the appearances of our Lord, including a long chapter on the empty tomb, and a discussion of "The Witness of the Grave Clothes," extending to 65 pages. Included is a good chapter on the relation of the resurrection to the Day of Pentecost.

George D. Boardman: *Our Risen King's Forty Days*, Philadelphia, 1902, pp. 214

H. B. Swete: *The Appearances of the Lord after the Passion*, 1907, pp. xviii, 151

James Orr: *The Resurrection of Jesus*. Originally published, 1908; later ed., Cincinnati: Jennings and Graham, n.d. pp. 292

Calvin Klopp Staudt: *The Idea of the Resurrection in the Ante-Nicene Period*, Un. of Chicago, Historical and Linguistic Studies in Literature related to the New Testament, 2nd series, Volume I, Part VIII, 1909, Chicago, pp. 90.

T. J. Thorburn: *The Resurrection Narratives and Modern Criticism*. London: K. Paul, Trench, Truebner, 1910. pp. xx, 217

William John Sparrow-Simpson: *The Resurrection and Modern Thought*. London, New York: Longmans, Green & Co., 1911, pp. ix, 464. This is definitely the most exhaustive and the most important work on the resurrection of Christ written in the English language. It is divided into four parts: "The Witness of the Twelve," "The Witness of St. Paul," "The Theology of the Resurrection," "The Resurrection and Modern Thought." The subjects under the third division are especially important and suggestive: "The Teaching of the Risen Lord in St. Matthew," "The Universality of the Risen Lord's Commission," "The Baptismal Formula," "Christ's Resurrection as Evidence of His Divinity," "Christ's Resurrection Instrumental in His Exaltation," "Christ's Resurrection the Means of Our Justification,"

"Christ's Resurrection Instrumental in the Moral Resurrection of Christians," "Christ's Resurrection Instrumental in the Physical Resurrection of Christians," "St. Paul's Conclusions on the Dogmatic Value of Christ's Resurrection," "St. Paul's Doctrine of the Resurrection Body," "Patristic Teaching of the Resurrection Body," "Formulas of the Church on the Resurrection Body," "Post-Reformation English Teaching on the Resurrection Body," "Modern Roman Teaching on the Resurrection Body," "Conclusions on the Doctrine of the Resurrection Body." An earlier volume by the same scholar, *Our Lord's Resurrection*, was published in the Oxford Library of Practical Theology (London, 1905, pp. 320), is still an excellent handbook.

Ralph William Harden: *The Evangelists and the Resurrection*, London, 1914

John Mackintosh Shaw: *The Resurrection of Christ*. Edinburgh, 1920, pp. viii, 215. Sir William Robertson Nicoll at the time this book was published said of it, "It is, we think, the best and most comprehensive handling of the august theme which is accessible to the English reader. Professor Shaw takes up every point, so far as we know, and does so with frankness, honesty, and cogency." The volume is an amplification of the author's article, "Resurrection of Christ," in James Hastings' *Dictionary of the Apostolic Church*.

Frank Morison: *Who Moved the Stone?* New York, 1930, pp. 294

Doremus A. Hayes: *The Resurrection Fact*. Nashville: Cokesbury Press, 1932, pp. 355, with extensive bibliography. One of the outstanding books on the Resurrection to be published during the twentieth century, too rarely referred to.

C. C. Dobson: *The Empty Tomb and the Risen Lord*, London, 1933, pp. xiv, 130; 2nd ed., rev., Marshall Morgan and Scott, 164 pages with many illustrations. Mainly occupied with the death of Christ, the entombment, the tomb itself, and the visit of the apostles and the women at the tomb Easter morning. Continued in, *The Risen Lord and His Disciples*, Edinburgh, n.d., pp. 108.

Arthur Michael Ramsey: *The Resurrection of Christ: An Essay in Biblical Theology*, London, 1st ed., 1945, 2nd ed., 1946, pp. 124. The author was the Van Mildert professor of Divinity at the University of Durham, England, now Archbishop of Canterbury. Among the best of *recent* works on the resurrection. It is a compact presentation of the major lines of evidence and manifests full acquaintance with the problems and the literature.

Merrill C. Tenney: *The Reality of the Resurrection*, N. Y., 1963, pp. 221. This is the most important conservative work on the Resurrection to appear in the last fifteen years.

SUPPLEMENTARY NOTE

In the vast Card Catalogue of the New York Public Library, I came upon a handwritten card carrying a reference placed there, no doubt, by some devoted bibliographer, calling attention to material to which in all these years, I had never previously seen a reference. This is to a series of bibliographies of published Easter sermons appearing in various issues of *Notes and Queries*. Upon an examination of the references, I would say that the following bibliographies are the most important: Series Seven, Volume III, pp. 286 and 325. Series Eight, Volume I, p. 310; Volume II, p. 282; and Volume VII, pp. 282 and 283. Series Ten, Volume V. (1906), pp. 281-283.

Though I have transcribed all the references, I have not felt that any of them needed insertion in the above bibliography, and most of them would be very difficult to discover in this country.

BOOKS DEVOTED TO AN EXPOSITION OF THE FIFTEENTH CHAPTER OF FIRST CORINTHIANS

John Worthington: *The Doctrines of the Resurrection and the Reward to Come,* London, 1690

Robert S. Candlish: *Life in a Risen Saviour,* Philadelphia, 1858, pp. 410. 3d ed., rev. Edinburgh, 1863, pp. 423

John Brown: *The Resurrection of Life,* Edinburgh, 1866, pp. 378

William Milligan: *The Resurrection of Our Lord,* London, 1881, pp. 304. 4th ed., New York, 1917, pp. 318

Samuel Cox: *The Resurrection,* London, 1881, pp. xx, 348

James M. Gray: *A Picture of the Resurrection,* New York, 1917, pp. 43

Philip L. Frick: *The Resurrection and Paul's Argument,* Cincinnati, 1912, pp. 348

Karl Barth: *The Resurrection of the Dead,* English translation, N. Y., 1938, pp. 213

Strange to say, and yet there are many reasons probably to account for the fact, while there are innumerable anthologies of material bearing upon the subjects of Christmas and our Lord's birth, there are very, very few similar volumes in relation to Easter and the Resurrection. The most important one is entitled *The Book of Easter,* published by Macmillan, New York, 1910, a work of some 260 pages, with a number of illustrations, a considerable amount of poetry etc. The book carries an introduction by Bishop William C. Doane, and presumably it was he that gathered this material together.

Frank Foxcroft: *Resurgit. A Collection of Hymns and Songs of the Resurrection,* Boston, 1879

Susan T. Rice: *Easter. Its History, Celebration,* etc., ed. by R. H. Schauffler, N. Y., 1916

Carl A. Glover: *The Easter Radiance,* Nashville, 1937, pp. 112

The Easter Book of Legends and Stories. Selected by Alice Isabel Hazeltine and Ella Saphronia Smith, N. Y., 1947. A large part of this volume consists of poetry.

WRITINGS OF THE CHURCH FATHERS

Of Justin Martyr's work on the Resurrection, only fragments remain. (*Ante-Nicene Fathers*, Vol. I, pp. 294-299). Tertullian, the great African theologian, wrote a famous treatise, *On the Resurrection of the Flesh*, near the beginning of the third century (ibid, Vol. III, pp. 545-595).

The work of Methodius (d. 311), *On the Resurrection*, was a refutation of Origen's strange views on the subject. (ibid, Vol. VI, pp. 364-377). St. Gregory of Nyssa (329-389 A.D.), wrote on *The Soul and the Resurrection* (Nicene and Post-Nicene Fathers, 2nd ser., Vol. V, pp. 430-468); and a contemporary of his, St. Ambrose (339-397) wrote *On the Belief in the Resurrection* (ibid, Vol. VI, pp. 364-377). See Calvin K. Staupt: *The Idea of the Resurrection in the Ante-Nicene Period*, Chicago, 1909, pp. 90. (A Ph.D. thesis presented to the University of Chicago).